ROUTLEDGE LIBRARY EDITIONS:
ENERGY ECONOMICS

Volume 24

A DYNAMIC MODEL OF THE U.S. ENERGY SYSTEM

A DYNAMIC MODEL OF THE U.S. ENERGY SYSTEM

A Tool For Energy R & D Planning

JOHN P. WEYANT

Routledge
Taylor & Francis Group
LONDON AND NEW YORK

First published in 1984 by Garland Publishing, Inc.

This edition first published in 2018
by Routledge
2 Park Square, Milton Park, Abingdon, Oxon OX14 4RN

and by Routledge
711 Third Avenue, New York, NY 10017

Routledge is an imprint of the Taylor & Francis Group, an informa business

British Library Cataloguing in Publication Data
A catalogue record for this book is available from the British Library

ISBN: 978-1-138-10476-1 (Set)
ISBN: 978-1-315-14526-6 (Set) (ebk)
ISBN: 978-1-138-50259-8 (Volume 24) (hbk)
ISBN: 978-1-315-14497-9 (Volume 24) (ebk)

Publisher's Note
The publisher has gone to great lengths to ensure the quality of this reprint but points out that some imperfections in the original copies may be apparent.

Disclaimer
The publisher has made every effort to trace copyright holders and would welcome correspondence from those they have been unable to trace.

A Dynamic Model of the U.S. Energy System

John P. Weyant

Garland Publishing, Inc.
New York & London, 1984

Library of Congress Cataloging in Publication Data

Weyant, John P. (John Peter)
A dynamic model of the U.S. energy system.

(Outstanding dissertations in economics)
Originally presented as the author's thesis (doctoral)—University of California, Berkeley, 1976.
Bibliography: p.
1. Energy development—United States—Mathematical models. I. Title. II. Series.
HD9502.U52W46 1984 333.79'0724 79-7941
ISBN 0-8240-4189-5

All volumes in this series are printed on acid-free, 250-year-life paper.

Printed in the United States of America

University of California
Berkeley

A Dynamic Model of the United States Energy System: A Tool for Energy R&D Planning

A dissertation submitted in partial satisfaction of the requirements for the degree Doctor of Philosophy in Business Administration

by

John Peter Weyant

1976

DEDICATION

This dissertation is dedicated to my parents for their patience, and continual support and encouragement.

CONTENTS

ACKNOWLEDGEMENTS

Without the help and encouragement of many people the writing of this dissertation would not have been possible. First and foremost, I am especially grateful to Professor Richard C. Grinold, my advisor, and Dr. Jean R. Gebman of the Rand Corporation for their constant guidance and encouragement, and for first suggesting the development of an energy policy model as a possible dissertation topic. In particular, Professor Grinold first made me aware of the seminal energy policy models of Professor Alan S. Manne and Brookhaven National Laboratory, made many helpful suggestions during the formulation of the algebra of the model, and convinced me of the necessity for carefully relating the policy conclusions to the results of the analysis. Dr. Gebman suggested the format for many of the tables and figures in the dissertation and proposed its final organization, but most importantly, showed me how sophisticated mathematical concepts can and must be explained in plain and simple terms in order to be useful in policy analysis. Finally, I am much more grateful to Jean and Richard for surely being better friends than I deserve than for being superb academic advisors.

I am also most indebted to the Rand Corporation for providing support not only for this dissertation, but also for four stimulating and thoroughly enjoyable summers during my graduate education.

Further, I would like to thank Dr. Edward S. Ojdana and Mr. Giles K. Smith of Rand for the many useful insights into the R&D planning process I gained from them during our work on a previous Rand study on the subject. Thanks are also due to William Stanley and Richard Fallon, with whom I worked on a Rand project on Air Force energy problems, for reading and commenting on the dissertation in its entirety and to Richard for suggesting the manner of presentation for most of the data used in the study.

I would also like to thank Professor John P. Holdren and Kirk R. Smith of the Energy and Resources Program at Berkeley for allowing me to assimilate a small portion of their incredible store of knowledge about energy issues during our work on a project for the Jet Propulsion Laboratory.

A special note of thanks should also be extended to Professors C. Bartlett McGuire and Hayne Leland who served on my doctoral committee and made helpful suggestions during the writing of the dissertation.

Although their busy schedules limited somewhat their contributions to this dissertation per se, I would like to extend special thanks to Mr. Giles K. Smith of Rand and Professor C. West Churchman of Berkeley for profoundly influencing my thinking on all matters these past 4-5 years, mostly as a consequence of their possessing more wisdom than I can ever hope to acquire.

Next, I would like to thank Lyn Raphael of Rand for typing at least a half dozen versions of the dissertation and for a superb job of laying out and typing all of the tables that appear in it, and Edith Kuhner for a super job on Figures B-10 and B-11.

Last, but certainly not least, I would like to thank Claudia Barber for taking the edge off of more long work days than I will ever admit to or care to remember. To all these people, and probably quite a few more, I am extremely grateful.

FIGURES

TABLES

Chapter 1

INTRODUCTION

This dissertation develops a quantitative model designed for use in the evaluation of the relative merits of alternative energy R&D programs. As an example of the type of problem that can be addressed with the model, it is used to compare some of the relative merits of three major energy-technology R&D programs that are currently being pursued by the Energy Research and Development Administration (ERDA). These programs are:

- o Liquid-metal fast breeder reactors
- o Synthetic fuels derived from coal and oil shale
- o Improved efficiency in end-use technologies.*

The relative merits are assessed in terms of the marginal benefit/disbenefit that would be attributable to the commercialization of the energy technologies developed by these programs. The benefits and disbenefits are stated in terms of:

- o Economics
- o Security
- o Environment.

The economic benefit is assessed in terms of the impact that commercialization of a particular energy-technology would have on the total 60-year cost of the United States energy supply system. The security benefit is measured in terms of the reduction in crude oil imports. Of the many possible measures of environmental disbenefit for the United States energy system, the measure used here is the total tonnage of coal and oil shale that is extracted each year.

This dissertation also provides a consistent methodology for evaluating the interaction between the benefits/disbenefits of these R&D programs.** It is the thesis of this dissertation that the benefits attributable to individual R&D programs should be evaluated in terms of

---

*E.g., more efficient automobile engines, space heaters, etc.

**Some of the individual merits of two of these programs have been evaluated in recent studies of the liquid-metal fast breeder reactor program (Atomic Energy Commission, 1974b) and the synthetic fuels commercialization program (Synfuels Interagency Task Force, 1975).

how they contribute as an integral part of the overall energy R&D effort, rather than in isolation as has typically been done in the past. A first attempt at such an integrated view of the benefits attributable to energy R&D was made in ERDA's recently formulated long-range energy R&D plan (ERDA-48, 1975). However, the associated analysis was seriously limited because an efficient and adequate dynamic model was not then available. The objective of this dissertation is to provide such a model.

The model developed here is dynamic in that it explicitly adjusts the rate of capacity buildup for energy conversion facilities (e.g., refineries, power plants, etc.) and the rate of resource depletion in order to minimize the cost of satisfying energy demands over a 60-year time horizon. This contrasts with the static model used in the ERDA-48 analysis, where the maximum capacity for energy conversion facilities and the cost of energy resources had to be assumed for future years of interest.

The characteristics and the assumptions that were incorporated in the present model were carefully tailored to reflect its intended use as an aid in evaluating the relative merits of major energy R&D programs. This is vitally important for a dynamic model because, in general, they tend to be quite cumbersome and expensive to use, since the relationships embodied in them must be repeated for a number of different time periods. The model developed here is extremely efficient* for a dynamic model because: 1) simplifying assumptions avoid nondecison-relevant features of the United States energy system; 2) some features of the system are represented in a way equivalent to, but more efficient than, previous representations; and 3) certain capabilities of the International Business Machines (IBM) 370/165 computer system and the Mathematical Programming System's (IBM, 1971) linear programming package were exploited in order to significantly reduce the computer costs.

The effective application of this model in the government's R&D planning process requires a familiarity with both the specific role

---

*The average computer cost for a single run of this model is about \$10. This compares to an average cost of about \$250 for other related dynamic models (Stanford Research Institute, 1975; Bodin, et al., 1974).

proposed for it and the part this role plays in the government's overall role in energy R&D. Following a discussion of this overall federal role in energy R&D, the specific role that is proposed for the model is described and the scope of the model is outlined.

THE GOVERNMENT'S ROLE IN ENERGY R&D

The rationale for government's role in energy R&D centers on the answers to the following interrelated questions:

- o Should government intervene in energy R&D?
- o How much government intervention in energy R&D is necessary?
- o How should government intervene in energy R&D?
- o What should be the relative priorities assigned to the various energy R&D programs?

In this analysis, it is assumed that government intervention in energy R&D is necessary at about the currently proposed level since the focus here is on evaluating the relative merits of major energy R&D programs. However, in the course of examining some of the relative merits of the three major energy R&D programs considered here, it is possible to draw some inferences about the appropriate absolute funding levels for them.

Rationale for Government Intervention

Should government intervene in energy R&D? Although the emphasis here will be on where government should place its emphasis in energy R&D, and not on whether it should intervene at all, it is relevant to note that Tilton (1974) has recently analyzed the following frequently-cited reasons for such intervention: 1) misappropriation of benefits, 2) the public good from environmental quality, 3) imperfect knowledge in the private sector due to high private information collection costs, 4) distortion of private R&D expenditures due to regulation and 5) distortion of private R&D expenditures due to monopoly power.

Whether these reasons are really the major ones is argued at some length by the reviewers of the Tilton monograph. Most of the reviewers argue that the government's basic role is to assure that the energy supply system operates as efficiently as possible, subject to appropriate accounting for nonmarketplace social goals. While recognizing the importance of this role, Holloman, et al. (1975) emphasize the need to consider "the goal of moderating those consequences of the operation of the energy system that produce significant social cost" as well. For example:

- o Operation of the system may lead to unacceptable consequences for the physical environment in the absence of positive government action of some sort;
- o Certain operations of the system may be subject to failure, leading to damage or loss of life;
- o The system may be subject to shocks beyond the control of any part of the system which would intolerably impair the ability to deliver energy to society or produce short-term unacceptable social costs.

Since private firms are very unlikely to take all of these social costs into account in their planning, these issues seem to fall within the province of governmental responsibility.

The Extent of Government Intervention

How much government intervention in energy R&D is necessary? One of the first widely publicized manifestations of increased governmental concern about energy R&D was the publication in December 1973 of the Ray report (Ray, 1973). This report was the AEC chairwoman's response to President Nixon's June 1973 request for a review of federal funding of energy R&D and recommendations for "...an integrated energy research and development program for the nation." The Ray report recommended how ten billion dollars should be spent on energy R&D over the five year period 1975 to 1979. Alternatively, Senator Henry Jackson, D-Washington, proposed the allocation of twenty billion dollars over ten years, primarily for nonnuclear energy R&D (Perry, 1973).

Already, there has been a sharp increase in the growth rate of government energy R&D expenditures from 3.2 per cent per year for the FY 1963-1973 time period to 48.8 per cent for the FY 1973-1975 time period based on a 1572 million dollar estimate of government expenditures in FY 1975 (Tilton, 1974). As a consequence of this growth, public expenditures on energy R&D have doubled from FY 1973 to FY 1975, exceeding private expenditures for the first time during FY 1975. This substantial expansion in government expenditures on energy R&D has increased the need for the development of efficient computational procedures that can be applied in a timely fashion in order to enhance the effectiveness of the government's energy R&D planning process.

Mode of Government Intervention

How should government intervene in energy R&D? Although present government policy seems to favor direct funding of energy R&D, it is important to realize that this is only one way in which the government can increase the nation's energy R&D effort. It can also directly stimulate private energy R&D funding by establishing joint industry-government R&D programs, guaranteeing loans for the construction of demonstration plants, issuing purchase contracts, etc. Finally, it can indirectly stimulate private funding of energy R&D by broader policy measures like import quotas, import tariffs, energy taxes, and the like. The pros and cons of these various means of stimulating the national effort in energy R&D have been discussed elsewhere (e.g., Tilton, 1974, and Holloman, et al., 1975), but the appropriate policy (or mix of policies) probably depends on both the nature of the technology being considered and its stage of development.

It is interesting to note that the Synthetic Fuels Task Force Report (1975) recommends almost no direct government funding of the synthetic fuels commercialization program, while the Liquid-Metal Fast Breeder Reactor Environmental Impact Statement (Atomic Energy Commission, 1974b) recommends almost complete federal funding of the liquid-metal fast breeder reactor program. These two programs are obviously at different stages of development. Nonetheless, there is considerable controversy at present over whether the recommended forms of government intervention in the two cases are based solely on fundamental differences in the technologies and their stages of development.

Although the establishment of ERDA was a first step towards the coordination of the nation's energy efforts, the close interplay between energy R&D policy and other energy policies probably necessitates an even greater level of coordination. Ultimately, not only a unified federal energy R&D program is desirable, but a unified overall federal energy program as well. In fact, many (e.g., Ray, 1973; Tilton, 1974; and Holloman, et al., 1975) have argued for the establishment of a single agency (a cabinet-level Department of Energy and Resources, say) with precisely this responsibility. However, such an agency would still be confronted with the problem of setting R&D priorities.

Determination of R&D Priorities

What should be the relative priorities of the various energy R&D programs? The final report of the Ford Energy Policy Project (1974) and the Federal Energy Administration's Project Independence Report (1974a) are neither decisive nor consistent in recommending how much to spend on energy R&D, who should spend it, when, or on what. Although a sizeable amount of data has been collected on some of the major energy technologies (e.g., Atomic Energy Commission, 1974b, on the proposed liquid-metal fast breeder reactor program, and the President's Synfuels Interagency Task Force, 1975, on the proposed synthetic fuels commercialization program), the conclusions that have been drawn from this information remain highly controversial.

This controversy has served to emphasize the need for the consistent evaluation of the interactions between the impacts which would stem from alternative energy R&D programs (c.f. ERDA-48, 1975). Furthermore, individuals who have been exposed to conflicting reports like "The Fast Breeder as a Cornerstone of Future Large Energy Supplies," (Haefele, 1973), and "Bypassing the Breeder: A Report on Misplaced Federal Energy Priorities," (Cochran, et al., 1975), have begun to appreciate the immensity of the problem of selecting appropriate R&D priorities. The model developed in this dissertation is designed to aid in the setting of these priorities by providing a consistent basis for the relative examination of the marginal benefits that would be accrued as a consequence of alternative energy R&D programs.

PROPOSED ROLE FOR THE MODEL IN THE ENERGY R&D PLANNING PROCESS

Figure 1-1 is a schematic representation of the proposed role for the model in the R&D planning process. A wide range of issues are considered in R&D planning deliberations. The model developed here can help to answer three of the many questions that typically arise during such deliberations: 1) Does the R&D on a new energy-technology concept need to start now? 2) How much would the new energy-technology

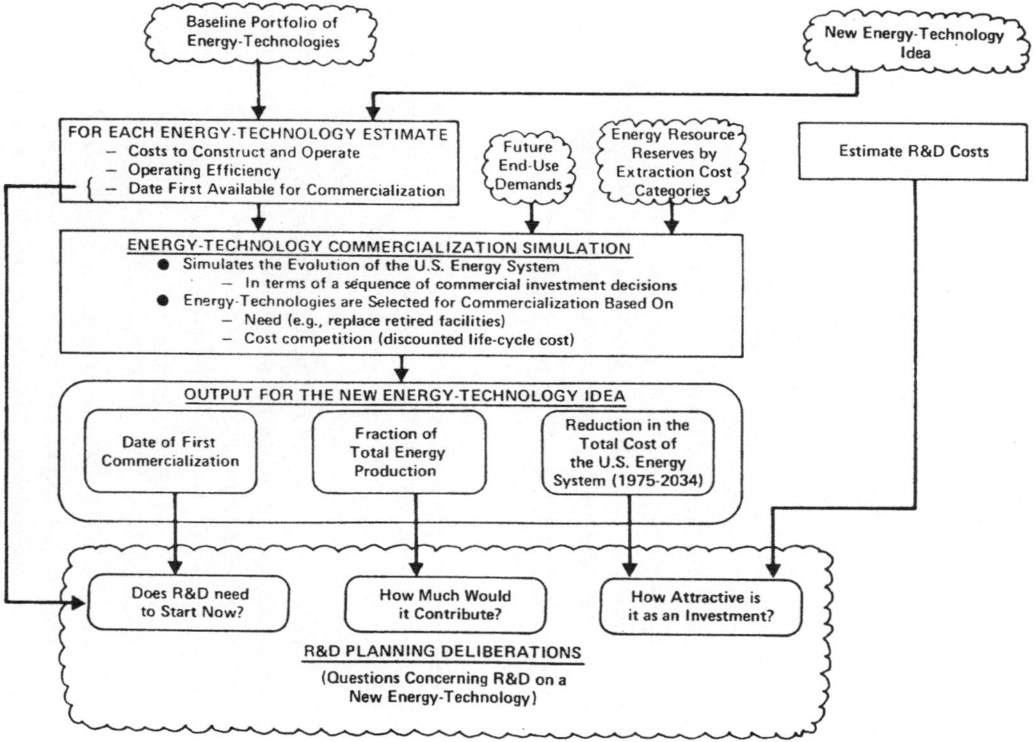

Fig. 1-1 — Proposed role of the model in the R&D planning process

ultimately contribute to total energy production? 3) How attractive is the R&D program as an investment in terms of the marginal benefits/disbenefits that would be attributed to the commercialization of the new energy-technology?

The model simulates the evolution of the United States energy system in order to provide relative information that is relevant to these three questions. First, the model provides the date at which the first actual commercialization takes place for the new energy technology. This simulated commercialization date can be compared to the availability date goals of the proposed R&D program to help ascertain whether the R&D program could be postponed without serious economic penalty. Second, the model determines the contribution of the new energy-technology to the total level of United States energy production. Third, the model can be used to determine the impact that the new energy-technology would have on the total discounted cost of running the United States energy supply system from 1975 through 2034.

The assigned R&D planning objective is the evaluation of the relative benefits/disbenefits of new energy conversion technologies and various combinations of these technologies. The present model assists in the accomplishment of this objective by computing the configuration of the United States energy system that minimizes the cost of meeting end-use demands both with and without inclusion of the new energy technology. The inclusion of a base case scenario in which no new technological incentives are assumed to be taken makes it possible to evaluate the marginal benefit of an R&D program that is intended to develop a particular technology or set of technologies, as well as to compare the relative merits of particular technologies or groups of technologies. This approach is used in the example application of the model (Chapter 4) in order to provide an illustration of the proposed role for the model in the R&D planning process. In that example, assessments are made of the relative benefits attributable to liquid-metal fast breeder reactors, synfuels derived from coal and oil shale, and improved end-use efficiency technologies.

One impact, the reduction in the total cost of the energy supply system that is attributable to the new energy-technology, can be compared with the projected R&D cost to help evaluate the R&D investment from an economic benefit standpoint. Security is another benefit from the R&D investment that is quantified by the model in terms of the reduction in energy imports. An environmental disbenefit that is calculated is the total annual tonnage of coal and oil shale that is extracted.

This general approach is similar to that used in ERDA's analysis of its long-range plan (ERDA-48, 1975). However, as previously indicated, the model employed here is dynamic as opposed to the static model used in ERDA-48. This dynamic model allows for consideration of the buildup of energy conversion capacity and - coupled with an extension of the year 2000 time horizon used in ERDA-48 through the year 2034 - allows for consideration of the impact of the depletion of low-cost domestic oil and gas reserves. The focus here is also more on the interplay between the impacts of the candidate R&D programs than the analysis in ERDA-48. For example, the impact of the development of a coal-synthetic fuels industry is evaluated with and without inclusion of nuclear breeder reactors.

THE SCOPE OF THE MODEL

Research and development planners face the exceedingly difficult task of trying to forecast four interrelated parameters: 1) project cost, 2) time of project completion, 3) performance of the project's product, and 4) the worth of the project's product once developed. Here the focus is on using values for the second and third parameters in order to assess the value of the fourth parameter. This is accomplished with a model that simulates the evolution of the United States energy system in terms of a sequence of commercial investment decisions that are occasioned by new energy demands or the retirement of old energy facilities.

The simulation of the sequence of commercial investment decisions requires that a new energy-technology compete with both existing technologies and other new technologies as well. The analysis of the benefits attributable to a new energy-technology may thus include an evaluation of the marginal economic benefit relative to a number of energy technology portfolios including existing and potential new energy-technologies.

Obviously, many tradeoffs exist between the funds allocated to a particular R&D project, when it is completed, and the performance characteristics of the resulting energy-technology. Rather than explicitly model all of these complex interrelationships, the approach taken here is to use technology availability dates (i.e., the date at which a technology is assumed to be first available for commercialization) and performance characteristics for energy-technologies as input to the model. The only other data required by the model are projections of the levels of future end-use demands and energy resource availabilities.

The energy-technology performance characteristics are stated in terms of: 1) the costs to construct and operate facilities to implement a given energy-technology (i.e., commercialization), and 2) the operating efficiencies of such facilities. These performance characteristics are assumed to be a direct consequence of the R&D that is proposed for the specified energy-technology.

The Goal for the United States Energy System

The assumed goal, or objective, represented in the model is minimization of the present value of the cost of the United States energy supply system over a 60-year period. The model, in effect, explores the impact of the introduction of alternative energy conversion technologies on this cost. Environmental and security factors may be externally considered through appropriate interpretation of the simulation results. Constraints which sum environmental impacts could also be added to aid in that endeavor if that was deemed to be desirable. Parameterization of such environmental constraints would allow for system-wide tradeoffs between costs and environmental impacts. Knowledge of such tradeoffs could be used in the setting of pollution standards.

Although minimization of the present value of the cost of the United States energy supply system is the explicit goal represented in the model, other energy system goals are implicitly considered. The three major goals for the United States energy R&D program outlined in the Ray report (Ray, 1973) and considered here are: 1) low cost energy (to ensure economic prosperity), 2) environmental quality, and 3) secure energy supplies. One might argue for directly reducing these three objectives to the single objective of low cost energy by assigning explicit costs for air pollution damages (c.f. Argonne National Laboratory, 1973) and for expected supply interruptions (c.f. Federal Energy Administration, 1974a).

In the present model, however, environmental goals are explicitly considered only insofar as they affect the cost of the various energy conversion facilities. Neither nonmarketplace socio-economic costs (e.g., costs for respiratory ailments caused by emissions of sulfur oxides), nor vulnerability costs (e.g., expected costs of an oil embargo as a function of the level of imports) are explicitly considered in the model. Nonetheless, such objectives can be externally considered, because the model outputs include the level of oil imports, coal production, oil shale production, etc. Such outputs can be used in the comparison of alternative R&D programs in order to account for various security, social, and environmental goals.

The Advantage of a Narrow Scope

The information generated by this model should be useful to decision makers in that it provides them with an assessment of the relative gross benefits of the various energy R&D programs which can be easily explained in terms of the inputs to the model. Thus, when the decision maker encounters results that conflict with his intuitive assessment of a particular issue, he can readily discern a simple explanation of why such results were obtained. This feature is a direct result of the narrow scope that was set for the present model.

Support for this approach can be found in a Rand study, by Weyant and Ojdana (1976), of R&D planning models that were considered for application by the Air Force. In that study, it was found that models that try to completely allocate an R&D budget are rarely implemented on a regular basis, primarily because the planner believes he is losing control of the planning process. R&D planning models designed to function as management information systems are much more likely to be adopted than those designed to function as budget allocators. Other contributing factors to this outcome are: 1) "comprehensive" R&D planning models tend to become so unwieldy that it is sometimes impossible to discern simple cause and effect mechanisms; and 2) it is probably not possible to include all relevant features of the R&D

planning process in any quantitative model. In light of these observations, the narrow scope of the model developed here seems to be a highly desirable characteristic for a model that is intended to assist in the R&D planning process.

ORGANIZATION OF THE DISSERTATION

This dissertation is organized to first meet the interests of the energy R&D planner. The main body provides a conceptual description of the model (Chapter 3), the results of the example application of the model to the evaluation of the three major energy R&D programs of interest (Chapter 4), and an R&D policy interpretation of those results (Chapter 5). The results and these policy interpretations are summarized in Chapter 2 in order to provide a condensed version of the essential rationale for using this type of model in the R&D planning process. Finally, Chapter 6 discusses some other potential applications for the model.

The energy modeling community will also be interested in the Appendices. Appendix A describes how the present model relates to other energy models. The algebraic formulation of the model is presented in Appendix B. The advantage of the representation of electrical generation capacity load sharing used in the model over previous representations is demonstrated in Appendix C. Finally, the data used in the example analysis (Chapter 4) is summarized in Appendix D.

Chapter 2

SUMMARY OF THE EXAMPLE APPLICATION

This dissertation provides a dynamic model of the United States energy system that is designed to be an efficient tool for comparing the potential economic, security, and environmental benefits/disbenefits attributable to alternative energy R&D programs. The use of the model is illustrated with an example application to three sets of new energy-technologies:

- o Liquid-metal fast breeder reactors
- o Synthetic fuels derived from coal and oil shale
- o Improved efficiency in end-use technologies.

These three sets of new energy-technologies are evaluated in terms of eight R&D program scenarios, each of which assumes the successful development of one of the possible combinations (including none) of the three sets of technologies. The model results for these eight scenarios are used to assess the relative benefits of the three sets of new energy technologies. Possible interactions among the benefits of the various programs are also considered.

NATURE OF THE RESULTS

Results are generated for each of the eight scenarios by employing an optimization model that explicitly adjusts the buildup of capacity for energy conversion facilities for both existing and new technologies that are assumed to be available. The model also adjusts the rate of depletion of domestic resources over time in order to minimize the cost of operating the U.S. energy supply system over the next 60 years. The relative differences in the minimum costs for the various scenarios are used to assess the gross economic benefits of each of the three energy R&D programs conditioned on the availability or lack of availability of the new technologies in the other programs.

Resource import and extraction rates are also compared to assess the validity of the scenarios and to provide other dimensions to the assessment of the benefits of the alternative R&D programs. For example, the level of imports is used to provide a quantifiable measure of the security benefit, and the total annual tonnage of coal and oil shale extracted is used to provide a quantifiable measure of one possible environmental disbenefit.

Finally, the sensitivity of the benefits/disbenefits to variations in the nominal oil and gas availability and imported oil price assumptions is investigated.

ENERGY R&D POLICY FINDINGS

The principal finding of the example application is that the economic benefits calculated for the three programs are in reverse order to the funding levels proposed in ERDA's FY 1976 budget. The liquid-metal fast breeder reactor currently has the largest share of the budget (301 million dollars), synfuels the second largest share (268 million dollars), and improved efficiency in end-use technologies the smallest share (148 million dollars). These budget requests are shown in the first column of Table 2-1 which summarizes the economic results of the example application.

In the base case scenario none of the three new technologies are assumed to be developed. If an improved efficiencies in end-use program is added to this base case scenario, a projected R&D investment cost of 1 billion dollars (in 1974 present value terms*) would be incurred assuming continued funding of this program at the currently proposed level for 12 years. Since the R&D investment is stated in present value terms (i.e., discounted), the estimate of the R&D program costs is not very sensitive to down-year changes in the funding level or the period of funding (e.g., the 12 years). Furthermore, it is found that the present value of the R&D program costs would have to change by an order of magnitude in order to effect the relative ordering of the economic benefits.

Improved End-Use Efficiencies

The marginal economic benefit attributable to the improved efficiencies in end-use program (relative to the base case scenario) would be from 279 to 334 billion dollars, depending upon alternative assumptions about the price of imported oil, and domestic oil and gas

---

*All present value calculations are based on a ten per cent annual "real" discount rate.

Table 2-1
Comparison of program R&D expenditures and marginal economic benefits

Energy-Technology R&D Program Scenarios	Federal Government R & D Expenditures: Proposed FY 1976 (Millions of 1976 Dollars)	Federal Government R & D Expenditures: Present Value for 1976-1987 (Estimate[b] in Billions of 1974 Dollars)	Marginal Economic Benefit: Reduction in the 60 Year Total Costs[a] of the U.S. Energy System (Billions of 1974 Dollars)	Marginal Economic Benefit Ratio (Marginal Economic Benefit / Present Value of FY 1976-1988 R & D Expenditures)
Base Case Scenario	0	0	0	—
+ Improved End-Use Efficiency Technologies	148	1	279-334[c]	279-334
+ Coal and Oil Shale Synthetics	268	1.8	0[d]-58	0-32
+ Liquid-Metal fast Breeder[e]	301	4.5	1-2	.2-.4

[a] Stated in 1974 present value terms at a 10% discount rate.

[b] Assumes continuation of FY 1976 funding level, except in the case of the breeder (see Atomic Energy Commission, 1974b).

[c] Range of values for the range of resource availability and import price assumptions (Synfuels Interagency Task Force Report, 1975; USGS Circular 725, 1975).

[d] There is zero benefit if oil import prices decline (e.g., less than $10/bbl until 2010; in 1974 dollars).

[e] Includes the Clinch River Program.

availability, which were derived from Synfuels Interagency Task Force (1975) and United States Geological Survey (1975) data. Finally, the resulting ratio of marginal economic benefit to the projected R&D investment cost is about 300 for the improved efficiencies in end use program on a stand-alone basis.

Synfuels

Now, if the synfuels program is added to a scenario that already includes improved end-use efficiencies, the present value of the incremental investment cost would be 1.8 billion dollars (again calculated by assuming continued funding at the currently proposed level for 12 years), and the marginal benefit-cost ratio would be 0-32 (corresponding to a 0-58 billion dollar range for the marginal economic benefits), with the zero value corresponding to a collapse of the world oil cartel. Notice that the marginal benefit-cost ratio for the synfuels program is an order of magnitude lower than that for the improved efficiencies in end-use program. Even if the synfuels program is added to the base case scenario on a stand-alone basis (i.e., no improved end-use efficiency technologies are assumed to be available), the marginal benefit-cost ratio is of the same order of magnitude. This is why the improved end-use efficiencies program (which has the higher benefit-cost ratio) was added to the base case scenario before the synfuels program.

The Breeder

Finally, if the liquid-metal fast breeder reactor (LMFBR) program is added to a scenario that already assumes development of improved end-use efficiency devices and synfuels, its marginal economic benefit ratio would be .4 or less (a marginal economic benefit of 1-2 billion dollars divided by a 4.5 billion dollar R&D investment cost). This means that less than one-half of the LMFBR R&D costs would be recovered in the form of economic benefits. If synfuels are not already in the R&D investment portfolio, the benefit-cost ratio for the LMFBR is .2. The subsequent addition of the synfuels program actually increases the ratio to .4, since the introduction of synfuels causes a shortage of low-cost coal for electric generation, which makes the breeder somewhat more attractive. Even if the LMFBR program had been added to the base case scenario on a stand-alone basis, its marginal benefit-cost ratio would still only have been 1.1-1.3.

Setting Energy R&D Priorities

The order of magnitude differences in the benefit-cost ratios shown here suggests, perhaps, that the federal energy R&D priorities should be set in terms of improved end-use efficiencies first, then synfuels, and finally, LMFBRs. Besides not being a very attractive financial investment, the LMFBR program also makes little contribution to the national goal of energy independence; breeder generated electricity can not be readily used in the petrochemical or transportation sectors, which are the only major consumers of petroleum products left by the time the LMFBR becomes economically competitive. Only with the introduction of electric or hydrogen powered transportation vehicles could the breeder make a contribution towards the independence goal. Development of these technologies to the point of economic competitiveness with conventional transportation vehicles does not seem plausible in this country until well into the next century.

A synfuels program can be further justified on the basis of national energy security. For example, without the synfuels program, the United States will either be paying very high extraction costs (e.g., \$25/bbl or more in 1974 dollars) for dwindling domestic crude oil, or otherwise be importing from 50 to 100 per cent of its oil within 25 to 50 years. Although the environmental disbenefits associated with synfuels may be significant (especially in the absence of appropriate R&D), they may be the price that must be paid for energy independence. Unfortunately, the fact that a marginal economic benefit of zero might result (e.g., if the cartel collapses) is probably discouraging private investment in synfuels and thereby retarding commercialization.

Finally, the improved efficiencies in end-use program appears to be an attractive investment opportunity regardless of the future resource supply situation. Furthermore, it makes significant contributions towards both the nation's energy security and environmental goals.

RECOMMENDATIONS

It is recommended that a model, such as the one developed here, be used to support future deliberations concerned with planning the relative R&D priorities for major activities like the three programs that were evaluated here. This recommendation is supported by the example application of the present model which has indicated that:

- Improved end-use efficiency technologies have both a short-run benefit through a reduction in the rate of energy consumption and a long-run benefit through the deferment of the depletion of the lower cost category domestic resources;
- Synthetic liquid fuels derived from coal and/or oil shale are essential to any effort towards energy independence and, consequently, have potentially large economic and security benefits;
- Breeder economic benefits have an extremely low present value, in part, because they will take many years to materialize, especially if improved end-use technologies are developed. Furthermore, the breeder makes no contribution towards achieving the goal of national energy independence.

Chapter 3

DESCRIPTION OF THE MODEL CONCEPT

The overview of the U.S. energy system model provided in this chapter is intended to familiarize the reader with the general concept of the model by providing an introduction and a general description of the model without getting involved with the precise details of the linear programming formulation. The details of the actual algebraic formulation are contained in Appendix B.

First, the model concept is introduced in terms of its time phasing, the activities of the United States energy system that are explicitly represented in it and its inputs and outputs. Next, the structure of the model is described in a little more detail in order to provide a conceptual description of how it works. The chapter closes with a brief discussion of how the model was simplified in order to make it an economical R&D planing tool. This involved the linearization of the total resource cost term and other simplifications that make the model a practical R&D planning tool.

INTRODUCTION TO THE MODEL CONCEPT

In this section, the model concept is introduced in terms of the selection of the time horizon and the lengths for the individual time periods used to represent that time horizon. Next, the activities of the United States energy supply system that are explicitly represented in the model are delineated. Finally, a description of the model's principal inputs and outputs is given.

Time Phasing of the Model

The time phasing of the model was handled in a manner suggested by Manne (1974b). In this approach, the time horizon of the model is broken up into several time periods, with the midpoint years of the periods termed "representative years." Demands are specified only for these representative years, which therefore, approximate the average rate of demand over the entire time period. The time period is identified by the subscript p.*

The total time frame selected for the model was based on a desire to consider the impact of the depletion of low-cost domestic oil and gas reserves. Recent United States Geological Survey (1975) estimates of the magnitude of these resources suggest that a sixty-year time frame is adequate for this purpose.

The lengths of the individual time periods that were used to represent this time frame were determined by consideration of the tradeoff between an adequate representation of new technology introduction (which argues for short time periods) and computational limits (which argues for long time periods). The present formulation consists of three seven-year time periods, followed by a nine-year period and two fifteen-year periods. The length of time period number p will be designated by L_p. The time-phasing for this six-period formulation is illustrated in Table 3-1. Note that this choice of time periods yields 1985 and 2000 as representative years. This allows for a comparison of the present results with the results of most of the analyses that have been performed to date using static models to compute equilibria for either or both of these two years (e.g., ERDA-48, 1975).

Representation of the U.S. Energy System

A delineation of the activities explicitly represented in the model is given in Fig. 3-1. The left-hand side of this figure gives a breakdown of the energy resource supply categories, while the right-hand side gives a breakdown of the end-use demands.

In the center of the figure, solid lines are used to represent activities explicitly represented in the model, while dashed lines are used to represent activities that are only implicitly represented in the model. Activities that are only implicitly considered are not allowed to compete with other activities on an economic basis. These activities do, however, have an impact on the evolution of the energy system in terms of the depletion of resources and the satisfaction of some of the

---

*The conceptual description of the model in this chapter will rely on a simplified set of nomenclature that was devised for the present illustrative purposes. The actual algebraic formulation that was used to implement the model (Appendix B) is necessarily developed in terms of a much more detailed nomenclature.

Table 3-1

TIME PHASING OF THE MODEL

Time Period (p)	Length of Time Period in Years (L_p)	Range of Calendar Years	Representative Calendar Year
1	7	1975-1981	1978
2	7	1982-1988	1985
3	7	1989-1995	1992
4	9	1996-2004	2000
5	15	2005-2019	2012
6	15	2020-2034	2027

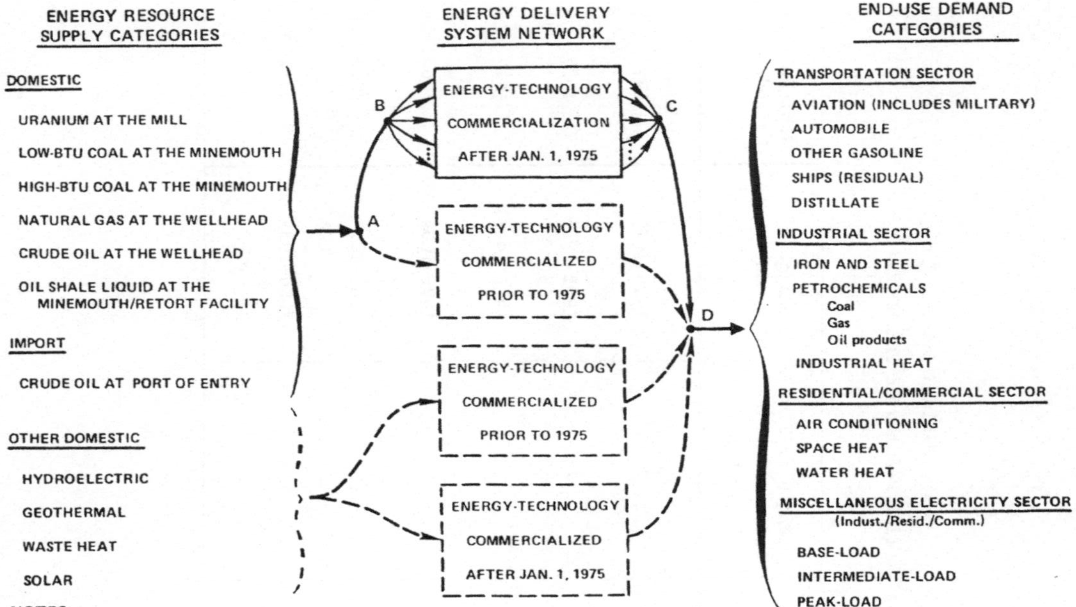

NOTES:

(1) Solid elements are explicitly represented in the simulation.

(2) Dashed elements are implicitly represented by accounting for their contribution to resource depletion (node A) and demand satisfaction (node D).

(3) Each arc connecting nodes B and C represents a new commercialization activity of some vintage (say p) that follows an energy-technology-trajectory (say t) through the network representing the energy delivery system.

Fig. 3-1 — Representation of the U.S. Energy System

end-use demands. These impacts are explicitly accounted for. Figure 3-1 shows that all energy conversion facilities existent before 1975, as well as new hydroelectric, geothermal, waste heat, and solar facilities, are only implicitly represented in the model.

Figure 3-1 also shows that demands are to be specified by end use (e.g., aviation, water heat, etc.). Demands are more realistically estimated by end use. Consideration of end-use demands necessitates the inclusion of appropriately aggregated utilization devices and their corresponding efficiencies in the model. Analyses based on historical data in which demands are considered by fuel (e.g., coal, electricity, etc.) may not capture the impact of the fundamental discontinuity in real fuel prices that occurred two years ago, when real fuel prices suddenly reversed their traditional downward trend. Historical data on fuel demands was gathered during an era when people were being replaced by machines. These machines required energy to run them and so energy and capital have historically been complements. Now that these machines have been developed, it is possible that in the face of rising fuel prices, the most favorable economic course to follow will be to make these machines more energy efficient by substituting capital for energy.

Consideration of demands by end use also allows for a more adequate representation of demands and demand elasticities as it allows for a more adequate projection of the impacts of satiation and subsistence effects. In addition, by specifying demands by end use, the efficiencies of the end-use utilizing devices can be explicitly represented, which is desirable as improved efficiencies in end-use is one of the major energy R&D programs considered in the example application of the model in Chapter 4.

Inputs and Outputs

The principal inputs and outputs which are specified for each time period are summarized in Fig. 3-2. The inputs include the supplies of the various energy resources at the beginning of the first period (i.e., the beginning of 1975), the levels of end-use demands (e.g., space heat) for each period, and the energy conversion process technologies that are assumed to be available for commercialization during each period. Resource availabilities are represented in two different manners in the model: domestic resources are classified by extraction cost category

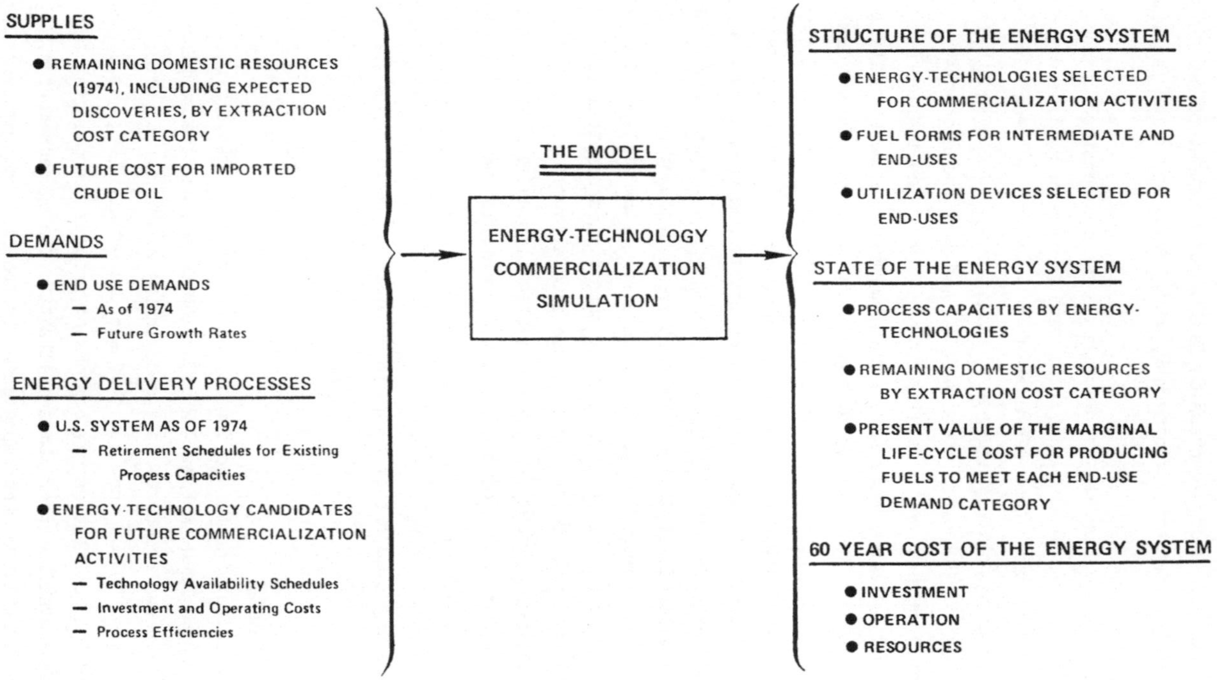

Fig. 3-2— Principal inputs and outputs

with the cost of the resource rising with cumulative extraction; the price of imported oil is input as a function of time.

The formulation of the end-use demand inputs starts with estimates for end-use demand growth rates that are applied to the 1974 levels of end-use demands. This yields a projection of gross end-use demands over time. This projection is then adjusted in order to subtract out the demands that will be satisfied by either: 1) energy conversion process facilities already in existence as of the end of 1974, or 2) facilities that process the "other domestic" energy resources listed in Fig. 3-1. In order to construct these "net end-use demands", retirement schedules are applied to energy conversion process facilities existing at the end of 1974 in order to represent their retirement from the United States energy system. The contribution of these facilities, as well as of the other non-explicitly represented elements of the energy supply system shown in Fig. 3-1, are then subtracted from the projected gross end-use energy demands to obtain net end-use demands that are provided to the model for each time period.

The final input category consists of the energy conversion process technology candidates which are represented in terms of their technology availability dates, investment and operating costs, and process efficiencies. This information gets combined with the costs for the basic resources in order to determine which energy conversion process technology candidates actually get commercialized.

The outputs of the model describe the evolution of both the structure and the state of the United States energy system for each time period, as well as the sixty year total cost of the United States energy system. The structure of the energy system is described in terms of the type of energy conversion facilities actually built, the fuel forms selected for intermediate* and end uses, and the utilization devices selected to satisfy the end-use demands. For each time period, the state of the energy system is described by: 1) the total capacity level for all of the energy conversion processes of each technology type

---

*For example, coal or uranium are sources for electricity, whereas crude oil or shale oil are refinery feedstocks. In these cases electricity generation and refining are viewed as "intermediate uses" as opposed to "end uses" such as space heat and automobiles.

(e.g., liquid-metal fast breeder reactors), 2) the supplies of domestic resources still remaining by cost category, and 3) the marginal life-cycle cost for producing fuels to satisfy each end-use demand (stated in 1974 present value terms).

GENERAL DESCRIPTION OF THE STRUCTURE OF THE MODEL

The structure of the model is described in terms of a generalized energy system network and the commercialization activities that provide for the construction and operation of energy processing facilities along trajectories through the generalized energy system network.

Generalized Energy System Network

The energy system network formulation used here is a generalized version of the energy system flow concept used by the Brookhaven National Laboratory in their Reference Energy Systems (Associated Universities, 1972). Figure 3-3 shows a simplified example of a Brookhaven-like energy system network. This diagram traces the flow of energy from resource extraction through a series of processing and conversion steps to final end use. For example, one can trace the flow of coal from the ground through cleaning and transport by unit train to combustion in an industrial burner to supply process heat.

A particular sequence of such conversion processes represents what is termed a trajectory through the energy system. These trajectories link nodes B and C in Figure 3-1. However, the specification of a resource and a demand does not uniquely define a trajectory. For example, if low-Btu coal and industrial process heat are specified as the resource and end-use demand of interest, then the coal could be first converted to electricity and used in an electric oven or it could be burned directly in an industrial coal-fired furnace. Thus, there can be several candidate trajectories that link a given end-use demand to a specific resource. This bookkeeping dilemma is resolved by resorting to the following generalized network specification.

The generalized energy system network adopted here is far more complex than the simplified network shown in Fig. 3-3. Thus, only the basic elements used in its formulation will be described here (Fig. 3-4). These elements consist of distribution, collection, and process functions which are arranged to provide generalized representations of

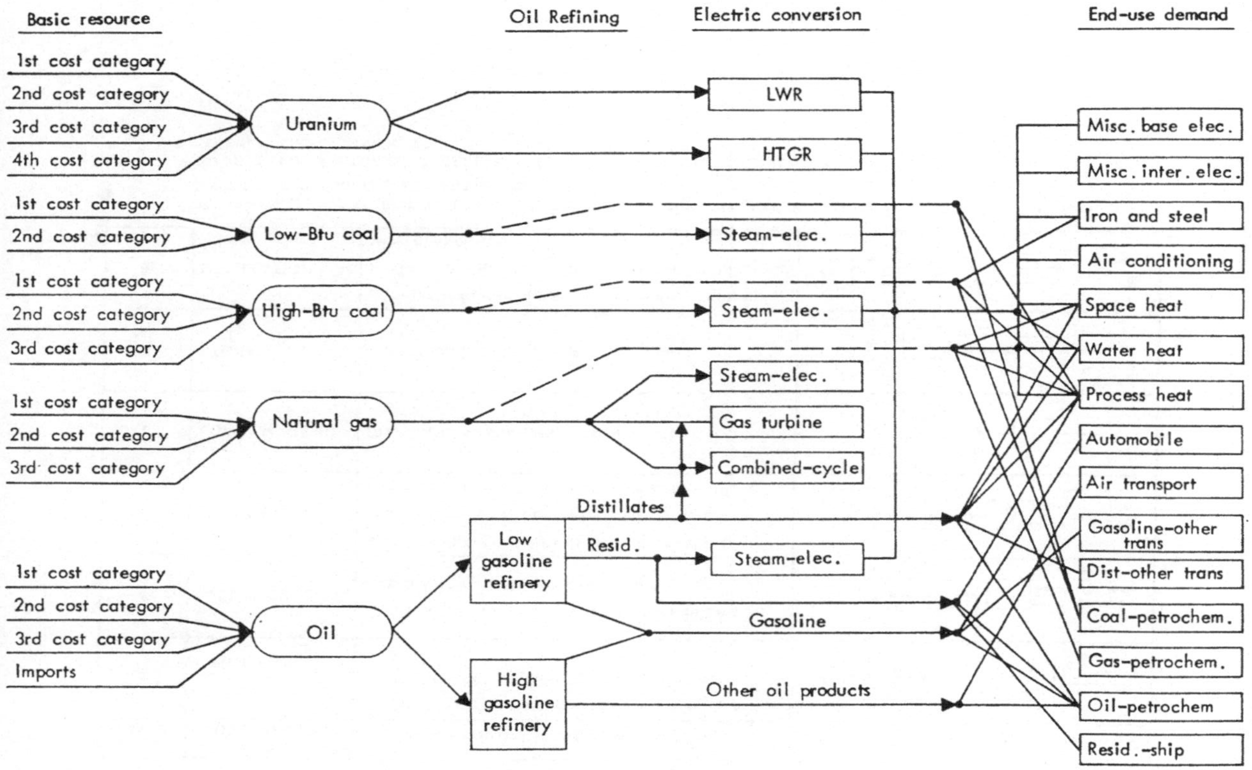

Fig. 3-3— Simplified example of an energy system network

STAGE NUMBER	STAGE DESCRIPTION	CLASSES OF ENERGY PROCESSING FACILITIES	FORMAT FOR STAGE ENERGY FLOW NETWORK[a]
3[b]	RAW MATERIAL PROCESSING	PLUTONIUM REPROCESSING; URANIUM CONVERSION; COAL LIQUEFACTION/GASIFICATION; SHALE OIL UPGRADING	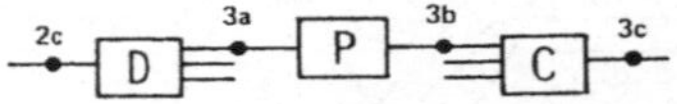
4	FUEL UPGRADING	BREEDER FUEL FABRICATION; URANIUM ENRICHMENT, FABRICATION AND REPROCESSING; REFINERIES	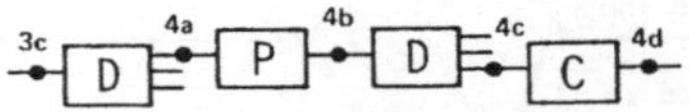
5	CONVERSION	NUCLEAR REACTORS (BREEDER, LIGHT WATER, HIGH TEMP. GAS COOLED); ELECTRICITY GENERATION (STEAM, COMBINED CYCLE, GAS TURBINE)	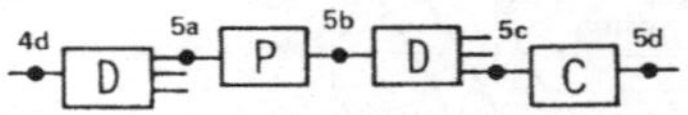
6	LOAD SHARING	DIURNAL LOAD SHARING, SEASONAL LOAD SHARING	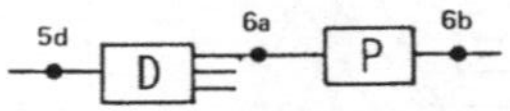
7	STORAGE	PLUTONIUM STORAGE, PUMPED STORAGE	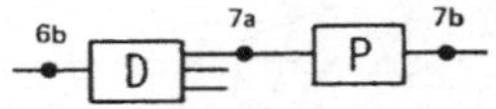
8	UTILIZATION	GAS TURBINES; GASOLINE ENGINES; DIESEL ENGINES; FURNACES; BURNERS; RESISTORS; VAPOR COMPRESSORS; MISCELLANEOUS	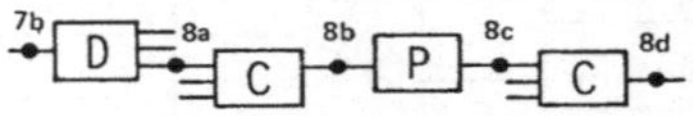

[a] BOXES REPRESENT DISTRIBUTION (D), PROCESS (P) AND COLLECTION (C) FUNCTIONS. LINES REPRESENT ENERGY FLOWS (LEFT TO RIGHT). NODES (e.g. 3a) ARE NETWORK REFERENCE POINTS.

[b] STAGES 1 AND 2 ARE FOR THE ARCS LEADING TO NODE B IN FIG. 3-1. SIMILARLY, STAGE 9 IS FOR THE ARCS LEADING TO NODE D IN FIG. 3-1.

Fig. 3-4 — Elements of the generalized energy system network

the various stages (e.g., fuel upgrading, conversion, etc.) in the energy system network. The energy conversion process trajectories must pass through each of the generalized conversion stages indicated in Fig. 3-4. Node reference points (e.g., 8dj) give the stage (8) and location (8d) in the network. For example, 8dj represents a notional collection of end-use energy forms from the various utilizing devices that satisfy a specific end-use demand category (say j). Thus the terminus of a trajectory is uniquely specified by the node designation 8dj. Each trajectory can then be identified by a sequence of such node designations which uniquely specify the path of the trajectory through the energy system.* However, a sequence of energy conversion facilities may be constructed along the same trajectory in different time periods. In order to incorporate this temporal distinction, the concept of a commercialization activity is now introduced.

The Commercialization Activity

A "commercialization activity" refers to a sequence of energy processing facilities that jointly initiate service in a particular time period (say $\overline{p}$) along a trajectory (say t).

Thus, a commercialization activity is uniquely specified by a vintage ($\overline{p}$) and a trajectory (t) and it is characterized by the capital cost, operating cost, and efficiency of the associated sequence of energy processing facilities. Because some energy is usually lost whenever its form is changed, the flow of energy that must be provided per unit of end-use demand increases from the end-use demand upstream towards the extraction of the resource for a particular commercialization activity. That the corresponding conversion facilities must be appropriately sized on account of these inefficiencies is reflected in the commercialization activity's cost characteristics.

Figure 3-5 provides a simplified example of a commercialization activity in terms of a chain of energy processing facilities that would be required to produce one unit of miscellaneous intermediate-load

---

*For example, the sequence of node designators 2c2, 3b4, 3c3, 4a4, 4c4, 4d9, 5b16, 5c20, 5d2, 6a2, 7b2, 8a19, 8c9, 8d7 represents the following trajectory: start with low-Btu coal, liquefy it, use the residual to generate electricity, use the electricity in a resistor to generate water heat.

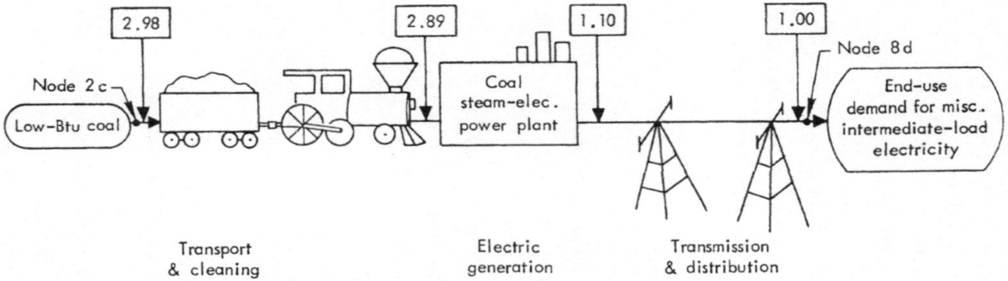

Profile of a "Commercialization Activity"

Energy Processing Facility	Energy flows to satisfy one unit of end-use demand	
	Input	Output
Coal transport and clean	2.98	2.89
Coal steam-elec. power plant	2.89	1.10
Electric transmission & distribution	1.10	1.00

The efficiency of the commercialization activity $= \frac{1.00}{2.98} = 0.34$

Fig. 3-5— Example of a "commercialization activity" along a trajectory through the generalized energy system network

electricity* from low-Btu coal. From this figure it is seen that, because of the inefficiencies of the various energy conversion processes, 2.98 units of energy in the form of low-Btu coal must flow by node 2c2 in order to provide one unit of energy in the form of miscellaneous intermediate-load electricity at node 8d2. The efficiency of a commercialization activity is defined as the amount of end-use energy that can be obtained from one unit of resource energy. In the present example, the efficiency of the commercialization activity may be calculated as 1.00/2.98 or .34.

The only energy flows that are explicitly considered here are commonly called primary energy flows, flows of the fuel resource itself. Ancillary energy flows, which are energy flows from outside the primary energy stream necessary for a particular energy conversion, are not explicitly modeled. Electricity needed to enrich (upgrade) nuclear fuels is an example of an ancillary energy requirement. Smith, Weyant, and Holdren (1975) have compiled data on the ancillary energy requirements for various energy conversion processes and found that only in the case of uranium enrichment and oil refining, are the ancillary energy requirements greater than one or two per cent and even then no greater than five percent of the corresponding primary energy flows. Furthermore, there is no reason to believe that these findings would be substantially altered for the new energy technologies considered in the next chapter. The energy required to construct the various energy conversion facilities is also not explicitly modeled here. Bullard, et al. (1975) have shown that these energy flows are not very significant as well. Thus, the impact of not explicitly modeling the ancillary and construction energy flows is not believed to be significant for the energy conversion processes considered herein.

The role of the commercialization activity as the model's basic building block is illustrated in Fig. 3-6. Construction of new energy facilities in period $\bar{p}$ is necessitated by either new end-use demands or the retirement of facilities used to satisfy a particular end-use

---

*Miscellaneous electric demands are those not included in the other end-use demand categories. These miscellaneous demands are further disaggregated according to the fraction of time over which they are assumed to occur. Base-load demands occur all the time; intermediate-load demands occur only about half the time; and peak-load demands occur only about ten per cent of the time.

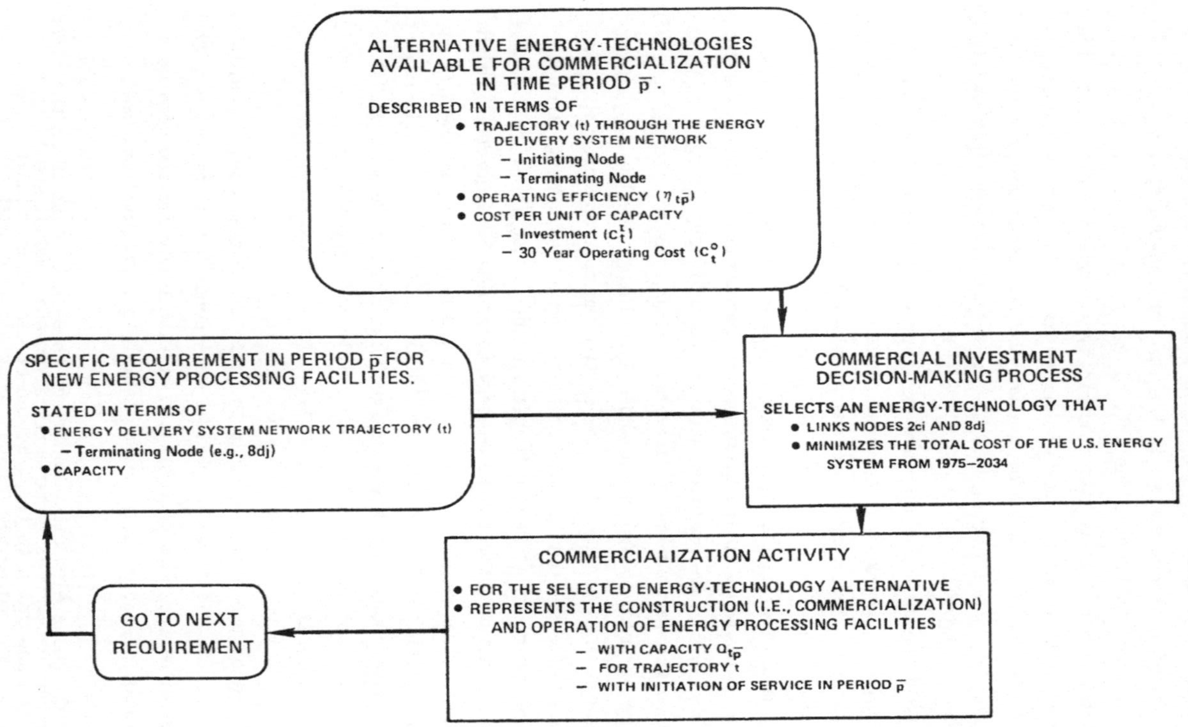

Fig. 3-6—Role of the "commercialization activity" as the model's basic building block

demand. The requirement for the construction of new energy processing facilities in period $\overline{p}$ is, in effect, stated in terms of the average annual energy flow for each terminating node (i.e., 8dj) that must be satisfied by facilities that comprise commercialization activities that are introduced into service during period $\overline{p}$.

The alternative energy technologies available for commercialization to satisfy these construction (or commercialization) requirements in period $\overline{p}$ are described in terms of a trajectory through the energy delivery system (t), the efficiency ($\eta_{t\overline{p}}$) of the commercialization activity, and the investment (C_t^I) and 30-year operating cost (C_t^O) for the commercialization activity.

The commercial investment decision-making process is in effect modeled by an algorithm that selects commercialization activities that provide the requisite energy flows at each terminating node (i.e., 8dj) in a way that minimizes the total sixty year cost of the United States energy system from 1975 through 2034. In aggregate, then, energy flows (or "capacities"), $Q_{t\overline{p}}$, are determined for each selected commercialization activity.

Selection of Commercialization Activities

Figure 3-7 is a schematic representation of the process whereby commercialization activities are selected. The representation here focuses on those activities that are explicitly represented in the model. The commercialization activity consists of a sequence of conversion facilities which are constructed to satisfy end-use demands that are driven by both the retirement of old energy conversion facilities and the growth in demands. The existence of these energy conversion facilities creates, in turn, demands for the various energy resources. The top portion of Fig. 3-7 shows that a commercialization activity's capacity is measured at its end point, so that the capacity $Q_{t\overline{p}}$ for a commercialization activity of vintage p and trajectory t requires the extraction of an amount of resource energy $Q_{t\overline{p}}^{2c}$ equal to the measured capacity, $Q_{t\overline{p}} = Q_{t\overline{p}}^{8d}$, divided by the efficiency, $\eta_{t\overline{p}}$, for the commercialization activity. The assumed 30-year lifetime for energy conversion facilities as well as the linear buildup and retirement of capacity assumptions are depicted in the center portion of the top of Fig. 3-7. The objective of the model is to select a least cost set

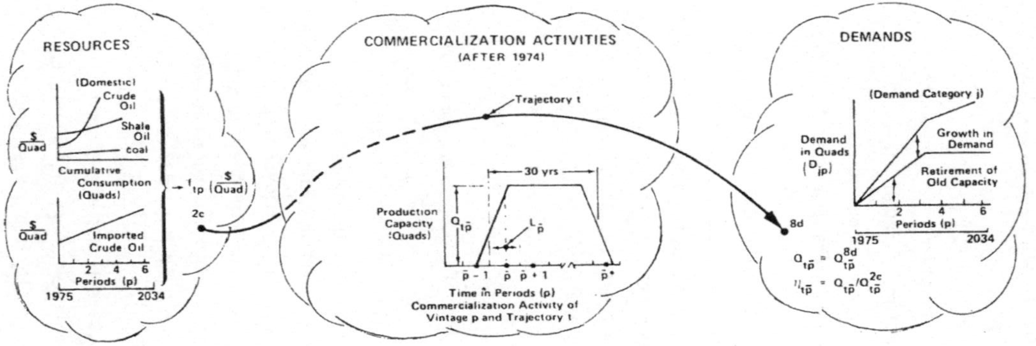

COMMERCIALIZATION ACTIVITY COST

$$\left\{\begin{array}{c}\text{Life-Cycle Cost for a Vintage } \bar{p} \\ \text{Activity Along Trajectory t} \\ \text{(in Terms of 1974 Present Value)}\end{array}\right\} = \left\{\left(\begin{array}{c}\text{Investment}\\ \text{Cost/Quad Out}\end{array}\right) + \left(\begin{array}{c}\text{30 yr Operating}\\ \text{Cost/Quad Out}\end{array}\right) + \left(\begin{array}{c}\text{30 yr Resource}\\ \text{Cost/Quad Out}\end{array}\right)\right\}\left(\begin{array}{c}\text{Activity}\\ \text{Capacity}\end{array}\right)$$

$$\overline{LCC}_{t\bar{p}} = \left\{ d_{\bar{p}} C_t^I + d_{\bar{p}\bar{p}^*} C_t^O + \frac{1}{\eta_{t\bar{p}}} \sum_{p=\bar{p}}^{\bar{p}^*} d_p L_p f_{tp} \right\} Q_{t\bar{p}}$$

(Discount at 10% from $\bar{p}$ to 1974) (Discount at 10% for the interval $\bar{p}$ through $\bar{p}^*$ to 1974)

COMMERCIALIZATION DECISION CRITERIA

THE SET OF COMMERCIALIZATION DECISIONS MADE BY THE SIMULATION YIELDS

- A Least Cost Set of Activities Over All Periods That
- Assures That All End-Use Demands are Satisfied through 2034

SIMULATION IMPLEMENTATION

$$\text{Min}\left(\sum_{\bar{p}=1}^{6}\left[\sum_{t\in T_{\bar{p}}}\left\{ d_{\bar{p}} C_t^I + d_{\bar{p}\bar{p}^*} C_t^O + \frac{1}{\eta_{t\bar{p}}}\sum_{p=\bar{p}}^{\bar{p}^*} d_p L_p f_{tp}\right\} Q_{t\bar{p}}\right]\right). \quad \text{Subject to} \sum_{\substack{\bar{p}=1 \\ \text{s.t. } \bar{p}^* \geq p}}^{p}\left[\sum_{t\in T_{\bar{p}j}} Q_{t\bar{p}}\right] \geq D_{jp} \; ; \left(\begin{array}{l} j = 1, 2, \ldots, 16 \\ p = 1, 2, \ldots, 6\end{array}\right).$$

Where $T_{\bar{p}}$ is the Set of Admissible Trajectories (i.e., Technologies) for Period $\bar{p}$, and $T_{\bar{p}j}$ is the Subset that Satisfy Demand Category j

Fig. 3-7— Selection of commercialization activities

of commercialization activity capacities over all periods that assures the satisfaction of end-use demands through 2034.

The cost for the construction of facilities for a particular commercialization activity is made up of three components: 1) the capital cost, 2) the operating cost, and 3) the energy resource cost. The sum of these three costs over the lifetime of the commercialization activity is referred to as its life-cycle cost ($\overline{LCC}_{t\overline{p}}$). This is depicted in the center portion of Fig. 3-7.

The bottom portion of Fig. 3-7 presents a conceptual representation of the model's implementation in terms of the minimization of an objective function subject to the constraint that all end-use demands are satisfied. The objective function is the sum of the life-cycle costs for all of the commercialization activities (i.e., the sum over all trajectories and time periods). Given values for the cost factors (C_t^I, C_t^O), the discount factors ($d_{\overline{p}}$, d_{pp*}), the commercialization activity efficiencies ($\eta_{t\overline{p}}$), the lengths of the time periods ($L_{\overline{p}}$), and the resorce costs as either a function of cumulative consumption (domestic resources) or time (imports), the model solves for the values of the commercialization activity production "capacities" ($Q_{t\overline{p}}$) for all trajectories and all time periods (i.e., for all of the candidate commercialization activities). A standard linear programming package is used to determine the solution.

SIMPLIFYING THE DYNAMIC MODEL

This section describes the key steps that were followed in order to formulate a viable and efficient linear programming implementation for this dynamic model of the United States energy system:

- o linearization of the total resource cost term
- o the commercialization activity concept
- o the full utilization of capacity assumption
- o the novel treatment of the load-sharing of electrical generation equipment.

Linearization of the Total Resource Cost Term

Those familiar with linear programming methods may have noticed that the function to be minimized at the bottom of Fig. 3-7 is nonlinear, since the total resource cost term involves the product of the resource cost variable (f_{tp}) and the commercialization activity production "capacity" variable ($Q_{t\overline{p}}$). This nonlinear term is linearized (see Fig. 3-8) by defining a new variable, E_{rip}, which represents the depletion of resource r in cost category i in period p. The total resource cost may then be alternatively represented in terms of the product of this new variable (E_{rip}) and the constant (C^R_{ri}) which represents the energy resource cost (e.g., domestic crude oil extraction cost). However, the introduction of this new variable also requires that constraints be added to assure that: 1) sufficient resources are extracted to meet the requirements of the U.S. energy system; and 2) the cumulative resources that are extracted in a given cost category do not exceed the total supply (S_{ri}) for that cost category.

Simplifying the Model

In general, in a dynamic model, it is necessary to define both production and capacity variables for each activity for each of several time periods. The size of such a model can very quickly become prohibitive. In order to cope with this problem, two simplifying assumptions were made. First, it was assumed that a set of dedicated energy processing facilities are constructed for entire paths through the energy system (e.g., from resource extraction to end-use) rather than for individual energy facilities. This assumption implies that individual energy facilities will be used to supply the same energy needs over their entire lifetime. This can be contrasted with the dynamic model of Bodin, et al. (1974), in which capacity is constructed for individual energy conversion facilities.

Second, it was assumed that once constructed, all capacity is fully utilized over its lifetime. This is a standard trick for simplifying dynamic models and, in fact, has been used in several recently formulated energy models (e.g., Haefele and Manne, 1975). This assumption eliminates the need for separate capacity and production variables for each activity as well as the need for any capacity constraints whatsoever. Several previous versions of the current model did allow for underutilization of capacity and capacity was, in fact, rarely underutilized. This was quite understandable since the underutilization of capacity tends to work against the objective of minimizing the total life-cycle cost of the United States energy system.

- INTRODUCE A NEW VARIABLE

E_{rip} = (AVERAGE ANNUAL EXTRACTION RATE (QUADS/YR) IN PERIOD p FOR RESOURCES OF TYPE r AND COST CATEGORY i)

AND TWO CONSTANTS

C^R_{ri} = (COST OF EXTRACTION ($/QUAD) FOR RESOURCES OF TYPE r AND COST CATEGORY i)

S_{ri} = (EXPECTED SUPPLY (QUADS) AS OF JAN 1, 1975 FOR RESOURCES OF TYPE r AND COST CATEGORY i)

- THEN THE TOTAL RESOURCE COST TERM MAY BE REPLACED WITH AN EQUIVALENT EXPRESSION IN TERMS OF E_{rip}

$$\sum_{\text{PERIODS}} \left\{ \sum_{\text{TRAJECTORIES}} \begin{pmatrix}\text{Life-cycle cost of resources}\\ \text{consumed by a vintage } \bar{p} \text{ activity}\\ \text{along trajectory } t\end{pmatrix} \right\} = \sum_{\substack{\text{RESOURCE}\\ \text{TYPES}}} \left[\sum_{\substack{\text{COST}\\ \text{CATEGORIES}}} \left\{ \sum_{\text{PERIODS}} \begin{pmatrix}\text{Cost in period } \bar{p} \text{ for the}\\ \text{extraction of resources of}\\ \text{type r and cost category i}\end{pmatrix} \right\} \right]$$

$$\sum_{\bar{p}=1}^{6} \sum_{t \in T_{\bar{p}}} \frac{1}{\eta_{t\bar{p}}} \left(\sum_{p=\bar{p}}^{\bar{p}^*} d_p L_p f_{tp} \right) Q_{t\bar{p}} = \sum_{r=1}^{5} \sum_{i=1}^{Nr} \sum_{\bar{p}=1}^{6} d_{\bar{p}} L_{\bar{p}} C^R_{ri} E_{ri\bar{p}}$$

SUBJECT TO THE CONSTRAINTS

$$\begin{pmatrix}\text{Total resources of}\\ \text{type r extracted in}\\ \text{period p}\end{pmatrix} - \begin{pmatrix}\text{Total resources of}\\ \text{type r consumed in period p}\end{pmatrix} \geqslant 0$$

$$\sum_{i=1}^{N_r} E_{rip} - \sum_{\substack{\bar{p}=1\\ \text{s.t.} \bar{p}^* \geqslant p}}^{p} \sum_{t \in T_{\bar{p}r}} \frac{1}{\eta_{t\bar{p}}} Q_{t\bar{p}} \geqslant 0 \qquad \begin{pmatrix} r = 1, 2, \ldots 5 \\ p = 1, 2, \ldots 6 \end{pmatrix}$$

$$\begin{pmatrix}\text{Total extraction}\\ \text{of resources of}\\ \text{type r and cost category i}\end{pmatrix} \leqslant \begin{pmatrix}\text{Expected supply of}\\ \text{resources of type r}\\ \text{and cost category i}\end{pmatrix}$$

$$\sum_{p=1}^{6} L_p E_{rip} \leqslant S_{ri} \qquad \begin{pmatrix} r = 1, 2, \ldots 5 \\ i = 1, 2, \ldots N_r \end{pmatrix}$$

Fig. 3-8—Linearization of the total resource cost term

Another simplification of the model involves the representation of the sharing of electic generation equipment by compatible pairs of peak and off-peak end-use demand categories. Previous models (e.g., in Bodin, et. al., 1974) represented this load sharing potential in terms of both a variable and a constraint for each type of electric generation technology for each type of load sharing considered for each time period. The present model only requires a variable (see Appendix C). Since the computational effort that must be expended to solve a linear program increases linearly with the number of variables, but with the cube of the number of constraints, the computational advantage of this representation is substantial. In fact, it reduced the computation cost of the model developed here by over fifty percent.

This completes the general description of the model concept. The details of the algebraic formulation of the model are given in Appendix B. The linearization of the total resource cost term, the simplifying assumptions that were made in formulating the model, and the computational efficiencies built into it, make it an extremely efficient dynamic energy system model. In fact, it requires at least an order of magnitude less computer time than similar dynamic models. These direct cost savings open up the interesting possibility of using the model in an interactive mode with solutions computed within a few minutes after the user has supplied the inputs. The model described here could, thus, potentially be a useful tool for those charged with energy R&D planning. The next chapter describes an example application of the model that is intended to illustrate this potential.

Chapter 4

RESULTS FROM THE EXAMPLE APPLICATION OF THE MODEL

This chapter presents an example application of the model in terms of the assessment of the relative benefits that could be attributed to the success of government sponsored R&D in the following three technology areas:

- o Liquid-metal fast breeder reactors
- o Synthetic fuels derived from coal and oil shale
- o Improved end-use efficiency technologies.

A set of government-sponsored, energy-technology R&D programs (Table 4-1) is assumed for each of these three technology areas. These three sets of R&D programs are presumed to produce three corresponding sets of energy-technologies that will be available for commercialization at the indicated dates. Table 4-1 also lists the FY 1976 ERDA budget requests for each of the energy R&D programs, as well as the assumed availability dates for the corresponding technologies.

SCENARIOS ANALYZED

The three sets of new energy technologies are evaluated by developing eight scenarios, each of which assumes the successful development of one of the possible combinations (including none) of the three sets of technologies. Each scenario is characterized by the set(s) of new technologies available in it. Each new technology is represented by its assumed availability date and the projected cost and efficiency parameters for the energy processing facilities that would implement it.

First, a base case scenario (referred to as BAS) is considered where there is no government R&D expenditures in these three technology areas. There is, however, a modest amount of technology advancement in end-use efficiencies which is presumed to be the result of industry R&D. Next, individual technology sets are added in isolation to the base case to form three more scenarios: breeders (BRE), synfuels (SYN) and improved end-use efficiency technologies (END). Finally, the introduction of all possible combinations of these sets of technologies are considered: synfuels and improved end-use efficiencies (SYN+END),

Table 4-1

ENERGY R&D PROGRAMS SELECTED FOR STUDY AND RELEVANT FY 1976 ERDA BUDGET REQUESTS[a]

(Millions of 1975 Dollars)

	Original Request	Revised Request
Liquid-Metal Fast Breeder Reactors (BRE)[b]		
LMFBR	212	194
CLINCH RIVER Breeder Reactor	153	107
TOTAL	365	301
Coal and Oil Shale Synthetics (SYN)[c]		
Liquefaction	98	98
High-Btu Coal Gasification	73	73
Low-Btu Coal Gasification	45	45
Demonstration Plants	37	37
Oil Shale	9	15
TOTAL	262	268
Improved End-Use Efficiency Technologies (END)[d]		
Electric Energy Systems	12	19
Transportation	10	13
Industry Conservation	2	5
Building Conservation	2	12
Storage, Waste, and Conversion	13	19
Geothermal (Hydrothermal)	6	6
Solar Heating and Cooling	26	29
Direct Fossil Combustion	38	45
TOTAL	109	148

[a]From ERDA (1975a).

[b]First available in 1985.

[c]First available in 1985.

[d]Solar heating and cooling, geothermal heat and waste heat utilization first available in 1978, other technologies available with small efficiency increases almost immediately and increasing efficiencies thereafter.

synfuels and breeders (SYN+BRE), improved end-use efficiencies and breeders (END+BRE) and all three sets of technologies (END+SYN+BRE). The top portion of Fig. 4-1 summarizes the combinations of new technology sets for each of the eight scenarios.

ALTERNATIVE RESOURCE CASES

Although many variations in the nominal parameter values assumed in this study would perhaps be of interest, time and resource constraints limited the investigation to only a few parameters that seemed a priori to be the most relevant. The parameters varied here are the domestic availability of low-cost oil and gas and the price of imported oil.

The nominal values for low-cost domestic oil and gas resources* are the "expected values" determined in a recent USGS study (United States Geological Survey, 1975). The values used for the sensitivity analysis here are the 5th and 95th percentile assessments made in that study. In other words, there is thought to be only a five per cent chance that the availability of low-cost domestic oil and gas will be less than the low availability case examined here, and similarly, only a five per cent chance that the availability of low-cost oil and gas will be greater than that assumed for the high availability case.

The nominal values assumed for the price of imported oil over time are the nominal values for this parameter given in the Synthetic Fuels Commercialization Task Force Report (Synfuels Interagency Task Force, 1975). High and low values for the price of imported oil were also included in that report and are used here in the high and low import price cases. The low price case involves a break in the world oil cartel; the nominal price case, the continuance of the current cartel; and the high price case, an immediate increase of 3 dollars per barrel in the price of imported oil. The bottom portion of Figure 4-1 summarizes the resource cases considered in the study.

Interestingly, the only variation of the nominal parameter values considered here that changes the results enough to effect the conclusions about the R&D program funding levels drawn in the next chapter, is a break in the world oil cartel. This tends to lower

---

*Includes demonstrated reserves, inferred reserves and expected undiscovered reserves.

- ENERGY R&D PLANNING SCENARIOS
  - BASELINE: NO NEW TECHNOLOGIES (BAS)
  - END-USE EFFICIENCIES (END)
  - SYNFUELS (SYN)
  - BREEDER (BRE)
  - END + SYN
  - END + BRE
  - SYN + BRE
  - SYN + END + BRE (CURRENT PROGRAM)
- RESOURCE ASSESSMENT CASES (OMB/USGS)

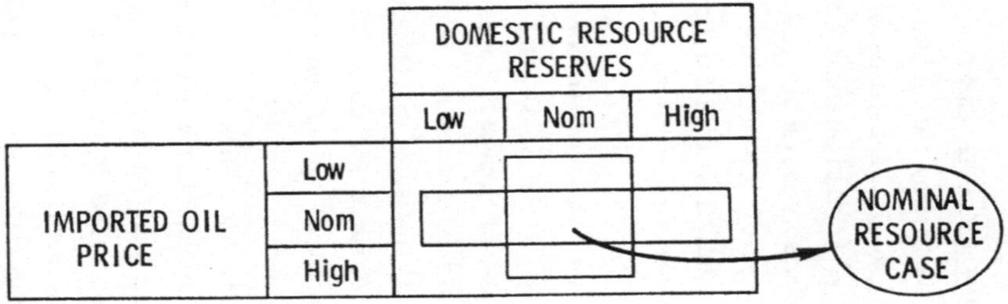

Fig. 4-1—Scenarios and resource cases

imported oil prices, which drastically reduces the gross economic benefits of the synfuels program in the absence of import restrictions.

The results presented here focus on interscenario comparisons which can be used to judge the relative merits of the three energy R&D programs. First, the scenarios are compared in terms of the level of total energy resources consumed, the amount of liquid fuels consumed, the amount of oil imported, the amount of coal consumed, the amount of gas produced, the amount of uranium extracted, and the amount of electricity generated. Then, a summary discussion of the economic benefits, security benefits, and environmental disbenefits of the three energy R&D programs concludes the chapter.

RESOURCE CONSUMPTION PATTERNS

Comparisons of the levels of the various resource consumptions help explain the differences in the economic benefits attributable to the various R&D programs and combinations of these programs. These resource consumption comparisons also provide further bases for judging the relative merits of the various energy R&D programs. For example, the level of imports constitutes a measure of security. Additionally, although U.S. coal reserves are immense, there is some question as to how fast the production rate for coal can be built up without incurring additional economic costs due to bottlenecks in the industries supplying the coal mining industry. A comparison of the buildup of coal production in each of the various scenarios, therefore, provides some insight into the potential for such bottlenecks as it depends on the availability of the new technologies.

Total Energy Resource Consumption

Figure 4-2 shows total resource energy consumption over time for the scenarios analyzed. Without the improved end-use efficiency technologies scenario (END), total energy consumption grows at about 3 per cent per year to the year 2000 (to about 155 Quads*) and slows to about 2 per cent per year thereafter. With improved end-use efficiency technologies, the growth rate of total energy consumption is slowed to about 2 per cent per year throughout the 60-year time horizon (reaching

*1 Quad = 1 quadrillion Btus = 10^{15} Btus.

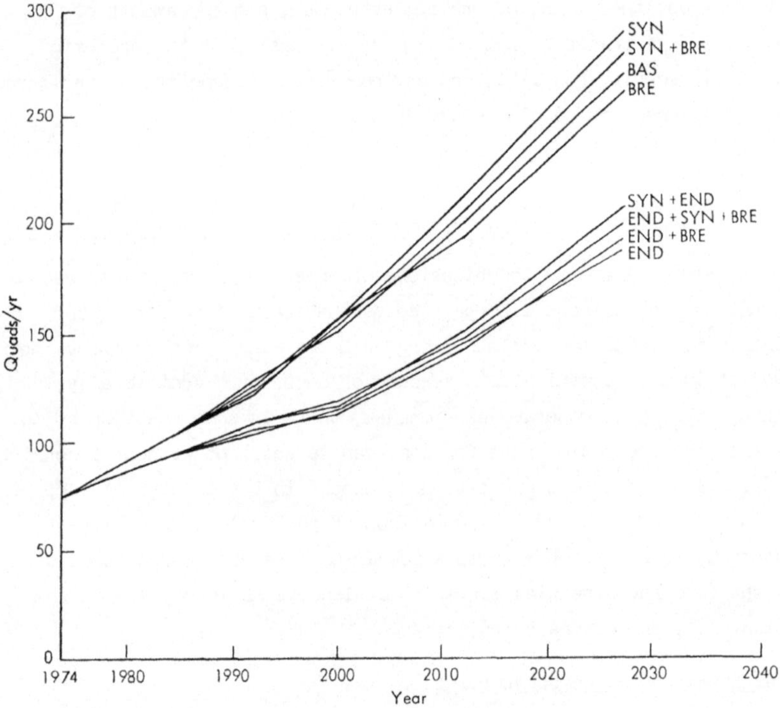

Fig. 4-2 — Interscenario comparison for total resource energy consumption (nominal resource case)

about 115 Quads in 2000). The higher demand rate slows after the turn of the century due to saturation effects (e.g., everybody who needs an air conditioner has one), while continued improvements in end-use efficiencies are less likely in the long run due to physical process limits. The SYN scenarios use more resources than the other scenarios because of the process inefficiencies that occur when coal is converted to liquid and gaseous fuels in these scenarios. However, the synthetic fuels scenarios provide the only possible paths to complete energy self-sufficiency (see below).

Liquid Fuels Consumption

Figure 4-3 summarizes total liquid fuels consumption as a function of the level of domestic oil and gas availability for the eight scenarios analyzed. Figures 4-3(a), (b), and (c) correspond to the low, nominal, and high domestic oil and gas availability cases, respectively. Two things are immediately interesting about these figures. First, only two levels of liquid fuels consumption obtain over all eight scenarios. The only determinant of the level of liquid fuels consumed is whether or not improved efficiencies in end-use technologies are available. Second, the overall level of increase in liquid fuels consumption is small in all cases, with the average rate of increase at about one per cent (as compared to a previously noted three per cent rate of increase in total energy resource consumption) for the non-END scenarios and .5 per cent (as compared to a two per cent rate of increase in total energy resource consumption) for the END scenarios. Thus there is a modest shift away from the liquid fuels.

The reason that only two levels of liquid fuels consumption occurred is that with the higher oil prices that have emerged as a result of the Arab oil embargo and ensuing cartel, liquid fuels are now less competitive for uses where interfuel competition possibilities exist (e.g., electric generation, space heat, water heat, and industrial process heat). Even when synthetic liquid fuels become available, they are competitive only with liquid fuels and not with other energy fuels. Consequently, the only new facilities that are constructed for oil products are constructed to satisfy stipulated petroleum product demands for transportation and petrochemicals.

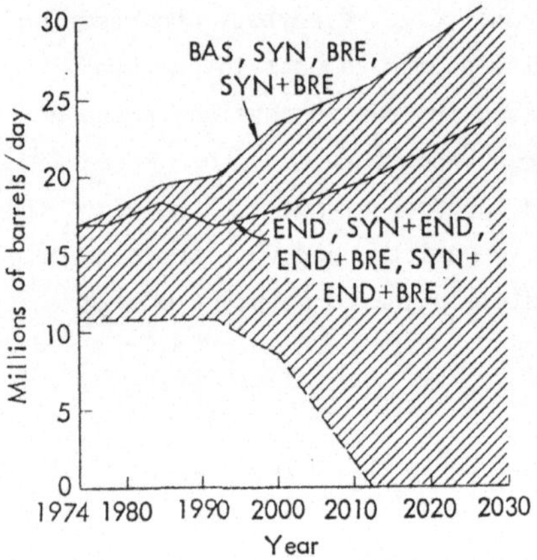

(a) Interscenario comparison for total liquid fuels consumption for the low domestic oil and gas availability case (nominal import price case)

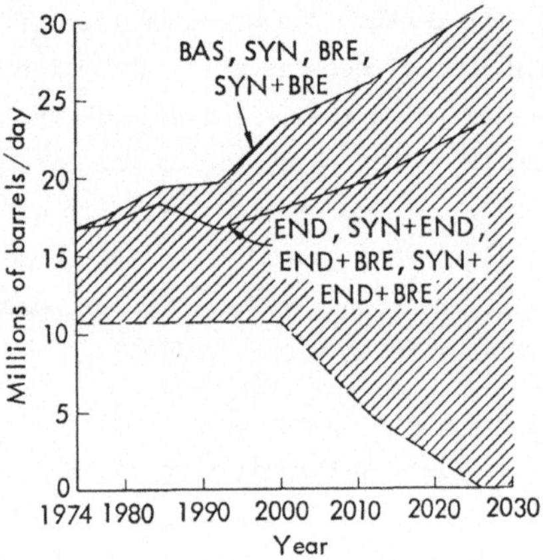

(b) Interscenario comparison for total liquid fuels consumption (nominal resource case)

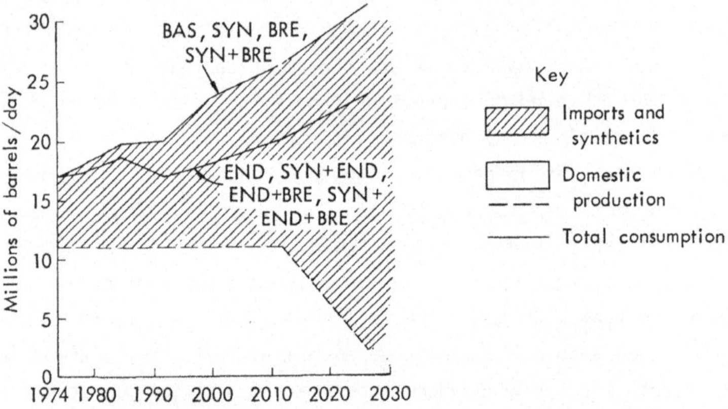

(c) Interscenario comparison for total liquid fuels consumption for the high domestic oil and gas availability case (nominal import price case)

Fig. 4-3—Sensitivity of total liquid fuels consumption to the availability of domestic oil and gas

The rate of increase of liquid fuels consumption is so low primarily due to the relative cost of liquid fuels. This fuel cost bias will cause improved efficiencies in transportation end uses (e.g., more efficient use of fuels by automobiles and aircraft) which are included in the base case scenario. The substitution of gas and coal for oil in the petrochemical industry serves to further suppress the rate of increase of liquid fuels consumption out to the year 2000. Indeed, with the improved efficiencies in end-use technologies scenario, the amount of petroleum consumed in 1992 is only about as much as was consumed in 1974.

As shown in Fig. 4-3(b), domestic oil production holds at about its current level of 11 million barrels per day until about the end of the century and then decreases rather dramatically with the depletion of low cost domestic reserves. The shaded area in the figure represents the amount of liquid fuels that must either be imported or produced synthetically. Figure 4-4(a) shows the amount of oil imported for each of the scenarios for the nominal import price case. As synthetic liquids are cheaper than imports starting in 1985, the SYN scenarios show a dramatic decrease in imports as soon as the synthetics are available to replace them. A second increase in synthetics occurs (at about the turn of the century) in order to replace the dwindling supply of low-cost domestic resources. In the absence of synthetics, imports grow rapidly and by the end of the time horizon (i.e, around 2030) constitute the entire supply of liquid fuels. Improved end-use efficiencies serve both to advance the date of energy independence from 2000 to 1992 in the event synfuels technologies are available and to delay the increase of imports to levels significantly above those that exist today from 1992 to 2000 in the absence of synfuels technologies. Further, the rate of growth of synthetics shown for the synfuels scenarios without improved end-use efficiencies may not, in reality, be achievable due to potential bottlenecks in both the synfuels industry and the coal mining industry (see below).

Figure 4-4(b) shows the imports required for the various scenarios for the low import price case. It is interesting to note that even with the breakup of the world oil cartel, the expected price of oil imports is still high enough to prevent them from competing with other fuels in

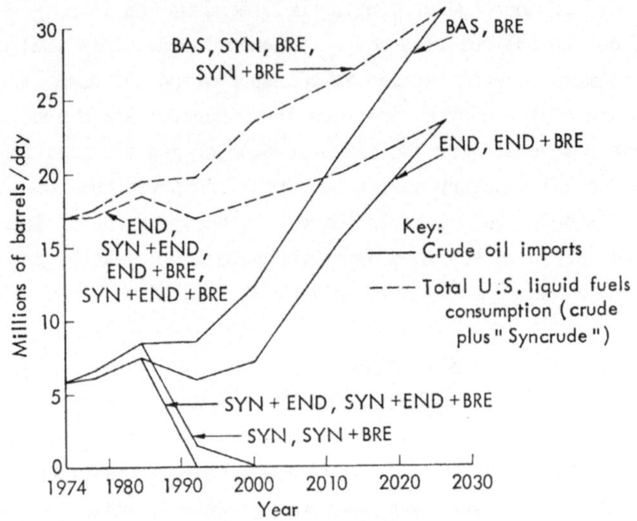

(a) Interscenario comparison for crude oil imports (nominal resource case)

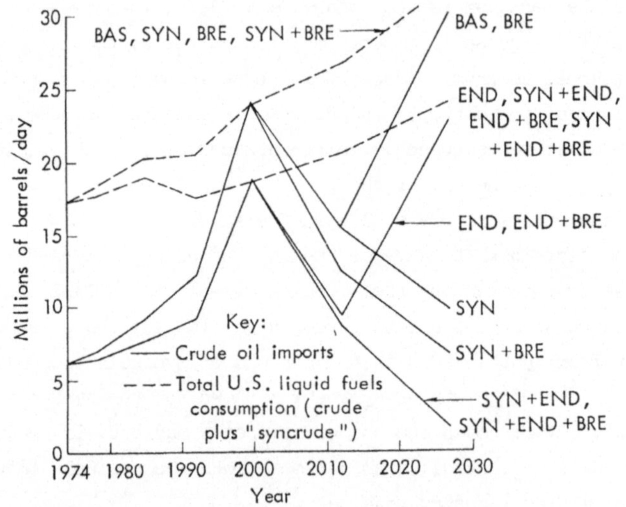

(b) Interscenario comparison for crude oil imports for the low import price case (nominal domestic resource availability case)

Fig. 4-4—Sensitivity of crude oil imports to import price

any end uses where such competition is possible. Up to 2012, the gap between imports and total liquid fuels is filled entirely by domestic oil production, while after this date, synfuels are used to fill most of the gap. There is serious doubt, though, that the level of imports will ever be allowed to grow to anywhere near the 100 per cent level shown in 2000. For example, imports may be restricted if the cartel breaks, thereby preserving the benefits of the synfuels program.

Coal Production

Figure 4-5(a) shows the drastic difference in coal requirements for the eight scenarios examined. In general, synthetics technologies lead to higher coal demands, while the breeder and improved end-use efficiency technologies tend to lead to lower coal demands. Up to the year 2012, the four END scenarios require less coal than the four non-END scenarios. The SYN, but non-END scenarios require the most coal. After 2012, the non-BRE scenarios require significant amounts of coal for electric generation since the depletion of low-cost uranium reserves causes coal-steam electric power generation to be cheaper than electric generation by conventional nuclear reactors.

To give some idea of the reasonableness of the rate of coal growth required for the various scenarios, the dashed line shown in Fig. 4-5(a) represents a yearly growth rate of seven per cent in coal production from 1974 through 2000. This is the maximum growth rate many feel to be attainable (e.g., Federal Energy Administration, 1974b). Growth rates for the SYN and SYN+BRE scenarios are about at this seven per cent level when averaged over the 1974 to 2000 interval. However, the growth rates for these two scenarios approaches 10 per cent during the 1985 to 1992 time period. During this period, the major increases in coal consumption are in new coal capacity for utilites and coal liquefaction. If such a growth rate is unattainable during this time period, additional oil imports may be required for a time, but the required cumulative growth in coal production during the 1985-2000 time interval would seem to be attainable since the growth rates for the 1993-2000 time period are only one or two per cent.

Coal production is sensitive to oil and gas availability as shown in Fig. 4-5(b) for the high-coal-requirements SYN scenario. The rapid

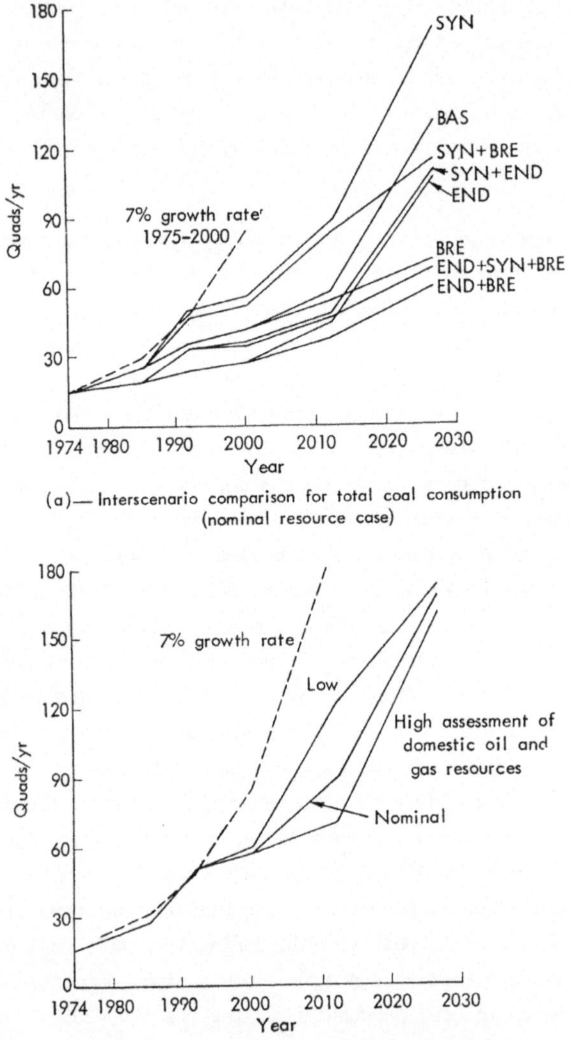

(a)— Interscenario comparison for total coal consumption (nominal resource case)

(b) — Sensitivity of total coal consumption to the availability of domestic oil and gas for the synfuels scenario (nominal import price case)

Fig. 4-5— Total coal consumption comparisons

growth in coal production during the 1985-1992 time period is not affected significantly by alternative oil and gas availability assumptions until after the year 2000.

Gas Consumption

Figure 4-6 shows natural gas consumption for the eight scenarios analyzed. The major determinant of the level of natural gas consumption is whether or not improved end-use efficiency technologies or synfuels are available. With neither improved end-use efficiency technologies nor synfuels, gas consumption declines very slowly as relatively high cost natural gas is still more economical than imported oil or electricity. With synthetics, but no improved end-use efficiencies, synthetic gas (not shown in Fig. 4-6) begins to replace natural gas in about 2000.

However, with improved end-use efficiency technologies, total gas consumption (including any synthetic gas) drops off quite rapidly after the turn of the century because: (1) the levels of end-use demands that gas can satisfy are reduced through improved efficiencies and (2) electricity from low-cost coal* or breeders competes effectively with high-priced gas (whether natural or synthetic). This is especially true for space heat, where heat pumps which are twice as efficient as current electric resistance heating systems, are assumed to be available. In these cases, synthetic gas is not produced until 2012 and then only in small amounts.

Uranium Extraction

Figure 4-7 shows cumulative uranium extraction for the eight scenarios. The lower horizontal dashed line represents the current best estimate (see, e.g., ERDA-1, 1975) of the amount of "low-cost" domestic uranium that is available. This quantity of uranium is thought to be extractable at a "forward cost" of $30 per pound or less. In this study, these "forward costs", which exclude return on investment and sunk costs, have been adjusted to include these true economic costs as suggested by Palmer, et al. (1975). The effect of this correction is to elevate the $30 per pound forward cost figure to an economic cost of

*There is still low-cost coal available as a result of improved end-use efficiencies.

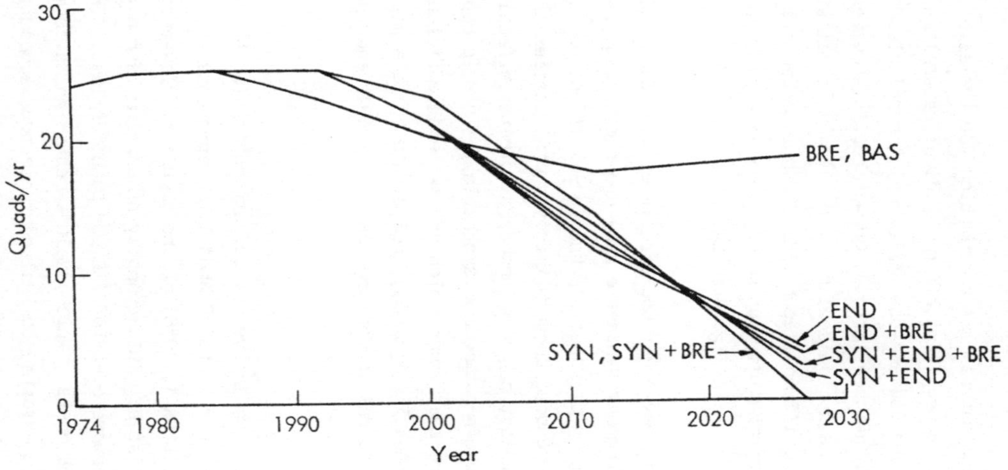

Fig. 4-6— Interscenario comparison for total natural gas consumption (nominal resource case)

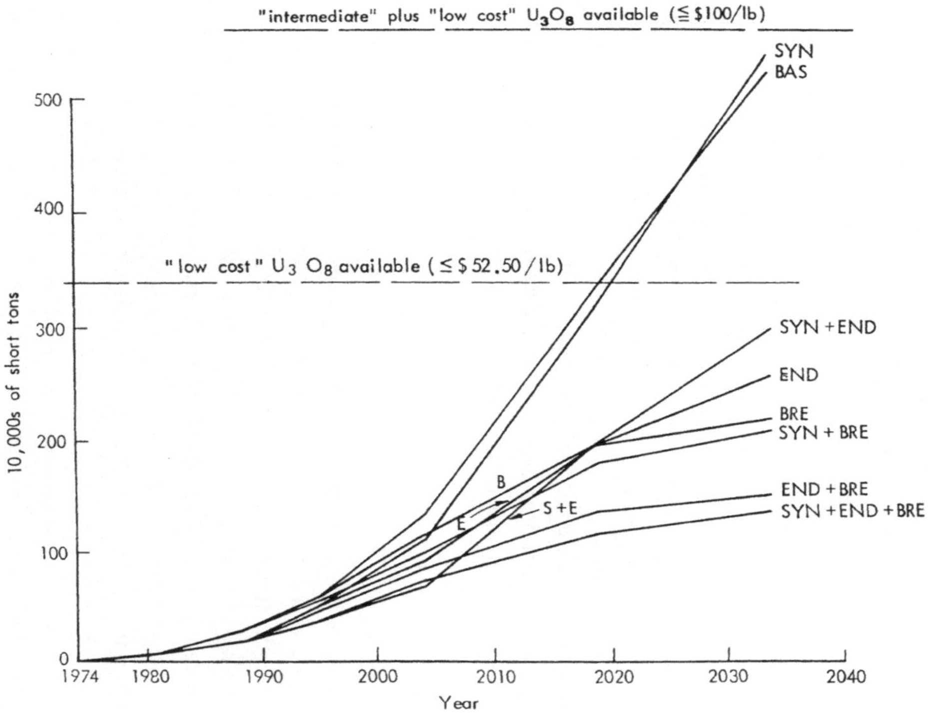

Fig. 4-7— Interscenario comparison for cumulative U_3O_8 extraction (nominal resource case)

$52.50 per pound. The possible depletion of "low-cost" uranium is typically used as an argument for the development of breeder reactors which use significantly less uranium than conventional reactors.

The upper dashed line represents the expected amount of uranium recoverable from known producing regions at an extraction cost of less than $100 per pound according to Searl, et al. (1974). The uranium availability question is far from settled (see, e.g., Atomic Energy Commission, 1974b; Holdren, 1974; Day, 1975; Hagerton, 1975; and Cochran, et al., 1975; for more on the debate), but the numbers used here are thought to reflect the most current best estimates.

From Fig. 4-7, it is seen that only when neither breeders nor improved end-use efficiency technologies are available, is the supply of "low-cost" uranium depleted, and then not until about 2020. In no case is the expected supply of $100/lb uranium exhausted within the model's time horizon. The availability of breeder reactors does lead to conservation of uranium supplies, but the savings are not significant until the 2020s. With improved end-use efficiency technologies, low-cost coal is used to generate electricity which delays significant introduction of breeders until after the turn of the century.

Electric Generation

Figure 4-8 shows that total electric generation is relatively insensitive to everything but whether or not improved end-use efficiency technologies are available. Although electric generation grows faster out to the year 2000 without increased end-use efficiencies (4.3 per cent to 2.5 per cent), it actually grows slower after 2000 without the improved end-use efficiency technologies (3.0 per cent to 3.7 percent). This occurs primarily because the improved end-use efficiencies enable electricity to more effectively substitute for other fuels in space heating and water heating end-use demands after the year 2000. This then stimulates the demand for electricity. Although the introduction of breeders provides a slightly lower cost source of electricity than conventional sources, the cost differential is not great enough to create significant new electricity demands. Actually, by the end of the time horizon, electricity already satisfies almost all new space heat

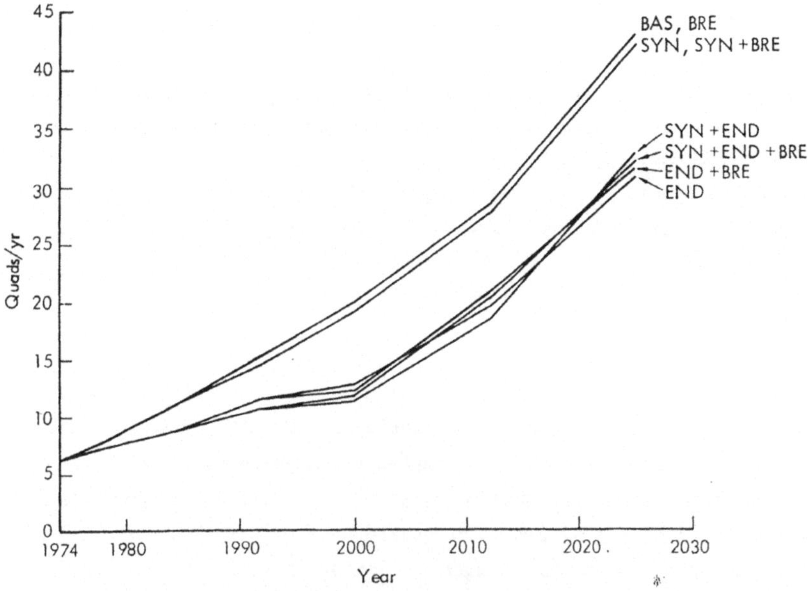

Fig. 4-8 — Interscenario comparison for total electricity generation (nominal resource case)

and water heat demands and could thus only make new contributions in the industrial process heat market, where, however, the inefficiency of electricity generation makes neither coal nor nuclear electricity generation cost competitive with the direct burning of coal.

SUMMARY OF BENEFITS/DISBENEFITS

This section summarizes the gross economic benefits, security benefits and environmental disbenefits of the three energy R&D programs. The gross economic benefits are stated in terms of both the reduction in the 60 year life-cycle cost for the United States energy system attributable to the programs and the ratio of this cost avoidance to the projected R&D cost for the programs.* The security benefit is stated in terms of the level of crude oil imports occuring in the year 2000 as a result of successful development programs. Finally, the environmental disbenefit of the programs is summarized by calculating the total tonnage of coal and oil shale mined in the year 2000 for each of the scenarios examined.

Economic Benefit

Figure 4-9 compares the 60 year life-cycle costs for the United States energy supply system for the eight scenarios analyzed. The numbers in the first column of the table are the life-cycle costs for the eight scenarios for the alternative resource cases. The other columns in the table give the reductions in the life-cycle cost for the United States energy system attributable to expanding the row R&D scenario to the column R&D scenario. For example, if the breeder program is the only program pursued, its marginal benefit would be from five to six billion dollars, while if the breeder program is added to a scenario that already assumes an on-going improved end-use efficiencies program, its marginal benefit would only be about one billion dollars. Since the latest cost estimate for the currently construed breeder R&D program (see, e.g., Atomic Energy Commission, 1974b) is about 4.5 billion discounted (at 10%) 1974 dollars, the availability (or lack of availability) of improved efficiency end-use devices would appear to be

*Recall that the life-cycle cost for running the United States energy system as defined here does not include R&D costs.

Given that this R&D scenario is already adopted		Then this is the reduction in the U.S. energy system's life-cycle cost that is attributable to the adoption of the new energy R&D scenario (Billions of 1974 dollars)						
Energy R&D Scenario	Total Life-Cycle Cost[a] (Billions of 1974 Dollars)	BRE + SYN + END (Current ERDA Program)	BRE + SYN	BRE + END	END + SYN	BRE	SYN	END
BAS (Baseline "do nothing")	1399; 1603 1563 1531; 1657	281; 360 351 338; 394	8; 62 57 48; 91	281; 322 316 312; 335	279; 358 350 337; 392	6; 6 6 5; 6	2; 55 50 41; 84	279; 321 315 311; 334
END (End-use efficiencies)	1120; 1282 1248 1220; 1323	2; 39 36 27; 60	—	2; 1 1 1; 1	0; 37 35 26; 58	—	—	
SYN (Synfuels)	1397; 1548 1513 1490; 1573	279; 305 301 297; 310	6; 7 7 7; 7	—	277; 303 300 296; 308	—		
END + SYN	1120; 1245 1213 1194; 1265	2; 2 1 1; 2	—	—	—			
BRE (Breeder (LMFBR))	1393; 1597 1557 1526; 1651	275; 354 345 333; 388	2; 56 51 43; 85	275; 316 310 307; 329				
BRE + SYN	1391; 1541 1506 1483; 1566	273; 298 294 290; 303	—					
BRE + END	1118; 1281 1247 1219; 1322	0; 38 35 26; 59						
BRE + SYN + END (Current ERDA program)	1118; 1243 1212 1193; 1263							

Key to resource cases

Imported Oil Price	Domestic Resource Reserves: LOW	NOM	HIGH
Low		■	
Nom	■	■	■
High		■	

[a] The 60 year life-cycle cost for the U.S. energy system is stated in terms of a 1974 present value using a 10% discount rate

Fig. 4-9—Economic benefit for marginal variations in the alternative R&D scenarios

a major determinant of the advisability of proceeding with the current breeder program.

The results in the top row of Fig. 4-9 show the existence of a moderate positive interaction between the breeder and synfuels technologies and a substantial negative interaction between the improved end-use efficiency technologies and both the breeder and synfuels technologies for the nominal resource case. The positive interaction between the breeder and synfuels technologies is due primarily to competition for coal between the electric generation sector and the liquefaction sector. In the absence of breeders, coal-fired power plants are cost competitive with conventional thermal nuclear reactors at about the turn of the century. If there are concurrent demands for coal as a feedstock for liquefaction, the cost of coal increases as reserves are depleted more rapidly.

The negative interaction between the improved end-use efficiency technologies and both the synfuels and breeder technologies is due to the slowdown of domestic resource depletion which results with the introduction of improved end-use efficiency technologies. Low-cost uranium and coal are available for a longer period of time to satisfy electric generation and liquefaction requirements. The economic benefits of the improved end-use efficiency technologies are two-fold. First, the resource requirements in any given year are less, and, second, the low cost resources last longer. Not only are less resources demanded per unit time, but those that are extracted are from the lower resource cost categories for a longer period of time.

Sensitivity to Domestic Oil and Gas Availability

Figure 4-9 also shows that the gross economic benefits of the R&D programs are relatively invariant to the availability of domestic oil and gas reserves. As the availability of oil and gas reserves is varied, the gross economic benefits of the synfuels program vary by about 10-20 per cent, those for the end-use technologies by only about 3 per cent, and for the breeder, less than 15 per cent. Benefits are, of course, higher when reserves are low, since synfuels and breeder generated electricity are needed as replacements for dwindling supplies of low-cost domestic oil and gas sooner. Synfuels benefits are not significantly affected by resource reserve availability, however, because the major portion of the benefits are garnered in replacing oil imports in the 1990-2000 time frame and not in replacing dwindling low-cost supplies of domestic oil and gas after the turn of the century. This phenomenon explains why the synfuels benefits are still relatively large when oil and gas availability is high. The breeder benefits are relatively insensitive to oil and gas reserve availability since they are garnered by replacing conventional nuclear reactors and coal-fired power plants that generate electricity.

Sensitivity to the Price of Imported Oil

Figure 4-9 also shows the sensitivity of the gross economic benefits for the various R&D programs to the imported oil price cases. For the high import price case, the solutions* for the scenarios do not change from the nominal resource case because imports are replaced by synfuels as rapidly as possible. The indicated life-cycle cost differences for a given scenario (i.e., comparing the high imported oil price case to the nominal case) in column two are attributable entirely to the high price paid for oil imports. Consequently, the benefits for the synfuels program, which saves the most imports increase by about 50 per cent when the high imported oil price case is compared to the nominal case.

The low import price case is the most significant sensitivity in that it is the only case examined that involves an order of magnitude change in the gross economic benefits of one of the R&D programs. Although the benefits of the improved end-use efficiency technologies program are little affected by a reduction in the price of imported oil, the benefits for the synfuels program are, as one might expect, drastically reduced. This occurs because synfuels do not compete with imported oil until the price of world oil rises due to the depletion of the world's supply of low-cost oil. This does not happen until the second decade of the next century according to the low imported oil price case.

Benefits Versus Costs

Thus far, only the economic benefits of the programs have been discussed. These results are interesting in their own right, but a

---

*The solutions are stated in terms of the commercialization activity "capacities."

better idea of the appropriateness of the R&D priorities assigned to the programs can be gained by comparing these benefits with the projected R&D program costs. Unfortunately, a projected total program R&D cost was available only for the breeder program. However, all three of the programs are allocated funds in the revised FY 1976 ERDA budget request: 301 million dollars for the LMFBR program, 268 million dollars for the synfuels program and 148 million dollars for the improved end-use efficiencies program (c.f. Table 4-1). The LMFBR program cost is expected to be about 4.5 billion discounted 1974 dollars through 1986. For comparison purposes, it is assumed here that the other two programs will receive funding at their currently proposed levels for about 12 years. This yields a 1974 dollar discounted R&D investment cost of $1.8 billion for the synfuels program and one billion dollars for the improved efficiencies in end-use program. This assumed funding stream coincides with the assumed synfuels availability date of 1986. A longer time stream would not change the present values significantly due to discounting. Furthermore, the focus here will be on order of magnitude differences among the benefit-cost ratios for the programs, so that with discounting, the actual funding levels for synfuels or improved end-use efficiencies could be an order of magnitude greater than the current budget expenditures without affecting the conclusions drawn from the results presented here.

Figure 4-10 shows the economic benefits divided by the projected R&D costs for each R&D scenario relative to all possible base scenarios for all the alternative resource cases. Without improved end-use efficiencies, the LMFBR looks like a marginally acceptable R&D investment; with them, it looks like a very poor investment. This observation should be coupled with the observation that the improved end-use efficiencies program looks like a tremendous R&D investment opportunity for all scenarios and all resource cases.

The synfuels program looks like a solid R&D investment if the cartel does not break, but a fairly poor investment if the cartel does break. It is interesting to note, however, that on a stand-alone basis (i.e., in comparison with the base case), even with the cartel breaking, the synfuels investment looks about as good as the LMFBR

Given that this R&D scenario is already adopted	Then this is the marginal benefit ratio associated with the adoption of the new scenario						
	BRE + SYN + END (Current ERDA Program)	BRE + SYN	BRE + END	END + SYN	BRE	SYN	END
BAS (Baseline "do nothing")	39 49 48 46 54	1.3 10 9 8 14	51 59 57 57 61	100 128 125 120 140	1.3 1.3 1.3 1.1 1.3	1.1 31 28 23 47	279 321 315 311 334
END (End-use efficiencies)	.3 6 6 4 10	—	0.4 0.2 0.2 0.2 0.2	0 21 19 14 32	—	—	
SYN (Synfuels)	51 55 55 54 56	1.3 1.6 1.6 1.6 1.6	—	277 303 300 296 308	—		
END + SYN	0.4 0.4 0.2 0.2 0.4	—	—	—			
BRE [Breeder (LMFBR)]	98 126 123 119 139	1.1 31 28 24 47	275 316 310 307 329				
BRE + SYN	273 298 294 290 303	—					
BRE + END	0 21 19 14 33						

Key to resource cases

Imported Oil Price	Domestic Resource Reserves: Low	Nom	High
Low		☐	
Nom	☐	☐	☐
High		☐	

Fig. 4-10 — Ratio of the economic benefit to the incremental R&D investment (the marginal benefit ratio)

investment. The ultimate economic attractiveness of the synfuels program as an investment depends on the likelihood of the collapse of the world oil cartel.

Security Benefit

One measure of the security of the United States energy supplies is the level of imported crude oil. In order to assess the relative contributions of the three energy R&D programs in terms of the national goal of energy security, the level of imports required in 2000 for all of the scenarios for all of the alternative resource cases are shown in column two of Figure 4-11. The remaining columns show the imports required for the scenarios listed at the heads of the respective columns. The emphasis here is on the marginal contribution of the R&D programs to the import posture of the United States in the year 2000.

In the absence of a break in the world oil cartel (i.e., low import prices), the message conveyed by Figure 4-11 is quite clear. Synfuels result in energy independence by the turn of the century, improved end-use efficiencies reduce the required level of imports significantly in the absence of synfuels and breeders make no contribution towards energy independence by 2000 at all.

If the cartel does break, neither domestic crude nor synfuels can compete with imported crude on an economic basis and, consequently, virtually all liquid fuels are imported in the year 2000. This would, however, probably be unacceptable from the point of view of national security. Therefore, imports might be restricted as a matter of national policy, which would thereby sustain/create a market for synfuels even in the event of a break in the world oil cartel.

Environmental Disbenefit

Many measures of environmental disbenefit for the United States energy system are possible. Regardless of the measure(s) chosen, though, improved end-use efficiencies reduce the overall disbenefit. Although the environmental disbenefit of breeder generated electricity has by no means been shown to be conclusively less severe than that of coal generated electricity, the measure of environmental disbenefit selected here is the total tonnage of coal and oil shale mined in the year 2000. This measure was selected partly because the analysis so far

Given that this R&D scenario is already adopted		Then this is the crude oil import level for the new R&D scenario						
Energy R&D Scenario	Crude Oil Imports (in millions of barrels/day)	BRE + SYN + END (Current ERDA Program)	BRE + SYN	BRE + END	END + SYN	BRE	SYN	END
BAS (Baseline "do nothing")	23 / 14 12 12 / 12	18 / 0 0 0 / 0	23 / 0 0 0 / 0	18 / 9 7 7 / 7	18 / 0 0 0 / 0	23 / 14 12 12 / 12	23 / 0 0 0 / 0	18 / 9 7 7 / 7
END (End-use efficiencies)	18 / 9 7 7 / 7	18 / 0 0 0 / 0	—	18 / 9 7 7 / 7	18 / 0 0 0 / 0	—	—	
SYN (Synfuels)	23 / 0 0 0 / 0	18 / 0 0 0 / 0	23 / 0 0 0 / 0	—	18 / 0 0 0 / 0	—		
END + SYN	18 / 0 0 0 / 0	18 / 0 0 0 / 0	—	—	—			
BRE [Breeder (LMFBR)]	23 / 14 12 12 / 12	18 / 0 0 0 / 0	23 / 0 0 0 / 0	18 / 9 7 7 / 7				
BRE + SYN	23 / 0 0 0 / 0	18 / 0 0 0 / 0	—					
BRE + END	18 / 9 7 7 / 7	18 / 0 0 0 / 0						
BRE + SYN + END (Current ERDA Program)	18 / 0 0 0 / 0							

Key to resource cases

Domestic Resource Reserves: Low, Nom, High

Imported Oil Prices: Low, Nom, High

Fig. 4-11 — Crude oil imports in the year 2000 (security)

has shown that the breeder program is the least attractive of the three programs according to the financial and security goals and partly to demonstrate the clear conflict a synfuels program creates between the security and environmental goals. The first column of Figure 4-12 shows the amounts of coal and oil shale mined in the year 2000 for all the scenarios for the alternative resource cases. The additional columns in the figure give the amount of coal and oil shale mined for the scenarios listed at the heads of the respective columns.

The environmental disbenefit of a synfuels program could be substantial. Improved end-use efficiencies would help ease the environmental disbenefit of the synfuels program considerably, but breeders would not help this situation by the year 2000. In fact, given any already adopted scenario, improved end-use efficiencies always reduce the environmental disbenefit in 2000, while breeders never help alleviate the disbenefit.

Given that this R&D scenario is already adopted		Then this is the coal and oil shale extraction level for the new R&D scenario (Billions of tons/yr)						
Energy R&D Scenario	Total Coal and Shale mined in 2000 (10^9 tons/yr)	BRE + SYN + END (Current ERDA Program)	BRE + SYN	BRE + END	END + SYN	BRE	SYN	END
BAS (Baseline "do nothing")	2.04 2.04 2.04 1.94 2.04	1.33 5.23 4.23 4.23 4.23	1.94 7.35 7.30 7.30 7.30	1.33 1.42 1.42 1.42 1.42	1.33 5.33 4.27 4.27 4.27	2.04 2.04 2.04 1.94 2.04	1.94 7.49 6.68 6.68 6.68	1.33 1.38 1.33 1.33 1.33
END (End-use efficiencies)	1.33 1.38 1.33 1.33 1.33	1.33 5.23 4.23 4.23 4.23	—	1.33 1.42 1.42 1.42 1.42	1.33 5.33 4.27 4.27 4.27	—	—	
SYN (Synfuels)	1.94 7.49 6.68 6.68 6.68	1.33 5.23 4.23 4.23 4.23	1.94 7.35 7.30 7.30 7.30	—	1.33 5.33 4.27 4.27 4.27	—		
END + SYN	1.33 5.33 4.27 4.27 4.27	1.33 5.23 4.23 4.23 4.23	—	—	—			
BRE [Breeder (LMFBR)]	2.04 2.04 2.04 1.94 2.04	1.33 5.23 4.23 4.23 4.23	1.94 7.35 7.30 7.30 7.30	1.33 1.42 1.42 1.42 1.42				
BRE + SYN	1.94 7.35 7.30 7.30 7.30	1.33 5.23 4.23 4.23 4.23	—					
BRE + END	1.33 1.42 1.42 1.42 1.42	1.33 5.23 4.23 4.23 4.23						
BRE + SYN + END (Current ERDA Program)	1.33 5.23 4.23 4.23 4.23							

Key to resource cases

		Domestic Resource Reserves		
		Low	Nom	High
Imported Oil Price	Low		☐	
	Nom	☐	☐	☐
	High		☐	

Fig. 4-12— Coal and oil shale extraction in the year 2000 (environment)

Chapter 5

R&D POLICY INTERPRETATIONS OF THE RESULTS

The intent of this chapter is to provide an example interpretation of the results of the previous chapter in terms of an assessment of the federal R&D priorities currently assigned to: 1) synthetic fuels from coal and oil shale, 2) liquid-metal fast breeder reactors, and 3) improved end-use efficiency technologies. The current R&D priorities are manifest in: 1) ERDA's FY 1976 budget and 2) proposals for two major energy R&D programs: the liquid-metal fast breeder reactor program (Atomic Energy Commission, 1974b) and the synfuels commercialization program (Synfuels Interagency Task Force, 1975). The present assessment is based primarily on the results given in chapter 4, although consideration of other oft-cited issues is integrated with the economic, security, and environmental results provided by the model. Both the total funds allocated to the three technology programs (see Table 4-1) and the allocation of funds to individual projects within each program are assessed. It is reassuring to note that although ERDA's current allocation of energy R&D funds differs substantially from the relative benefit assessment made herein, virtually all the revisions in ERDA's proposed FY 1976 budget since its original request to Congress (see ERDA, 1975a) have been in the direction of the reallocations suggested here.

THE ECONOMIC COMPARISON

The principal finding of this example application is that the economic benefits calculated for the three programs are in reverse order to their funding levels proposed in ERDA's FY 1976 budget. The liquid-metal fast breeder reactor currently has the largest share of the budget (301 million dollars), synfuels the second largest share (268 million dollars), and end-use technologies, the smallest share (148 million dollars). These budget requests are shown in the first column of Table 5-1 which summarizes the economic results of the example application.

In the base case scenario none of the three new technologies are assumed to be developed. If an improved efficiencies in end-use program

Table 5-1

Comparison of program R&D expenditures and marginal economic benefits

Energy-Technology R&D Program Scenarios	Federal Government R & D Expenditures		Marginal Economic Benefit:	Marginal Economic Benefit Ratio
	Proposed FY 1976 (Millions of 1976 Dollars)	Present Value for 1976-1987 (Estimate[b] in Billions of 1974 Dollars)	Reduction in the 60 Year Total Costs[a] of the U.S. Energy System (Billions of 1974 Dollars)	(Marginal Economic Benefit / Present Value of FY 1976-1988 R & D Expenditures)
Base Case Scenario	0	0	0	—
+ Improved End-Use Efficiency Technologies	148	1	279-334[c]	279-334
+ Coal and Oil Shale Synthetics	268	1.8	0[d]-58	0-32
+ Liquid-Metal fast Breeder[e]	301	4.5	1-2	.2-.4

[a] Stated in 1974 present value terms at a 10% discount rate.

[b] Assumes continuation of FY 1976 funding level, except in the case of the breeder (see Atomic Energy Commission, 1974b).

[c] Range of values for the range of resource availability and import price assumptions (Synfuels Interagency Task Force Report, 1975; USGS Circular 725, 1975).

[d] There is zero benefit if oil import prices decline (e.g., less than $ 10/bbl until 2010; in 1974 dollars).

[e] Includes the Clinch River Program.

is added to this base case scenario, a projected R&D investment cost of 1 billion dollars (in 1974 present value terms*) would be incurred assuming continued funding at the currently proposed level for 12 years. Since the R&D investment is stated in present value terms (i.e., discounted), the estimate of the R&D program costs is not very sensitive to down-year changes in the funding level or the period of funding (e.g., the 12 years). Furthermore, it is found that the present value of the R&D program costs would have to change by at least an order of magnitude in order to effect the relative ordering of the economic benefits.

The marginal economic benefit attributable to the improved end-use efficiencies program relative to the base case scenario would be from 279 to 334 billion dollars depending upon the resource case considered. Finally, the resulting ratio of the marginal economic benefit to the projected R&D investment would be about 300 for the improved end-use efficiencies program when it is compared to the base case on a stand-alone basis.

Now, if the synfuels program is added to a scenario that already includes improved end-use efficiencies, the present value of the incremental investment cost would be 1.8 billion dollars (again, calculated by assuming continued funding at the currently proposed level for 12 years), and the marginal benefit-cost ratio would be 0-32, with the zero value corresponding to a collapse of the world oil cartel. Notice that the marginal benefit-cost ratio for the synfuels program would be an order of magnitude lower than that for the improved efficiencies in end-use program. Even if the synfuels program is added to the base case scenario on a stand-alone basis (i.e., no improved end-use efficiency technologies), the marginal benefit-cost ratio would be of the same order of magnitude.

Finally, if the liquid-metal fast breeder reactor (LMFBR) program is added to a scenario that already assumes development of improved end-use efficiency devices and synfuels, the marginal economic benefit ratio is .4 or less. This means that less than one-half of the LMFBR

---

*All present value calculations are based on a ten percent annual "real" discount rate.

R&D costs would be recovered in the form of economic benefits. If synfuels are not already in the R&D investment portfolio, the benefit-cost ratio for the LMFBR would be .2. The subsequent addition of the synfuels program actually increases the ratio for some resource cases to .4, since the introduction of the synfuels causes a shortage of low-cost coal for electric generation, which makes the breeder somewhat more attractive. Even if the LMFBR program is added to the base case scenario on a stand-alone basis, its marginal benefit-cost ratio would be 1.1-1.3. This might make it a marginally acceptable investment, albeit less attractive than the other two programs.

The order of magnitude differences in the benefit-cost ratios shown here suggests, perhaps, that the federal energy R&D effort should be thought of in terms of improved end-use efficiencies first, then synfuels, and finally, LMFBRs. With this view, the currently proposed LMFBR program looks like an unattractive investment on economic grounds. The synfuels program looks like a reasonable national investment, especially in view of energy independence considerations. However, the fact that a marginal economic benefit of zero might result is probably discouraging private investment in synfuels and thereby retarding commercialization.

Each of the next three sections of this chapter analyzes the economic, environmental, and security results attributable to one of the three R&D programs. Consideration of security and environmental issues does not alter the suggested R&D program priorities suggested here based on economic considerations. In fact, consideration of these issues, as well as several supplementary issues, actually reinforces the suggested priorities.

LIQUID-METAL FAST BREEDER REACTORS

Although the FY 1976 allocation to the liquid-metal fast breeder reactor program was revised downwards from 365 million dollars to 301 million dollars, the results obtained here suggest that an additional significant reduction is perhaps warranted. This could possibly involve cancellation or delay of the Clinch River Breeder Reactor demonstration plant.

It is observed here that the budget allocation for the breeder reactor program could be reduced because:

- The gross economic benefits that accrue to this program are relatively small, especially if improved end-use efficiency technologies are developed (as is strongly suggested here);
- The breeder program provides little help in reaching and maintaining energy independence until well after the turn of the century;
- Besides having their own environmental disbenefits, breeders do not help alleviate the environmental disbenefit attributable to mining coal and oil shale until after the turn of the century;
- A full-scale breeder development program may be premature at this time (c.f. Cochran, et al., 1975);
- Advanced breeder technology may be importable well before needed (c.f. Metz, 1975).

The gross benefits calculated for the breeder program here are only: six billion dollars without synfuels or improved end-use efficiency technologies, seven billion dollars with synfuels but no improved end-use technologies, one billion dollars with improved end-use efficiencies but no synfuels and one billion dollars with both improved end-use efficiencies and synfuels. Further, these results are not very sensitive to the alternative resource assumptions considered here. Since the currently construed breeder program (Atomic Energy Commission, 1974b) has a projected total cost in 1974 present value terms of 4.5 billion 1974 dollars and the results here suggest a strong emphasis on improved end-use technologies, the breeder program appears to be receiving a disproportionate emphasis. The gross economic benefits of the breeder program are relatively small because:

- A commercial breeder will not compete with either conventional thermal nuclear reactors or coal-fired steam-electric power plants for electric generation until the mid-1990s without improved end-use efficiency technologies and not until after the turn of the century with improved end-use efficiency technologies;

- o Uranium availability is not a problem until the 2010s at the earliest (unless significant quantities are exported);
- o Electric generation growth rates were found to be in the range of 2.5 to 4.3 per cent and not the 5-7 per cent that is sometimes claimed in order to justify an aggressive breeder R&D program.

The breeder also does little to help achieve energy independence before the turn of the century as the transportation and petrochemical end uses claim all new liquid fuels production. It appears that it would take an exotic new technology, like electric cars, to sufficiently stimulate electricity demand to a level that would justify the widespread introduction of breeders in this century.

Without improved end-use efficiencies, breeders would be introduced in the 1990s. With improved end-use efficiencies, breeders are not introduced until the turn of the century. Breeders consequently do not help alleviate the environmental disbenefit attributable to the mining of coal and oil shale until after the turn of the century.

Since breeder benefits don´t even start to accrue until the mid-1990s without improved end-use efficiency technologies, and after 2000 with them, a large scale development program designed to lead to a commercial breeder in 1986 seems premature. Cochran, et al. (1975) and Alexander and Rice (1975) have argued that the Clinch River Breeder demonstration plant may be obsolete before it is operational. The breeder is just one option for providing essentially unlimited electrical energy. Fusion power, solar electric generation, and other breeder concepts (i.e., the light-water breeder) are all in the applied technology stage of development. There seems to be no compelling economic reason why the liquid-metal fast breeder deserves to be advanced past this level of development at this time.

Finally, in countries not endowed with a large and diverse nonrenewable energy resource base (e.g., Britain, France, and West Germany), breeder development is much more needed than in this country. These countries will likely develop breeders, nuclear-based hydrogen generation and electric cars much sooner than they will become economical necessities in this country. Indeed, the French and British already have an operational breeder demonstration plant (c.f. Metz, 1975). The prospects for the importation of such technology by the United States are thus quite real. Further, although U.S. supremacy in space exploration and fusion research is probably a necessity for national defense, a leadership position in breeder technology does not appear to be a crucial national security requirement.

SYNTHETIC FUELS FROM COAL AND OIL SHALE

Although the FY 1976 allocation to fossil synthetics was revised upwards from 262 million dollars to 268 million dollars, a moderate further increase (perhaps involving the proposed synthetic fuels commercialization program) seems to be indicated. Further, the 73 million dollars allocated to high-Btu coal gasification could be too high, while the upward revision in the oil shale allocation from 9 to 15 million dollars was probably too small, albeit a step in the right direction.

It is concluded here that the budget allocation to the fossil synthetics program could be moderately increased because:

- In the absence of a break in the world oil cartel, the gross benefits of the program are relatively large, while in the event of a break in the cartel, import restrictions would still yield program benefits;
- Synthetic liquids from coal and oil shale provide the only hope for energy independence before the turn of the century;
- Federal support for synfuels appears to be required because of uncertainty about the future world price of oil.

For the nominal resource case, the gross economic benefits calculated for the synfuels program here are 50 billion dollars if they are the only new technologies developed, 51 billion dollars if breeders are also developed, 35 billion dollars if improved end-use efficiency technologies are available, and 35 billion if both improved end-use efficiency technologies and breeders are developed. The low domestic oil and gas availability assumptions would increase these figures by 10 to 20 per cent, while the high domestic oil and gas availability assumptions would decrease them by a similar amount. If the cartel breaks, the benefits of the synfuels program drop to nearly zero, as introduction of the new technologies does not occur until the 2010s, when global depletion drives up the world price of oil. If imports are restricted, however, some of the benefits may be recovered. In the absence of a break in the cartel, the synfuels program has moderately large economic benefits because:

- Synthetic fuels replace increasingly costly imports, both to achieve energy independence and to substitute for dwindling low-cost domestic oil and gas supplies;
- Availability of low-cost coal for liquefaction won't be a problem, especially if improved end-use efficiency technologies are developed;
- Coal and oil shale extraction costs will increase less rapidly than oil extraction costs due to the larger available resource bases for coal and oil shale.

Synthetic liquids from coal and oil shale are essential for energy independence any time before the turn of the century. Due to the rapid depletion of low-cost domestic oil reserves, it is extremely unlikely that domestic oil production can be increased enough to significantly replace imports. Although the environmental disbenefits of a large synthetic fuel industry could be considerable, it appears to be the price that must be paid for energy independence.

Many argue that fossil fuel synthetics are close enough to commercialization to warrant adequate R&D funding from the private sector. However, uncertainty about the world price of oil is probably preventing adequate funding by risk-averse industrial firms. The federal government should perhaps bear this risk since the expected payoffs, both economic and security, are large. The synthetic fuels commercialization program (see Synfuels Interagency Task Force, 1975) could be implemented at least at the informational level (350 thousand barrels per day by 1985). An additional one or two hundred more million dollars per year might be warranted for this program based upon the present results.

There are two parts of the synfuels program where the analysis performed here suggests that the federal funding levels might require adjustment. First, although high-Btu coal gasification technology is well developed, natural gas reserves with lower extraction costs than synthetic gas production costs are adequate to meet demands until 2000. In industry, coal will substitute for gas, particularly if the gas must be produced synthetically from coal. Only if gas is regulated and allowed to be consumed by low-priority users (i.e., industry as opposed to residences) at artificially low prices, could low-cost domestic reserves be depleted rapidly enough to make synthetic gas attractive by the 1980s.

The second program which may need adjustment based on the analysis performed here is the oil shale program, whose budget allocation was revised up from 9 million to 15 million dollars. Oil shale promises to be the least-cost marginal source of premium refined petroleum products by the mid 1980s. On a Btu-per-pound basis, coal is easier to mine than oil shale, but once mined, the oil shale is much cheaper to liquefy and refine into gasoline, jet fuel and other petroleum products.
Since large demands will be placed on coal as a nonliquid fuel feedstock (for electric generation and direct burning), the oil shale program could provide an environmentally acceptable alternative to coal. However, the spent shale disposal and water availability problems inherent in first generation oil shale processing technologies need to be solved (e.g., by developing in-situ processes). Thus, the R&D funds allocated to the oil shale program could be as much as an order of magnitude too low if one places a high priority on both environmental objectives and the achievement of national energy independence.

IMPROVED END-USE EFFICIENCY TECHNOLOGIES

Although the FY 1976 budget allocation to improved end-use efficiency technologies was revised upward from 109 million dollars to 148 million dollars, the results presented here seem to indicate a several-fold increase in this allocation might be warranted because:

- The benefits from an improved efficiency in end-use technologies program are potentially very large and are virtually independent of whether the other programs are pursued;

- o An improved efficiencies in end-use technologies program makes energy independence easier to achieve with synfuels and delays increases in imports to levels significantly above those that exist today from 1992 to 2000 in the absence of synfuels;
- o An improved efficiency in end-use technologies program helps to significantly reduce the environmental disbenefit of a synfuels program;
- o Improved efficiency in end-use technologies help prevent bottlenecks in new technology and resource extraction industries;
- o Private funding for R&D on these technologies may not be forthcoming in a timely manner, due to market structure in the industries supplying end-use devices and uncertainty about the future world price of oil;
- o Development of improved efficiency in end-use technologies provides additional time to develop new technologies.

Although the economic benefits of improved end-use efficiency technologies include acceptable capital cost differentials for the new end-use devices, it may be that near zero capital cost differentials should be the goal for R&D on such technologies. This would involve, for example, designing buildings and engines that are more energy conservative, but not significantly more expensive, than current ones. Indeed, difficulties in private capital acquisition may necessitate near-zero capital cost differentials in order for the new technologies to be rapidly introduced on a widespread basis. At any rate, the economic benefits of improved end-use technologies are potentially an order of magnitude greater than those for synfuels and two orders of magnitude greater than those for breeders. These gross economic benefits are: 315 billion dollars on a stand-alone basis, 310 billion with pre-existing breeders, 300 billion with pre-existing synfuels, and 294 billion with both pre-existing synfuels and breeders. These gross economic benefits are relatively insensitive to alternative resource assumptions and other programs because:

- o The benefits start accruing sooner for improved end-use technologies than for the other programs;

- o The amount of energy resources required in any time period are less;
- o As resources are depleted less rapidly, the low extraction cost resources last for longer periods of time;
- o With improved end-use efficiency technologies, uranium availability is not a problem for the next sixty years.

The improved end-use efficiencies also allow achievement of energy independence sooner in the event synfuels are developed and reduces the amount of imports required in the future in the absence of synfuels. They also help prevent bottlenecks in both new technology industries (e.g., synfuels) and resource extraction (e.g., coal mining) industries by slowing the required growth rates in these industries. The development of improved efficiency end-use devices would also help alleviate the environmental disbenefit attributable to a synfuels program by slowing the rate of growth of demand for liquid fuels and reducing the competing demands for coal for direct burning and electric generation. Further, regardless of how the environmental disbenefit is measured, this program would help alleviate it relative to any base scenario for any resource case.

The main argument against federal funding of improved end-use efficiency technologies claims that private funding will eventually be adequate. There are several counters to that claim. First of all, "eventually" may not be soon enough to gain a substantial portion of the potential R&D benefits. Market structures in many of the industries supplying end-use devices (e.g., the automotive, construction, steel, and aircraft industries) are not perfectly competitive. Furthermore, uncertainty about future petroleum prices may also be dampening the R&D effort towards energy conservation in these industries. Unfortunately, it is probably not possible for end users themselves (e.g., private citizens, commercial firms, and airlines) to fund the necessary R&D themselves. Thus, substantial government funding of such R&D would appear to be warranted.

Development of improved end-use efficiency technologies would also provide more time to develop and compare alternative new technologies, more time to decide whether a plutonium-based electric economy is worth its potential risks, more time to decide which of the many possible renewable energy sources should be exploited first, and more time to decide whether energy independence is a practical or necessary goal.

In summary, an increase in federal funding of energy conservation R&D would appear to be desirable, particularly where prevailing market structure and uncertainty may dampen the timeliness of the private sector's R&D response. This conclusion is in concert with a major conclusion of the congressional Office of Technology Assessment's recent critique of ERDA's FY 1976 budget (c.f. Boffey, 1975).

In conclusion, the analysis performed here has compared three alternative energy R&D programs according to several criteria. The results of this analysis seem to be quite useful in suggesting both possible reallocations of the federal energy R&D funds allocated to these programs, and areas where future research might prove profitable. Since the model employed here was quite useful in this analysis, a discussion of some other potential applications for this model is contained in the next chapter.

FACTORS THAT COULD POTENTIALLY ALTER THESE CONCLUSIONS

There are several factors that were not considered in the present analysis that could have a significant impact on the policy conclusions drawn here. These factors include lower availability of uranium than expected, the development of economical electric cars, and the interaction of the United States energy system with the world energy system.

The availabilty of low-cost uranium may be significantly less than expected. This would tend to increase the economic benefits attributable to the LMFBR. The sensitivity of the conclusions drawn here to the availability of low-cost uranium needs to be explored.

Significant introduction of electric cars before the turn of the century may be possible. This would tend to increase the growth rate of electricity demand, which would increase the economic benefits attributable to the LMFBR. A study of the potential benefits of an electric car R&D program and especially of the interactions between the benefits of such a program and other energy R&D programs needs to be undertaken.

Finally, the present analysis has assumed the relative insulation of the U.S. energy system from the world energy system. The only interactions between the United States energy system and the world energy system were the potential for unlimited imports of foreign oil and the stipulation of continued United States coal exports at the rate of 1.5 Quads per year. The interaction of the United States energy system with the world energy system, as tempered by the role of the United States in the global political economy may, however, necessitate the export of considerable amounts of uranium, coal, and perhaps even synfuels. The potential for these higher export levels, as well as their impact on the benefits of the various energy R&D programs may merit closer scrutiny.

Chapter 6

OTHER POTENTIAL MODEL APPLICATIONS

The model used in the foregoing analysis may be applicable to energy problems other than the problem analyzed here. The model developed here was designed to specifically focus on the comparison of the relative merits of three major energy R&D programs. However, by the selection of the characteristics of the U.S. energy system included in it, as well as the simplifying assumptions that were made in designing it, the model was tailored with the hope that it could also prove useful in analyzing the relative merits of other existing and proposed energy R&D programs. Applications to other classes of energy problems may also be possible, but the model would likely require modification in order to adequately deal with them.

MAJOR ENERGY R&D PROGRAM EVALUATIONS

The list of existing and proposed major energy R&D programs that could be evaluated using the model is substantial: fusion, solar electric generation, electric cars and thermochemical watersplitting are just a few of the alternatives. The case for electric cars is particularly interesting; an accelerated development program for this technology to the point where electric cars become economical in large numbers before the turn of the century might have a favorable impact on the value of an advanced technology electrical generation (e.g., fusion or the breeder) program. The gross economic benefits of the development of an economical electric car could be calculated using the model and compared with its projected cost.

One major conclusion drawn here is that R&D on improved end-use efficiency technologies is quite possibly being underemphasized at this time. A major study of improved efficiency end-use devices seems long past due. Congress has already expressed considerable interest in these technologies (see, e.g., Committee on Commerce, 1974a, 1974b; Congressional Research Service, 1975; Committee on Aeronautical and Space Sciences, 1974).

If it is found that improved end-use efficiency devices would realistically have to cost significantly more than existing devices, a precise evaluation of the improved end-use technologies would have to include consideration of the relative costs of the currently utilized and improved efficiency end-use devices. It is conceptually easy to include the costs of utilizing devices in the model. The cost of the appropriate utilizing device could be added to the cost of each of the commercialization activities.

The estimation of costs for the utilizing devices is probably easiest in the residential sector, since the problems of aggregation are, in general, less severe here than in the other sectors. For example, the cost of a "representative" home water heating system is probably easier to estimate than the cost of "a representative" industrial process heat generating system, simply because of the greater variety of the latter. In fact, Mutch (1974) has compiled data that is probably sufficient for costing electric, gas, and solar water heaters. Additionally, some data for air conditioners is given in Berg (1974) and Moyers (1973), and for space heaters in Morrow (1973), EPA (1973) and Bechtel (1975). A concerted effort to develop data on the acquisition costs of current end-use devices, and the development and acquisition costs of potential improved efficiency end-use devices in the residential sector would seem to be both not exceedingly difficult and extremely worthwhile. This data could then be used in the model to ascertain the relative merits of the requisite R&D projects.

OTHER ENERGY PROBLEMS AND POSSIBLE MODEL EXTENSIONS

Although the model formulated in this dissertation was designed to help compare major energy R&D programs, it could prove useful for analyzing other energy problems. It might, however, require some modification in order to be useful for analyzing these other problems. This section discusses some possible extensions of the model that could prove useful for analyzing non-R&D energy problems.

Table 6-1 lists some possible extensions to the model, including the reasons these extensions were not incorporated in the original model, the actions required to incorporate the extension and the resulting computer cost projected for one run of the model with the inclusion of the corresponding extension.

The model, as currently formulated, costs about $10 for one run. The capability for including price elastic demands in the model could be

Table 6-1

POTENTIAL MODEL EXTENSIONS

Description of the extension	Reason extension was not incorporated in the original model		Actions required to incorporate the extension		Computer cost for one run
	Data Availability	Computer Cost	Data Collection	Model Modification	
1. Model as is					$10
2. Add elastic demands	X	X	X	X	~35
3. Include cost of utilizing devices	X		X		~10
4. Allow for under-utilization of capacity		X		X	~200
5. Stochastic specification for the world price of oil		X		X	~120
6. Time-stream representation for resource discoveries	X	X	X	X	~25
7. All of the above extensions	X	X	X	X	~2000

handled in a manner suggested by Manne (1974b), where linear approximations to nonlinear demand curves are employed. This would involve the addition of one new constraint per demand category for each time period. The cost of running the model with these constraints included is projected to be approximately $35. This feature was not included in the current model for several reasons. First, the elasticity of demand was not felt to be crucial to the decision being analyzed. In a similar application, SRI (Synfuels Interagency Task Force, 1975) found that the elasticity of end-use demands was not significant to the synthetic fuels commercialization program decision. Second, comprehensive data on the elasticity of all of these end-use demands is not currently available. Finally, the additional computer cost for including such a capability was not thought to be cost effective for the purpose of comparing major energy R&D programs.

The inclusion of utilization device costs in the model was not accomplished primarily due to the lack of adequate data. This modification would involve no real modification to the model (only the input data) and no additional computer cost.

In order to allow for the underutilization of capacity, separate variables for both installed capacity and actual utilization must be defined for each energy commercialization activity. Constraints relating the capacity and utilization variables must also be included. Inclusion of these constraints increases the cost of the model by at least one order of magnitude. The additional realism bought by this facility is probably not worth its cost for the purpose of comparing major energy R&D programs.

Uncertainty about the future world price of oil is a significant factor determining the evolution of the U.S. energy system. However, stochastic programming formulations tend to be quite expensive. Further, the advantage of a stochastic specification over extensive sensitivity analyses on a cost effectiveness basis is not clear. Computer costs are an order of magnitude greater for a minimal stochastic treatment for the world price of oil than for the current model formulation.

Inclusion of a time-phased representation of resource discoveries by cost category could potentially make the model more realistic at a minimal increase in computer cost. However, data on the projected temporal discovery of resources by cost categories is not available.

Finally, inclusion of all the above model extensions would not simply involve a computer cost obtained by summing the costs for the individual modifications. Since the algorithm used to optimize the configuration of the U.S energy system is a linear programming algorithm, the model's computational cost increases with the cube of the number of constraints. Consequently, the inclusion of all the above extensions would involve a computer cost of approximately $2000 per run.

Appendix A

RELATION TO OTHER WORK

This appendix relates the model developed in this dissertation to other energy models and the analysis performed here to some of the analyses that have been performed with these other models. In particular, an attempt is made to justify the need for the new energy model developed here for the specific purpose of evaluating major energy R&D programs. It is concluded that dynamic energy models that consider all the major energy resources and emphasize the technical aspects of energy conversion rather than the economy-wide implications of cost/price fluctuations in the energy sector are best suited to the task of assessing major energy R&D programs at the present time. Consequently, the model developed here is subjected to a more detailed comparison with several other energy models of this type.

The manner in which certain aspects of the energy supply system are handled in the model developed in this dissertation, as well as its relative inexpensiveness, allows it to compare favorably with other energy system-wide dynamic energy models for the purpose of R&D planning. It is also pointed out, however, that for applications other than R&D planning many of these other models are potentially superior. Finally, some previous applications of the other energy models are described and some unresolved issues involved with the use of energy system models in general are discussed.

ENERGY SYSTEM MODELS

A sizable number of quantitative energy models have been developed and recent world and domestic events seem to be leading to an exponential increase in this number. Limaye, et al. (1974) have summarized 94 such studies, while Anderson (1972) contributes 86 additional references. Add to this the proceedings of the 1973 Resources for the Future seminar on energy modeling (Searl, 1973), the MIT conference "Energy: Demand, Conservation and Institutional Problems" (Macrakis, 1974), the 1973 energy modelling workshop at Queen Mary College in London (National Science Foundation, 1973), the 1973 IIASA planning conference on energy systems (International Institute for Applied Systems Analysis, 1973), and the 1974 Electric Power Research Institute (1974) and Lawrence Berkeley Laboratory (Benenson, et al., 1974) conferences on energy modeling and one starts to gain some appreciation for just how much energy modeling has been done.

Since there are in existence such a large number of energy models, it would be impossible to contrast them all with the model developed here. Consequently, the distinction is first made between models that consider less than the entire energy economy (e.g., just oil and gas production, just electricity generation, etc.) and models that consider the entire energy economy. These latter models will be referred to as energy system models. Energy system models were designed primarily to study the complete spectrum of energy resources and conversions for the United States as a whole. Since the current United States energy system is characterized by a high degree of potential inter-fuel substitution and new technologies promise to increase this potential even further, consideration of all of the major energy resources seems a logical prerequisite for a model intended for use in national energy R&D planning. The next section attempts to narrow the domain of models appropriate for energy R&D planning by arguing that only a certain class of energy system models are appropriate for this purpose.

A CLASSIFICATION SCHEME FOR ENERGY SYSTEM MODELS

In the last section the distinction between models that consider less than the entire energy economy and models that consider the entire energy economy was made. For the purpose of identifying model types that are most apppropriate for energy R&D planning, energy system models are next categorized according to: (1) whether or not the model includes explicitly the interaction between the energy economy and the rest of the U.S. economy (i.e., whether it is a general or a partial equilibrium model) and (2) whether the model is static or dynamic. Static models consider the system in equilibrium at given points in time (and therefore are analogous to snapshots of the system), while dynamic models follow the system from one point in time to the next (and, therefore, are analogous to motion pictures of the system). Table A-1 gives examples of energy system models that fit into the four partitions defined by these two criteria.

Table A-1

A SIMPLE CLASSIFICATION SCHEME FOR ENERGY SYSTEM MODELS

	STATIC	DYNAMIC
Energy Economy Only	Hoffman (1972) PIES (FEA, 1974) Michigan (Bushnell, et al., 1974)	Haefele-Manne (1975) Baughman (1972) TERA (American Gas Association, 1974) SRI (1975) RAND (Anderson, 1976) Brookhaven (Bodin, et al., 1974) Weyant
Entire Economy	CAC (Herendeen, 1974) CAC-Brookhaven (Hoffman, 1974) Just (1972) Hudson-Jorgenson (1974)	Hudson-Jorgenson (1974)

Static Versus Dynamic Energy System Models

The static models shown in Table A-1 include the U.S. energy system model of Hoffman (1972), the FEA's project independence evaluation system (PIES) model (Federal Energy Administration, 1974a), the Michigan fuel energy policy model (Bushnell, et al., 1974), an input-output model developed at the Center for Advanced Computation (CAC) at the University of Illinois (Herendeen, 1974), a model that combines the CAC economic model and the energy system model developed at Brookhaven by Hoffman, et al. (1974) and the generalized, input-output, new energy technology model of Just (1973). The Hudson-Jorgenson model (1974) is hard to classify as either dynamic or static since its macroeconomic growth sub-model is, of course, dynamic, while its inter-industry input-output sub-model (which uses the output of the macro-growth model as input) is static. Recall that these static models calculate equilibria for the energy system at given points in time.

Static models are useful in two contexts: (1) in very short run analyses where appropriate capacity constraints are easy to project (e.g., since for most activities in the energy sector capacity takes at least 3 years to build, existing capacities could be used as constraints on the operation of the system for several years into the future) and (2) in very long run analyses where projections are made far enough into the future that the assumption that the requisite capacity will be built is not too bad (even so, the operation of the system at the future date will be influenced by the actual buildup of capacity between now and then). Some appreciation for how long it can take for the effect of presently existing capacity to be dampened can be gained by recalling that a nuclear power plant built today could well be in service thirty years from now, while a home heating system installed in a new home today could still be relied on for forty years or more). As many energy R&D projects take only a few years to bear fruit and only a few take over 30 years, it probably makes great sense to use a dynamic representation of the energy system to assess potential energy R&D programs.

The dynamic models listed in Table A-1 include the "Transition from Fossil to Nuclear Fuels" policy model of Haefele and Manne (1975), the "Dynamic Inter-Fuel Competition" model of Baughman (1972), the American

Gas Association's "Total Energy Resource Analysis" (TERA) Model (1974), the Brookhaven dynamic model (Bodin, et al., 1974), the Rand model (Anderson, 1976) and Stanford Research Institute's economic equilibrium model (1975). These models consider how the energy system moves from an equilibrium at one point in time to equilibria at successive points in time. They, therefore, implicitly or explicitly consider the requisite capacity adjustments necessary to move from one state of energy system operation to another.

Economy-Wide Versus Technically-Oriented Energy System Models

Of the example models listed in Table A-1, the CAC, CAC-Brookhaven, Just and Hudson-Jorgenson Models consider explicitly the link between the energy economy and the rest of the U.S. economy, while the Hoffman, PIES, Michigan, Haefele-Manne, Baughman, Brookhaven dynamic, Rand, SRI and TERA models do not. However, it is important to note that expected general economic conditions are partially reflected in the projected levels of demand and the price sensitivities of these demands that are provided as input. Besides, the feedback effect of prices in the energy sector on the rest of the economy may not be very significant in the future*, as was implied by the Hudson-Jorgenson analysis (Ford Energy Policy Project, 1974, Appendix F). However, although the Hudson-Jorgenson model does allow the input-output coefficients to vary in response to the prices of inputs and outputs, thereby simulating technical change within the energy sector, the level of aggregation of this model (as well as of the CAC model) does not allow one to observe the details of the nature of this change.

To summarize, econometric models like the Hudson-Jorgenson model treat technical change in the energy sector in a very aggregate manner, while endogenously considering several gross economic indicators. In "process analysis" models such as that of Hoffman, this emphasis is reversed in that general economic conditions are assumed and the specifics of technical advances in energy conversion technologies are explicitly dealt with. The CAC-Brookhaven model does promise to consider both general economic conditions and the details of the energy

*Of course the discovery of a cheap and abundant source of energy (e.g., a simple process to fuse dueterium molecules that are in abundant supply in sea water) could alter this.

conversion processes, however, it is not a dynamic model. Models that are dynamic and that explicitly consider the interaction of the energy economy with the rest of the economy are difficult to formulate because of computational limits (consider, for example, the extreme level of aggregation utilized in the "Limits to Growth" study; Meadows, et al., 1972).

In conclusion, it appears likely that no existing energy model (including the one presented herein) adequately captures the impact of the evolution of the U.S. energy system (and especially of rising prices in this sector) on the U.S. macro-economy. The Hudson-Jorgenson approach seems to be headed in the right direction (subject perhaps to some of the additional caveats mentioned later in the "Applications" and "Unresolved Issues" sections), but more meaningful results will be obtained from this type of analysis only when technical data on the efficiencies and costs of emerging energy technologies are integrated with historical fuel price trends to form a firmer foundation upon which to make future energy price projections. It would seem that at the present time a model that emphasizes the technical aspects of the energy conversion system rather than the interaction of the energy economy with the rest of the United States economy would be more useful for energy R&D planning. The next section discusses and contrasts a number of such models as to their appropriateness for energy R&D planning.

DYNAMIC TECHNICALLY-ORIENTATED ENERGY SYSTEM MODELS

In this section the seven dynamic and technically-orientated energy system models identified in the last section (and shown in the upper right-hand quadrant of Table A-1) are compared as to their appropriateness for national energy R&D planning. The emphasis here is on charateristics that are thought to be particularly relevant to the assessment of alternative energy R&D programs. Table A-2 shows six such characteristics and identifies the models that possess them.

In Weyant and Ojdana (1976) it is argued that it is inadvisable to use this type of comparison scheme to "rate" alternative R&D planning models. Thus, the purpose of Table A-2 is more to provide an outline for the subsequent discussion rather than a "report card" on the alternative models.

Table A-2

COMPARISON OF ALTERNATIVE DYNAMIC TECHNICALLY ORIENTED ENERGY MODELS RELATIVE TO NATIONAL ENERGY R&D PLANNING

	Demands Specified by End-Use	Depletion of Domestic Resources Modeled	Commercial Investment Decisions Based on Minimum Life-Cycle Cost	Refinery Sector Modeled	Cost/Run
Haefele-Manne		Limited	X		?
Baughman		X			?
TERA		X			?
SRI	X	X	X		~$250
RAND		X			~$10
Brookhaven	X		X		~$250
Weyant	X	X	X	X	$10

Specification of Demands by End Use

It is of interest to contrast the manner in which demands are specified in the various energy system models. There seem to be three levels at which demands are specified: (1) by basic fuel (e.g. oil, gas, electricity, etc.), as in the Baughman (1972) model, (2) by basic fuel disaggregated by sector (e.g., oil to residential consumers, coal to industrial users, etc.), as in the Rand model (Anderson, 1976) and (3) by energy end-use form (e.g., residential space heat, industrial process heat, etc.), as in the Brookhaven (Bodin, et al., 1974) and SRI (1975) models. Consideration of demands by end use allows for a more adequate representation of demands and demand elasticities since it enables one to more adequately project the impacts of satiation and subsistence effects. In addition, by specifying demands by end use, the efficiencies of the end-use utilizing devices can be explicitly represented. This is highly desirable since improved end-use efficiencies is one of the major energy R&D programs considered in this study.

Cost Escalation of Depleting Resources

An adequate representation of the cost escalation of energy resources due to depletion is a necessary prerequisite for an energy R&D planning model. The costs of the basic resources over time determines when a new technology product like liquefied coal will compete with domestic petroleum. Although the Haefele-Manne model uses the most detailed breakdown of U_3O_8 costs and hence is better able to deal with the uranium availability question than any of the other models, it does not include consideration of the cost escalation of the fossil fuel resources. The Brookhaven dynamic model does not consider any resource depletion cost escalation at all. Both the Haefele-Manne and Brookhaven dynamic models could, however, be modified to include multiple cost categories for each non-renewable energy resource.

Minimization of Life-Cycle Cost as the Objective

The Haefele-Manne, Brookhaven dynamic and Weyant models all use minimization of the life-cycle cost of the energy conversion facilities necessary to supply the nation's energy needs over a specified time horizon as the objective function for a mathematical programming model of the United States energy system. This implies that the individual firms in the energy economy make commercialization decisions with perfect foresight on a minimum life-cycle cost basis. This assumption allows a simple calculation of the gross benefits of a new energy technology to be made by comparing objective function values obtained by optimizing with and without inclusion of the new technology.

Whether the minimization of life-cycle cost objective allows for an adequate aggregate representation of the decision processes engaged in by the many diverse firms in the energy economy is an open question. The designers of the other models listed in Table A-1, in fact, expended considerable modeling effort trying to simulate these individual decision processes in a more detailed manner. For the type of assessment carried out in this dissertation, this type of effort was not thought to be worth its cost. The greater cost of using these other models is a reflection of the desire on the part of their architects to develop general purpose models, which attempt to model reality. In contrast, the Weyant model is an example of a special purpose model that focuses only on those elements of the energy system that are relevant to the particular class of decision problems of immediate interest (i.e., R&D planning).

Detailed Technical Representation of the Electric Generation Sector

An adequate technical representation of the electric generation sector is crucial to any representation of the United States energy system that is to be used for R&D planning purposes. This is the sector where the greatest potential for inter-fuel substitution exists. The Weyant model uses the Brookhaven representation of the electrical load-duration curve, as well as its scheme for including the potential for the sharing of electric generation equipment by compatible pairs of demands. However, the modeling of the load sharing is done more efficiently in the Weyant model than in the Brookhaven formulation. To represent this load sharing potential, the Brookhaven model requires both a variable and a constraint for each type of electric generation equipment for each time period, while in the Weyant model only variables are required.* Since the computational effort that must be expended to solve a linear program increases only linearly with the number of variables, but with the cube of the number of constraints, the computational advantage of this representation are substantial. In fact, it reduced the computational cost of the present model by about fifty per cent.

Liquid Fuels Refineries Modeled

Although some of the input-output type of energy models have included a refining industry, most of the models of the energy system and also most energy system flow diagrams (e.g., Associated Universities, 1972; Austin, et al., 1973), treat oil as a single homogeneous product. In reality, however, not all of the various oil products are perfect substitutes for each other in all end uses and there are limits to the yield of a particular oil product that can be refined from a barrel of crude at reasonable cost. For example, residual fuel oil (which is a by-product of the refining process) can not presently be utilized to power automobiles or to heat homes. In view of these considerations and since maintaining an adequate supply of low-cost liquid fuels seems to be the biggest problem facing energy R&D planners, the simple refinery model included in the present model is thought to be well worth its cost.

In summary, it is seen from Table A-2 that the model developed in this dissertation is the only one of those listed that includes consideration of all aspects of the U.S. energy system thought to be required for a representation adequate for energy R&D planning. Other models that come close cost significantly more to use. Some of the other models are, of course, better suited for analyzing problems other than R&D planning problems. To illustrate this point and to provide some additional insight into the motivation for the development of the current model, prior applications of three of these energy models are summarized in the next section.

---

* See Appendix C for a discussion of the computational advantage of this scheme over previously employed schemes.

SOME APPLICATIONS OF ENERGY SYSTEM MODELS

In this section some actual applications of three representative energy system models are discussed. Since all of the representative models have been developed quite recently, documentation even for the three applications discussed here is still somewhat meager.

The three applications discussed here are: (1) the use of the Brookhaven (static) model in the formulation of ERDA's energy R&D plan (as manifest in ERDA-48,1975), (2) the use of the Hudson-Jorgenson model to support several contentions made in the final report of the Ford Energy Policy Project concerning the potential impact of energy conservation on the U.S. macro-economy and (3) the use of the SRI model in the president's Synfuels Interagency Task Force study of the proposed synthetic fuels commercialization program.

The Brookhaven Model

The first application discussed here is the use of the Brookhaven static model* (c.f. Cherniavsky, 1974) in the Energy Research and Development Administration's R&D plan submitted to Congress on June 30, 1975 (ERDA-48, 1975). In this study, experts were asked to project resource consumption levels and distribution patterns to satisfy end-use demands for each of six representative energy demand and technology scenarios for the years 1985 and 2000. The resource consumption patterns projected by these experts were used as input to the Brookhaven model, which was then used to calculate the minimum cost set of energy conversion and distribution activities to satisfy specified end-use demands. The minimum cost for the base case scenario, in which no new technological incentives were assumed to be taken for the rest of the century was then compared with the costs for the other scenarios in order to ascertain how much the development of the corresponding new technologies might be worth.

Three possible shortcomings of this analysis were: (1) no consideration was given to the uncertainties associated with the future evolution of the U.S. energy system (e.g., those associated with the amounts of economically recoverable resources of the various types); (2)

*This model is originally due to Hoffman (1972) and, consequently, was referred to as the "Hoffman" model above.

the model utilized was a static rather than a dynamic model and (3) since costs for energy utilizing devices (e.g., space heaters and industrial furnaces) were not considered, a direct comparison of the relative worths of R&D dollars spent on end-use devices (such as solar heating and cooling, and heat pumps) and R&D dollars spent on supply technologies (such as nuclear breeder reactors) may not be completely valid. Resolving these deficiencies is, needless to say, a high priority area for future research. The first two deficiencies have been resolved with the model developed in this dissertation. Resolution of the third deficiency can be accomplished by augmenting the present model's input data base.

The Hudson-Jorgenson Model

The Hudson-Jorgenson model was used to support several allegations made by the Ford Foundation Energy Policy Project in their final report (Ford Energy Policy Project, 1974). Basically, it was the Energy Policy Project's conclusion (for a critique of this study, see Institute for Contemporary Studies, 1975) that energy conservation is an often neglected and effective means for combating the shortages and rapidly escalating energy prices that are the essence of the "energy crisis." The usual counter to pro-conservation arguments is that conservation measures would tend to lead to a reduction in GNP and an increase in unemployment, as it is alleged that a high level of energy consumption promulgates a healthy growth rate of GNP. The Hudson-Jorgenson model was used in an attempt to show the incorrectness of this allegation. For example, even under the conditions of the project's "zero energy growth" scenario (in which energy consumption was projected to grow at a leisurely pace until 1985 and then to hold steady for the rest of the century) the Hudson-Jorgenson model predicted no adverse effects on GNP or employment.

Possible deficiencies of this analysis were: (1) the econometric model used is estimated using data gathered during a time when real energy prices were declining, while today real energy prices are rising rapidly; such a fundamental discontinuity in real energy prices makes the utilization of such historically estimated parameters highly suspect and (2) the technology of the energy sector is represented in a highly aggregated form so that many critical factors (such as the buildup of nuclear reactor generating capacity) must be assumed as inputs. Researchers at Harvard are, however, attempting to integrate the Brookhaven energy system model with the Hudson-Jorgenson model. It should prove interesting to compare the results of this effort with the results of the CAC-Brookhaven study (Hoffman, et al., 1974).

The SRI Model

The SRI model has been used: (1) to help Gulf Oil evaluate its synthetic fuels program (Stanford Research Institute, 1975), (2) to help the Council on Environmental Quality perform a resource assessment (study still in progress) and (3) by a presidential task force on synthetic fuels to provide background analysis for the presidential decision on the nature of a possible federally supported synthetic fuels commercialization program (Synfuels Interagency Task Force, 1975). Since the documentation for the synthetic fuels study is the most complete at present, this application is discussed next.

The Synfuels Interagency Task Force used the SRI model to aid in a decision analysis of a synthetic fuels commercialization program that would provide government support (in the form of price supports and guaranteed loans, etc.) for the accelerated commercialization of synthetic fuels (primarily from coal and oil shale).

The analysis focused on the selection of an appropriate level of government involvement in such a commercialization program. The alternative goals considered for such a program were: 1) zero, 2) 350,000, 3) 1,000,000, and 4) 1,700,000 barrels per day by 1985. The SRI model was used to simulate the evolution of the U.S. energy system under a number of alternative assumptions thought to be relevant to this decision. The model was used to construct a demand curve for synthetic fuels based upon price-quantity pairs from some of the scenarios analyzed. Then, expected values were calculated external to the model for certain measures of performance (e.g., consumer's surplus, producer's surplus, expected embargo loss, and socio-economic costs) for each alternative program level. The values for these measures of performance were then added in order to provide an aggregate measure of performance which was used to compare the alternative program goals.

Some possible deficiencies of this analysis were: (1) the demand curve for synthetic fuels that was used to calculate values for consumer's and producer's surplus was based upon a number of assumptions (e.g. the usual ceteris paribus assumption that underlies the construction of a demand curve) that were never really verified; (2) the adequacy of consumer's surplus and producer's surplus as benefit measures and producer's surplus as a commercial investment criteria were never discussed; (3) the impact of the descretization of certain parameters and decision variables necessitated by the decision analysis approach is never really considered and (4) the complexity and additional computer costs of using the SRI model relative to other simpler models was never justified for this particular application.

The SRI model probably includes consideration of more aspects of the U.S. energy system than any other existing energy model. Consequently, it also requires more input data and is more costly to use than most other models. Whether reliable data of the sort required by this model is available and whether its considerable computational costs are justified relative to simpler models are open questions, whose answers probably depend on the particular problem being analyzed. Actually, it is probably most justified for studying programs that have a short term (say pre-1985) and potentially significant impact on the energy system (like the synfuels commercialization program) and least justified for long-run problems like the R&D decisions analyzed in this dissertation. In fact, a model such as that developed here could possibly be used to examine a large number of energy R&D policy issues in order to delineate those that merit a more detailed treatment with a model like the SRI model. There are, however, several unresolved issues involved with the use of any energy system model. A brief discussion of some of these issues concludes this appendix.

SOME UNRESOLVED ISSUES INVOLVED WITH THE USE OF ENERGY SYSTEM MODELS

In concluding this appendix, several unresolved issues that seem to be inherent to varying degrees with the use of most energy system models are discussed. These issues include the assumption of perfect competition utilized in many of the models, the lack of attention usually given to the selection of appropriate levels of aggregation for the energy resources and products represented in the models and the lack of consideration of political and organizational factors by the designers of the models.

The Perfect Competition Assumption

One critical unresolved issue involved with the use of these models is that many of them are based on the assumption of perfect competition. This implies that demands are always satisfied by the least cost energy supply alternative. As many energy industries are characterized by a high level of concentration (e.g., oil and coal) and others have been subsidized or operated by the federal government (e.g., uranium enrichment), competition in the real energy economy may be far from perfect. Whether the current increased attention gained by the energy economy will lead to legislation designed to make competition in the energy industries more perfect and whether the assumption of perfect competition allows one to adequately represent an imperfectly competitive energy economy are both questions that additional research should help to answer (see e.g., Duchesneau ,1974, for an analysis of the level of competition existing in the U.S. energy industries).

Selection of Appropriate Levels of Aggregation

A second unresolved issue has already been touched upon in the discussion of an appropriate level of aggregation for oil products. The determination of the appropriate level of aggregation for other energy products is equally as unresolved. For example, should coal be represented as a single homogenous product? strip-mine versus deep-mine coal? or high-sulfur versus low-sulfur coal? It is undoubtedly true that the appropriate level of aggregation depends on the particular energy problem being addressed, but it is equally as true (as has been noted by Manne, 1974a) that not much thought has gone into the selection of the level of aggregation chosen for any particular study.

Lack of Consideration of Political and Organizational Factors

A third unresolved issue involved with the use of these models is their lack of consideration of political and organizational factors. Many argue that all major governmental decisions are actually based on political considerations, rendering quantitative systems analysis of dubious value. The systems analysts counter that, while the models are far from perfect, they are the best available means for helping decision makers to arrive at rational public policy decisions. Whether and how quantitative models are actually used in making public policy decisions seems to be an area of research that may be, in the final analysis, more relevant than the refinement of the characteristics of existing models. The Stanford Research Institute is presently performing a study for ERDA on the utility of energy models.

Appendix B

ALGEBRAIC FORMULATION OF THE MODEL

This appendix presents a description of an algebraic formulation of the model that is intended to provide a general view of how the model works. In the interest of brevity, the present discussion will focus on the primary elements of the model. Details on data sources and the values assumed for the various model input parameters are presented in Appendix D. It is assumed that the reader has already read Chapter 3 and is familiar with the model´s concepts. Unfortunately, however, the simplistic nomenclature used in Chapter 3 must be virtually discarded.

The model formulation for the base case scenario will be developed first in order to make clear precisely what activities and constraints are included in the model. After this task has been accomplished, the modifications that must be made to the base case scenario formulation in order to represent the other scenarios are described. The final section of the chapter presents an algebraic summary of the linear programming implementation of the model for all of the R&D scenarios. The reader well versed in both energy modeling and linear programming may want to skip directly to the last section and omit the development of the model´s nomenclature, objective function and constraints that follows.

The network orientation of the model was described in Chapter 3 and was illustrated in the example in Fig. 3-3. That figure is repeated here as Fig. B-1 in order to initiate the discussion of the nomenclature used in the algebraic formulation of the model. Keep in mind, however, that Fig. B-1 is only a simple example that is intended to provide a link with Chapter 3 and thereby initiate the present description of the model´s algebraic formulation. This formulation follows the classical linear programming format in that there are variables, coefficients, constants, constraints and an objective function.* However, some of the coefficients used in the formulation are actually combinations of several more fundamental parameters; these more fundamental parameters are referred to as "coefficient parameters" in what follows. Given a

*Both the objective function and the constraints are linear functions of both the variables and the coefficients. The constraints also include a constant.

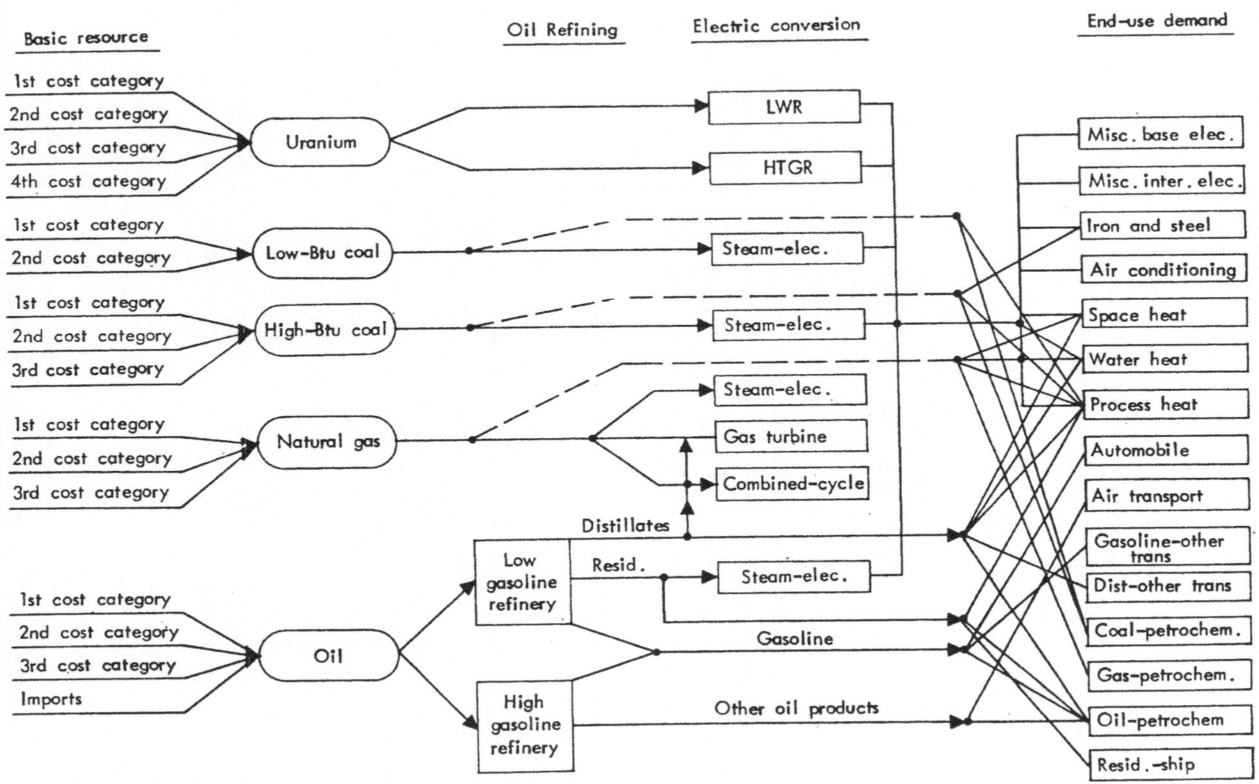

Fig. B-1 — Simplified example of an energy system network

user specified set of values for the coefficients and the constants, the standard linear programming package solves for the values of the variables by minimizing the objective function subject to the satisfaction of the constraints. Before the constraints and objective function are presented, there is a brief description of some of the more significant variables, coefficient parameters and constants that are used in the formulation.

PRINCIPAL VARIABLES, COEFFICIENT PARAMETERS AND CONSTANTS FOR THE BASE CASE SCENARIO

The model concepts described in Chapter 3 used the "commercialization activity" as the basic conceptual building block. The commercialization activity represented the construction in a specified period of an appropriately sized sequence of energy conversion facilities along a trajectory through the generalized energy system network. In order to represent certain features of the energy system in the algebraic formulation of the model, it is necessary to break some of the trajectories (commercialization activities) up into several segments. Furthermore, some of the commercialization activities are allowed to share certain energy supply/processing facilities. Thus, the simplistic concept of a "commercialization activity" must be replaced by a more sophisticated concept which embodies the essential features of the former concept as well as certain new features that allow a particular sequence of energy processing facilities (now termed an "energy supply enterprise") to supply energy to other "supply enterprises" as well as to end-use devices as appropriate.

A supply enterprise is analogous to a commercialization activity in that it is characterized by cost and efficiency coefficients in addition to an energy production "capacity" (PC or RC) variable which represents the average annual energy output from the supply enterprise. The "PC" and "RC" variables, therefore, provide the links between the basic energy resources and the end-use demands.

The Resource Variables, Coefficient Parameters and Constants

There is only one resource variable type; it represents the annual depletion of the supply ("DS") of a given kind of basic resource. The basic resources considered in the base case scenario are uranium, low-Btu (predominantly strip-mine) coal, high-Btu (predominantly deep-mine) coal, natural gas and crude oil. Each of these resources is subdivided into several supply cost categories depending upon the difficulty of recovery. Thus, the resource variables are indexed by resource type (i) and supply cost category (j) according to the scheme outlined in Table B-1. The resource depletion variables are also indexed by period (t), that is DS(i,j,t).

The principal resource coefficient parameter is the supply cost coefficient parameter ("CDS"), which gives the unit cost for the resource supply category for each period. Since the annual resource costs are discounted to reflect consumption during alternative periods of varying lengths, the supply cost coefficient parameters are indexed on t.

The only resource constant is the remaining resource supply constant (R), which represents the total remaining resources in a given cost category (j) for a specified resource type (i) thought to be ultimately available as of the beginning of 1975. Both the cost and remaining resource coefficients are indexed on both i and j (i.e., CDS(i,j,t) and R(i,j)).

The End-use Demand Constants

The end-use demand categories represent the four principal sectors of the United States energy economy: namely, transportation, industry, residential/commercial and miscellaneous electricity which is not explicitly included in the representation for the other sectors (see Fig. 3-1). The demand categories used in the model are described in Table B-2 in terms of the nature of the end-use demand and the candidate fuel forms (and associated utilizing devices) that can satisfy that end-use demand. The net demand for a given end-use demand category (say n) is represented by the constant D(n,t), where t is the period (see Chapter 3 and Appendix D for discussions of how the net demands are determined).

The end-use demands are related to the resources by means of the supply enterprises. It is not sufficient to simply pair up a basic resource with an end-use demand in order to specify a supply enterprise for two reasons. First, each supply enterprise must be uniquely defined. For example, if just the basic resource "low-Btu coal" and the

Table B-1

BASIC ENERGY RESOURCE TYPES AND SUPPLY CATEGORIES FOR THE BASE CASE SCENARIO

Resource Type		Supply Cost Categories[a]		
Index i	Description	Index j	Cost Basis	Cost Category Basis
1	Uranium (U_3O_8) as output by the mill	1	Domestic extraction	1
		2	Domestic extraction	2
		3	Domestic extraction	3
		4	Domestic extraction	4
2	Low-Btu coal at the mine-mouth	1	Domestic extraction	1
		2	Domestic extraction	2
3	High-Btu coal at the mine-mouth	1	Domestic extraction	1
		2	Domestic extraction	2
		3	Domestic extraction	3
4	Natural gas at the wellhead	1	Domestic extraction	1
		2	Domestic extraction	2
		3	Domestic extraction	3
5	Crude oil at the wellhead/ port of entry	1	Domestic extraction	1
		2	Domestic extraction	2
		3	Domestic extraction	3
		4	Imports (port of entry price)	-

[a]All supply categories are for domestic resource supplies unless otherwise indicated. Each supply category includes demonstrated reserves plus both inferred and expected undiscovered reserves for that category.

Table B-2

END-USE DEMAND CATEGORIES AND UTILIZING DEVICES FOR THE BASE CASE SCENARIO

End-Use Demand Category		Utilizing Devices	
Index[a] n	Description	Fuel Form Used	Type of Device
1	Miscellaneous base-load electricity	Electricity	Miscellaneous
2	Miscellaneous intermediate-load electricity	Electricity	Miscellaneous
3	Peak-load electricity	Electricity	Miscellaneous
5	Iron and steel	High-Btu coal	Blast furnace
6	Air conditioning	Electricity	Vapor compressor
7	Space heat	Electricity	Resistor
		Gas	Gas burner
		Distillate	Distillate burner
8	Water heat	Electricity	Resistor
		Gas	Gas burner
		Distillate	Distillate burner
9	Industrial process heat	Electricity	Electric oven
		Gas	Gas burner
		High-Btu coal	High-Btu coal furnace
		Low-Btu coal	Low-Btu coal furnace
		Distillate	Distillate burner
		Residual oil	Residual boiler
10	Automobile	Gasoline	Internal combustion engine
11	Air transportation	Jet fuel	Gas turbine
12	Other gasoline transportation	Gasoline	Internal combusion engine
13	Other distillate transportation	Distillate	Diesel engine
14	Coal for petrochemicals	Coal	Miscellaneous
15	Gas for petrochemicals	Gas	Miscellaneous
16	Refined oil products for petrochemicals	Refined oil products	Miscellaneous
17	Residual oil for ships	Residual oil	Residual boiler

[a]Index 4 was not used.

end-use demand "industrial process heat" are specified, it is impossible to ascertain whether the coal is burned in an industrial furnace (one supply enterprise) or whether it is first converted to electicity that is used in an electric oven (a second supply enterprise). Second, a single supply enterprise may be used to satisfy more than one end-use demand. Thus a system of two types of variables, each described by a fairly sophisticated nomenclature, must be established in order to provide for the unique identification of supply enterprises. These variables represent paths through the energy supply system network.

Supply Enterprises Represented by "PC" Variables

The variables of the first type, termed "PC", are related directly to the end-use demand constants (D) via a constraint that is subsequently introduced. The supply enterprises that are represented by the "PC" variables are uniquely identified by three subscripts (m,k,t) which reference: 1) the input-and-process path for the energy supply enterprise (m), the output path for the supply enterprise (k), and the period (t) during which the enterprise is first introduced into service.* The relevant input and output paths are described in Tables B-3 and B-4, along with the corresponding index values for m and k.

In order to illustrate the concept of an energy supply enterprise of variable type "PC", a sequence of three increasingly complex example models are now described. These three examples are illustrated schematically in Figs. B-2 through B-4. In these examples, only the basic resources low-Btu coal and oil are considered. In the first example, no oil refining or electricity generation is included, in the second example, oil refining is added and, finally, in the third example, electricity generation is added.

Figure B-2 shows a simple example that includes only the basic resources low-Btu coal and oil, and the end-use demands for industrial process heat and automotive gasoline. The subscript i refers to the basic resource category (Table B-1), m to the input-and-process path for the supply enterprise (Table B-3), k to the output path for the supply enterprise (Table B-4), and n to the end-use demand category (Table B-2)

---

*Recall that the nomenclature in this Appendix is different from that used in Chapter 3.

Table B-3

DESCRIPTION OF THE INPUT-AND-PROCESS PATHS FOR THE TYPE "PC" SUPPLY ENTERPRISES

(For the Base Case Scenario)

Index m	Input Resource Supply		Principal Process (electricity generation/transportation)	Admissable Output Paths (Index k; see Table B-4)
	Energy Form	Point of Delivery		
1	Uranium	Mill output	Light-water reactor	1-4,7,8,11,12,14,16,17
2	Uranium	Mill output	High-temperature gas-cooled reactor	1-4,7,8,11,12,14,16,17
3	Low-Btu coal	Minemouth	Transportation	17,22
4	Low-Btu coal	Minemouth	Steam electric	1-4,7,8,11,12,14,16,17
5	High-Btu coal	Minemouth	Transportation	10,17,22
6	High-Btu coal	Minemouth	Steam electric	1-4,7,8,11,12,14,16,17
7	Natural gas	Wellhead	Transportation	12,16,17,23
8	Natural gas	Wellhead	Combined cycle	1-4,7,8,11,12,14,16,17
9	Natural gas	Wellhead	Gas turbine	1-4,6-8,11,12,14,16,17
10	Natural gas	Wellhead	Steam electric	1-4,7,8,11,12,14,16,17
11	Gasoline	Low gasoline refinery[a]	Transportation	18,20,24
12	Distillates	Low gasoline refinery[a]	Transportation	12,16,17,21,24
13	Residual oil	Low gasoline refinery[a]	Transportation	17,24,25
14	Distillates	Low gasoline refinery[a]	Combined cycle	1-4,7,8,11,12,14,16,17
15	Distillates	Low gasoline refinery[a]	Gas turbine	1-4,6-8,11,12,14,16,17
16	Residual oil	Low gasoline refinery[a]	Steam electric	1-4,7,8,11,12,14,16,17
17	Gasoline	High gasoline refinery[a]	Transportation	18,20,24
18	Jet fuel + Other[b]	High gasoline refinery[a]	Transportation	19,24

[a]Output side of refinery.

[b]Other jet fuel grade products.

Table B-4

DESCRIPTION OF THE OUTPUT PATHS FOR THE TYPE "PC" SUPPLY ENTERPRISES[a]

(For the Base Case Scenario)

Index[b] k	Pumped Storage	Utilizing End-Use Demand Categories		Admissable Paths for the Input-and-Process Side of the Supply Enterprise (Index m; see Table B-3)
		Index n (see Table B-2)	Description (Primary / -- Secondary[c])	
1		1	Miscellaneous base-load electricity	1,2,4,6,8-10,14-16
2		2	Miscellaneous intermediate-load electricity	1,2,4,6,8-10-14-16
3	X	2	Miscellaneous intermediate-load electricity	1,2,4,6,8-10,14-16
		3	-- Peak-load electricity	
4		2	Miscellaneous intermediate-load electricity	1,2,4,6,8-10,14-16
		8	-- Water heat	
6		3	Peak-load electricity	9,15
7	X	3	Peak-load electricity	1,2,4,6,8-10,14-16
		3	--Peak-load electricity	
8		3	Peak-load electricity	1,2,4,6,8-10,14-16
		8	-- Water heat	
10		5	Iron and Steel	5
11		6	Air conditioning	1,2,4,6,8-10,14-16
12		7	Space heat	1,2,4,6-10,12,14-16
14		7	Space heat	1,2,4,6,8-10,14-16
		8	-- Air conditioning	
16		8	Water heat	1,2,4,6-10,12,14-16
17		9	Industrial process heat	1-10,12-16
18		10	Automobile	11,17
19		11	Air transportation	18
20		12	Other gasoline transportation	11,17
21		13	Other distillate transportation	12
22		14	Coal for petrochemicals	3,5
23		15	Gas for petrochemicals	7
24		16	Refined oil products for petrochemicals	11-13,17,18
25		17	Residual oil for ships	13

[a]The type "PC" supply enterprise delivers the output energy form to the utilizing device.

[b]Indices 5, 9, 13, and 15 were not used.

[c]A "secondary" utilization demand category can share underutilized electricity generation facilities that are otherwise dedicated to the associated primary demand categories.

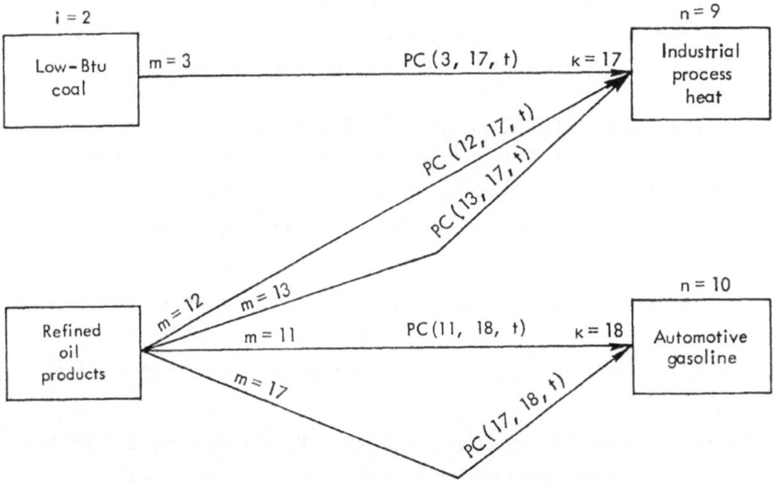

Fig. B-2—Type "PC" supply enterprises

that is ultimately satisfied. The variable PC(m,k,t) represents the average annual energy production for the enterprise. Thus, PC(3,17,t) = PC(low-Btu coal, process heat, t) represents the average annual production of industrial process heat from low-Btu coal facilities that were first introduced into service at the beginning of period t. These facilities are assumed to be available for thirty years. However, this time interval is more a reflection of the useful lifetime of the utilizing device (in this case, industrial furnace) than of the associated transport system. The supply enterprise costs do, however, include the cost of setting up the requisite transportation capacity.

Note that a type "PC" supply enterprise is uniquely identified by the set of indices (m,k,t). Furthermore, note that only the type "PC" supply enterprise is allowed to directly satisfy an end-use demand.

<u>Supply Enterprises Represented by "RC" Variables</u>

In Fig. B-3, two refinery types have been added to the system, as well as the petrochemical end-use demand for oil. These refineries input crude oil and output the various oil products, which now become the energy supply sources for the type "PC" supply enterprises considered in Fig. B-2. The refinery supply enterprise is represented by the variable RC(p,t), which represents the crude oil input requirement for refinery type p first available at the beginning of period t.

Figure B-4 adds electricity generation from low-Btu coal, as well as the end-use demand categories: 1) miscellaneous intermediate-load electricity and 2) water heat. Two things are noteworthy in this diagram. First, the electrical generation enterprises include appropriately sized facilities to transport the coal to the power plant, convert it to electricity, and transmit and distribute the electricity to the user (e.g., Fig. B-5 represents the entire chain of facilities required to supply miscellaneous intermediate-load electricity generated from low-Btu coal). Second, the electrical generation supply enterprise facilities may be shared by the miscellaneous intermediate-load electricity and water heat end-use demands.

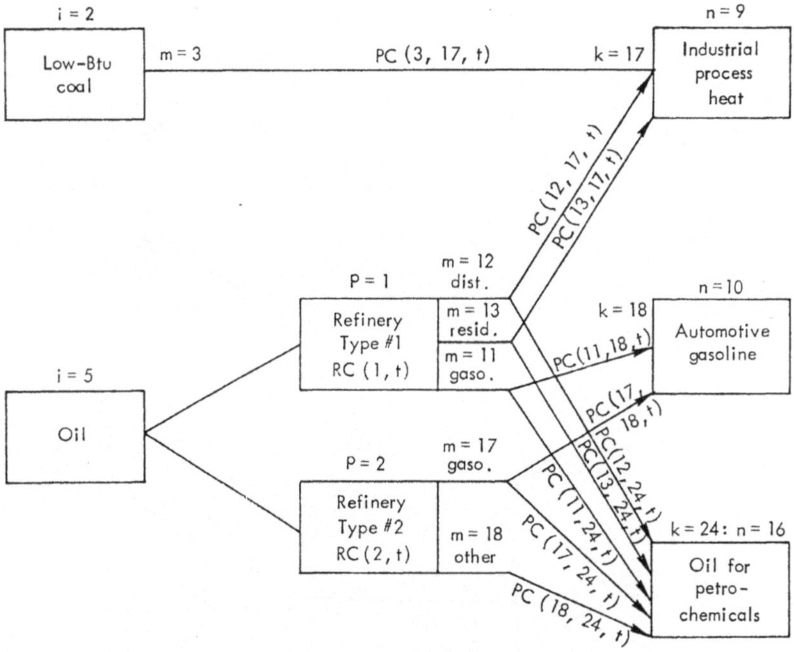

Fig. B-3—Type "PC" and "RC" supply enterprises: a simple example

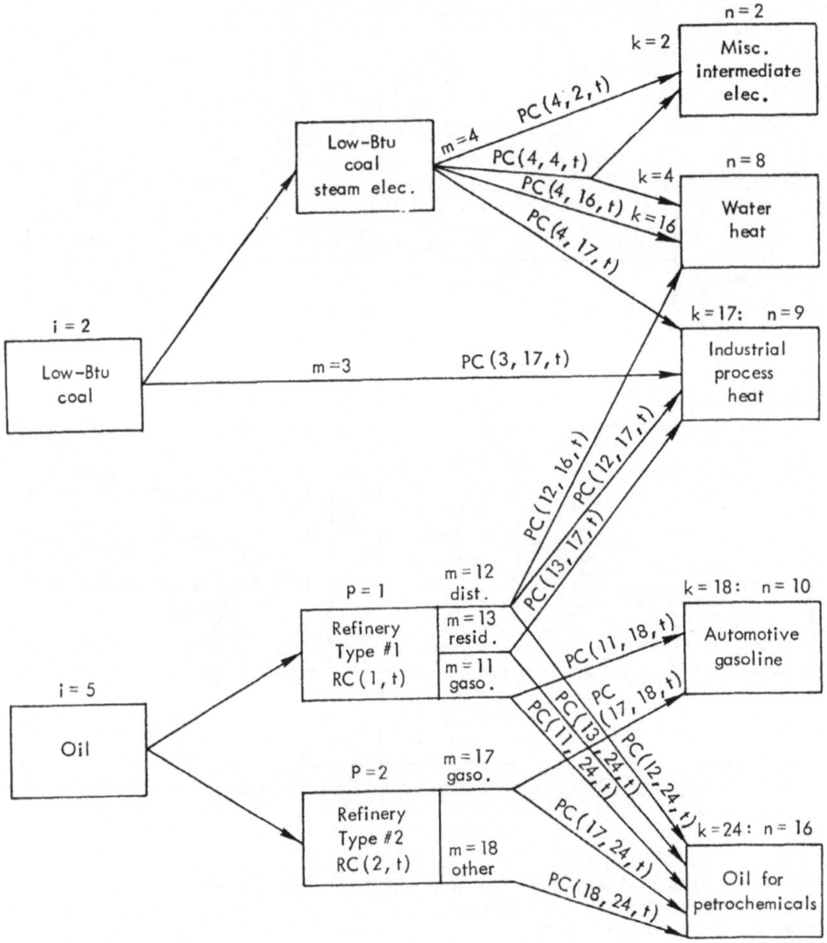

Fig. B-4—Type "PC" and "RC" supply enterprises: a more complex example

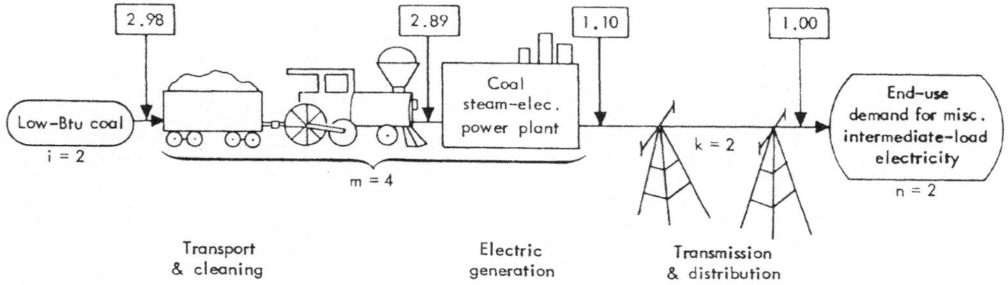

Profile of an "energy supply enterprise"

	Energy Processing Facility	Energy flows to satisfy one unit of end-use demand	
		Input	Output
m = 4	Coal transport and clean	2.98	2.89
	Coal steam-elec. power plant	2.89	1.10
k = 2	Electric transmission & distribution	1.10	1.00

The efficiency of the supply enterprise

$$= \frac{1.00}{2.98} = 0.34$$

Fig. B-5 — Example of an "energy supply enterprise" along a trajectory through the generalized energy system network

CONSTRAINTS FOR THE BASE CASE SCENARIO

Constraints are required in the formulation of the model in order to either relate variables (e.g., the PC's to the RC's) or to represent some physical limit (e.g., the limited supplies of basic energy resources).

There are five basic types of constraints in the model: 1) supply constraints - which ensure that enough of each basic resource is extracted in each period to fuel all of the facilities requiring that fuel type; 2) demand constraints - which ensure that all of the end-use demands are satisfied in each period; 3) refinery balance constraints - which ensure that the various oil products are produced in the right proportions for each refinery type; 4) resource constraints - which ensure that the total extraction of each basic resource in each extraction cost category does not exceed the total amount of the resource in that cost category; and 5) growth constraints - which limit the growth of certain energy system activities.

Supply Constraints: A Simple Example

The supply constraints require that the total amount of a basic resource extracted in any period be sufficient to meet the requirements of all facilities that require that resource in that period. Figure B-6 shows the low-Btu coal sector (i = 2) for a single period t. As shown on the left-hand side of the figure, there are two different extraction cost categories for low-Btu coal (j = 1,2). The average annual amounts of coal extracted during period t are represented by DS(2,1,t) and DS(2,2,t), respectively, for extraction cost categories 1 and 2. Thus, DS(2,1,t) + DS(2,2,t) is the total amount of low-Btu coal extracted annually during period t.

The PC(m,k,u) variables on the right-hand side of the figure represent the annual production capacity of supply enterprises first introduced into service at the beginning of period u. It is assumed that a fraction r(u,t) of the capacity first available for use in period u will still be available for use in period t. Furthermore, s(m,u) represents the efficiency of the facilities for the energy supply enterprise identified by the (m,k) pair that are first introduced into service at the beginning of period u. The coefficient parameter s(m,u) is the amount of energy (as a fraction of one Quad) that can be supplied

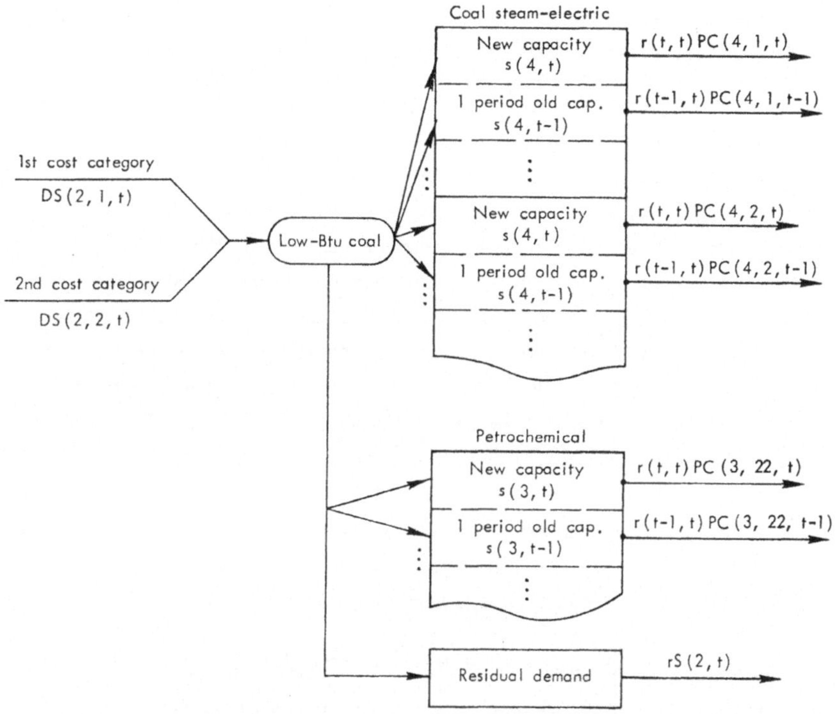

[Annual low-Btu coal extraction in period t.] ≥ [Annual low-Btu coal requirement in period t for facilities built since 1975.] + [Annual low-Btu coal requirement in period t for facilities built before 1975.]

$$\sum_{j} DS(2, j, t) \geq \sum_{\substack{u \leq t \\ (m,k) \in MKI(2)}} \frac{r(u, t)\, PC(m, k, u)}{s(m, u)} + r\, S(2, t)$$

Fig. B-6 — Example supply constraint for low-Btu coal

by a supply enterprise (e.g., PC(m,k,u)) from one Quad (i.e., one quadrillion Btus) of low-Btu coal (i.e., i = 2). In addition, there is a <u>residual demand</u> for low-Btu coal during period t, (say, rS(2,t)) which represents the annual consumption of low-Btu coal by energy conversion facilities that were constructed prior to the beginning of the modeled time horizon (i.e., prior to 1975).

<u>Supply Constraints: The General Case (Except Crude Oil)</u>

Having defined the necessary notation, it is now possible to write the supply constraint for low-Btu coal for period t as shown at the bottom of Fig. B-6. The right-hand side of this inequality represents the amount of low-Btu coal required during period t. This includes the low-Btu coal required to satisfy all of the enterprises and end-use devices that use low-Btu coal as well as the low Btu-coal required to fuel capacity built prior to the start of the model's time horizon, rS(2,t). The set MKI(2) is the set of all (m,k) pairs that represent the enterprises and end-use devices that use low-Btu coal. The supply constraint for low-Btu coal for period t simply requires that this annual "demand" (i.e., the right-hand side) for low Btu-coal not be more than that which is extracted annually during period t (i.e., DS(2,1,t) + DS(2,2,t)). In general, the supply constraint for resources other than crude oil (which is treated subsequently) is

$$\begin{bmatrix}\text{Average annual}\\ \text{consumption of}\\ \text{basic resource}\\ \text{i in period t.}\\ \\ \\ \\ \end{bmatrix} \geq \begin{bmatrix}\text{Average annual}\\ \text{requirement for}\\ \text{basic resource}\\ \text{i in period t}\\ \text{for facilities}\\ \text{built before}\\ \text{1975.}\end{bmatrix} + \begin{bmatrix}\text{Average annual}\\ \text{requirement for}\\ \text{basic resource}\\ \text{i in period t}\\ \text{for facilities}\\ \text{built since}\\ \text{1975.}\end{bmatrix}$$

$$\sum_{j} DS(i,j,t) \geq rS(i,t) + \sum_{\substack{u \leq t \\ (m,k) \in MKI(i)}} \frac{r(u,t)PC(m,k,u)}{s(m,u)},$$

$$i=1,\ldots,4;\ \forall t. \qquad \text{(B-1)}$$

Where:

Indices

t = a subscript corresponding to the time periods;

u = a subscript corresponding to the time periods when supply enterprises are first introduced into service;

i = a subscript corresponding to the basic resource categories;

j = a subscript corresponding to the extraction cost categories for the basic resources;

m = a subscript corresponding to the energy supply enterprise's input-and-process path (used in defining the supply enterprises of type "PC");

k = a subscript corresponding to the supply enterprise's output path (used in defining the supply enterprises of type "PC");

Set

MKI(i) = the set of supply enterprises (m,k) that use basic resource i;

Coefficient Parameters

r(u,t) = the fraction of capacity first available for use in period u that remains available for use in period t;

s(m,u) = for non-nuclear supply enterprises: the efficiency of energy resource supply facilities for the supply enterprise with input-and-process path m that was first introduced into service at the beginning of period u;

s(m,u) = for nuclear supply enterprises: the U_3O_8 requirement (10,000s of short tons/year) for one Quad of delivered electricity from the supply enterprise with input-and-process path m that was first introduced into service at the beginning of period u;

Constant

rS(i,t) = the average annual consumption (Quads/year) of basic resource i in period t by facilities built prior to 1975;

Variables

PC(m,k,u) = the average annual energy production (in Quads/year) for the supply enterprise specified by the (m,k) pair first introduced into service at the beginning of period u;

DS(i,j,t) = the average annual consumption (in Quads/year) during period t of basic resource type i in supply cost category j.

Supply Constraints: Crude Oil

In order to develop the supply constraint for crude oil, the oil-refining sector needs to be briefly described. The refining sector creates a requirement for crude oil, while certain of the "PC" type supply enterprises create requirements for the products from the refineries. Only two different refinery types are included. These refineries differ in their output product mixes and possess different cost and efficiency coefficient parameters. Let RC(p,u) be the capacity for refinery type p that first becomes available for use in representative year u. This capacity is measured at the input to the refinery. Since it is assumed that there are no losses at all between the well-head and the refinery, the demand for crude oil in period t is

$$\sum_{\substack{u \leq t \\ p}} r(u,t)RC(p,u).$$

Consequently, the supply constraints for crude oil may be written as

$$\begin{bmatrix}\text{Average annual}\\ \text{crude oil}\\ \text{requirement}\\ \text{in period t}\\ \text{for refineries}\\ \text{built since}\\ \text{1975.}\end{bmatrix} + \begin{bmatrix}\text{Average annual}\\ \text{crude oil}\\ \text{requirement}\\ \text{in period t}\\ \text{for refineries}\\ \text{built before}\\ \text{1975.}\end{bmatrix} \leq \begin{bmatrix}\text{Average annual}\\ \text{consumption of}\\ \text{crude oil during}\\ \text{period t.}\\ \\ \\ \\ \end{bmatrix}$$

$$\sum_{\substack{u\leq t\\ p}} r(u,t)RC(p,u) + rS(5,t) \leq \sum_{j} DS(5,j,t), \quad \forall t. \qquad \text{(B-2)}$$

Where:

Index

p = a subscript corresponding to oil refinery types;

Variables

$RC(p,u)$ = the annual crude oil requirement (in Quads/year) for refinery type p that is first introduced into service at the beginning of period u.

Demand Constraints: A Simple Example

The demand constraints ensure that the end-use energy demands are satisfied in every time period. For example, consider the demand for automotive gasoline depicted schematically in Fig. B-7. The variables $PC(m,k,u)$ and coefficients $r(u,t)$ have previously been described. The coefficient parameter $d(k,10,u)$ is the end-use efficiency for period u that represents the amount of end-use energy (e.g., $n = 10$ for automotive gasoline) that can be delivered from one unit of energy that is supplied from a supply enterprise having an output path k. Consequently, if $MKN(10)$ is the set of supply enterprises (m,k) that supply automotive gasoline, the amount of gasoline produced in period t

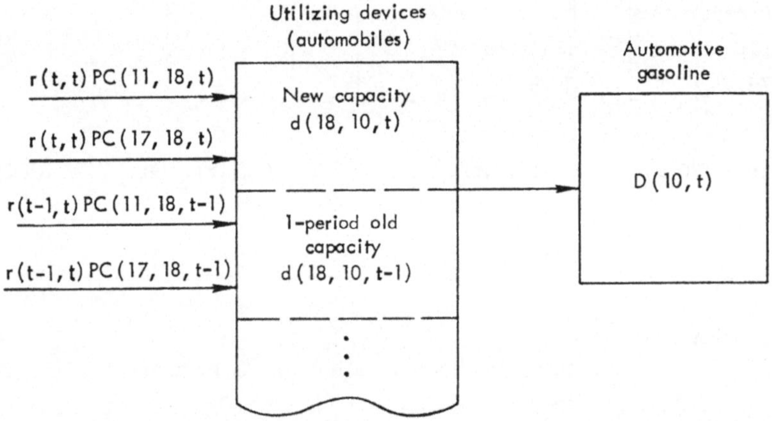

$$\left[\begin{array}{l}\text{Annual automotive gasoline}\\ \text{production in period } t \text{ by}\\ \text{facilities constructed since 1975.}\end{array}\right] \geq \left[\begin{array}{l}\text{Annual net demand}\\ \text{for automotive gasoline}\\ \text{in period } t.\end{array}\right]$$

$$\sum_{\substack{u \leq t \\ (m,k) \in MKN(10)}} d(k, 10, u)\, r(u, t)\, PC(m, k, u) \geqq D(10, t)$$

Fig. B-7— Example demand constraint for automotive gasoline

to meet the demand that can't be satisfied by facilities constructed prior to 1975 is

$$\sum_{\substack{u \leq t \\ (m,k)\in MKN(10)}} d(k,10,u)r(u,t)PC(m,k,u).$$

The demand constraint for automotive gasoline in period t ensures the satisfaction of this net demand as shown at the bottom of Fig. B-7.

Demand Constraints: A Special Case (Excluding Electricity)

The general demand constraint for demands that can not be satisfied by electricity (electricity is treated subsequently) can be written as

$$\begin{bmatrix}\text{Average annual} \\ \text{production of} \\ \text{end-use energy} \\ \text{category n} \\ \text{by facilities} \\ \text{constructed} \\ \text{since 1975.}\end{bmatrix} \geq \begin{bmatrix}\text{Average annual} \\ \text{net demand for} \\ \text{energy in} \\ \text{category n in} \\ \text{period t.} \\ \\ \\ \end{bmatrix}$$

$$\sum_{\substack{u \leq t \\ (m,k)\in MKN(n)}} d(k,n,u)r(u,t)PC(m,k,u) \geq D(n,t),$$

$$\forall n, \text{ non-electric}; \forall t. \qquad (B-3)$$

Where:

Index

n = a subscript corresponding to end-use demand categories;

Set

MKN(n) = the set of supply enterprises (m,k) that satisfy end-use demand category n;

Coefficient Parameters

d(k,n,u) = the efficiency for the supply enterprise with output path k that is first introduced into service at the beginning of period u and can deliver energy to end-use demand category n;

Constant

$D(n,t)$ = the average annual net demand (in Quads/year) for end-use energy form n in period t.

Demand Constraints: Peak-Load Electricity

The demand constraints necessary for end-use demands that can be satisfied using electricity include two additional features. Both of these features arise from consideration of the non-storability of electrical energy, which necessitates consideration of the time profile of energy demand rates. Several analytical techniques for approximating this time profile have been suggested in the literature (c.f., Anderson, 1972; Hoffman, 1972; and Manne, 1974b). The representation chosen here is due to Hoffman (1972).

Figure B-8 shows the general temporal profile used for end-use demand category n. This demand rate (energy/unit time) versus time profile is repeated during each "demand period" (e.g., week or year). A rate of demand PA(n) occurs over a fraction DDA(n) of this demand period, while a demand rate PB(n) occurs over a fraction DDB(n) of the demand period. Thus, the rate profile for end-use demand category n is represented in terms of two demand blocks; a "base-block" demand with area EA(n) and a "peak-block" demand with area EB(n). The area EA(n) + EB(n) represents the total energy that is demanded in one demand period whose length is one unit of time. The ratio $f(-,n) = EB(n)/EA(n)$ represents the ratio between the amount of energy supplied to the "peak-block" and the energy supplied to the "base-block." Finally, DDA(n), DDB(n), and f(-,n) specify the time profile for end-use demand category n, as treated in the present model. This demand block energy ratio representation is required because the total amount of electrical energy supplied to demands that can be satisfied by either electrical or non-electrical energy is itself variable. The present formulation ensures that any electrical energy supplied to a particular end-use demand is supplied with the requisite time profile (i.e., the required split between "peak-block" and "base-block" demands).

Table B-5 presents the temporal characteristics for the end-use demand categories that may be satisfied by electricity. For example, the demand for industrial process heat (n=9) has a one week period. The

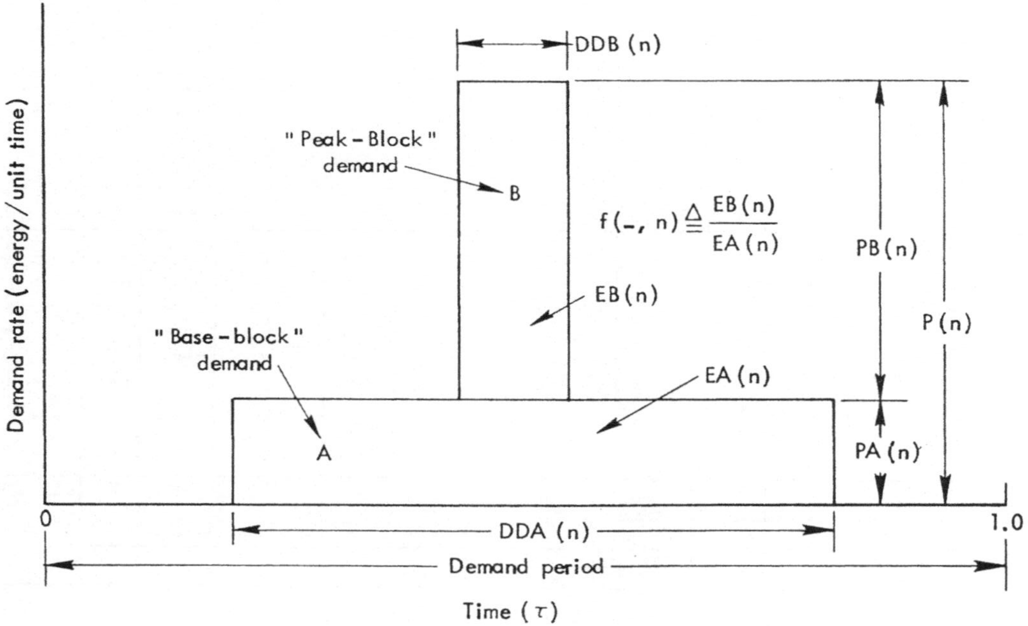

Fig. B-8—Temporal representation of the demand for end-use category n

Table B-5

TEMPORAL CHARACTERISTICS FOR END-USE DEMAND CATEGORIES THAT MAY BE SATISFIED BY ELECTRICITY

End-Use Demand Category		TEMPORAL CHARACTERISTICS								End-Use Demand Categories that May Share Any Under-Utilized Electrical Generation Facilities[a]			
			The Demand Cycle					Constraints					
			Base-Block Demand Duration		Peak-Block Demand Duration		Peak-Block to Base-Block Energy Ratio f(_,n)	The Demand Must Be Satisfied		End-Use Demand Category		Load Sharing Facility	
Index n	Description	Period	Time Interval	Fraction of the Demand cycle's period DDA(n)	Time Interval	Fraction of the Demand cycle's period DDB(n)		At Fixed Times	Any Time Within One Period	Index n	Description	Type	Efficiency
1	Miscellaneous base-load electricity	None	Continuous	1.00	Random	0.10	0.05	X		None	-	-	-
2	Miscellanous intermediate-load electricity	1 week	Random	0.50	Random	0.10	0.10	X		3 8	Peak-load electricity Water heat	Pumped Storage None	.25[b] -
3	Peak-load electricity	1 week	-	-	Random	0.10	-	X		3 8	Peak-load electricity Water heat	Pumped Storage None	.25[b] -
5	Iron and steel	None	Continuous	1.00	Random	0.10	0.05	X		None	-	-	-
6	Air conditioning	1 year	Summer	0.33	Random	0.10	0.20	X		None	-	-	-
7	Space heat	1 year	Winter	0.42	0	0	0	X		6	Air conditioning	None	-
8	Water heat	1 week	-	-	-	-	-		X	None	-	-	-
9	Industrial process heat	1 week	Random	0.75	Random	0.10	0.05	X		None	-	-	-

[a]These are said to be "secondary" end-use demand categories

[b]Includes the efficiencies of both the pumping of the water uphill and the subsequent hydroelectric generation.

base-block demand occurs randomly during 75 per cent of the week (DDA(9)=.75) and the peak-block demand occurrs randomly during 10 per cent of the week (DDB(9)=.10). Additionally, the ratio of the peak-block to the base-block energy demands for industrial process heat is .05 (f(-,n)=.05). Notice that the demand duration factor, DDB(n), is always equal to .1 for all of the end-use demand categories that have a peak-block. Thus, the so-called "peak-load" electricity generation requirement (n=3) is endogenously determined by the heights (i.e., PB(n)) of the peak-blocks for the end-use demand categories that are satisfied by electricity. The expression for the peak-load electricity demand will be determined subsequently.

First, the manner in which the model allows for the sharing of electrical generation (i.e., supply enterprise) capacity by compatible pairs of end-use demand categories is considered. Two different types of so-called electrical "load-sharing" are possible. First, electrical generation facilities that are sized to meet end-use demands with a demand period of one week and a random demand duration interval (e.g., miscellaneous intermediate-load electricity and peak-load electricity) can be used to satisfy end-use demand categories that can be satisfied at any time during the week. The two relevant cases (see Table B-5) are water heat* and pumped storage facilities. Pumped storage facilities are used to store electrical energy for subsequent hydroelectric electricity generation to satisfy peak-load electicity demands. The second type of load-sharing involves electrical generation facilities that are sized to meet the winter space heat demands that can also be used to satisfy air conditioning demands in the summer.

The end-use demand for which the electrical generation facilities are sized will be called a "primary" demand, while the sharing end-use demand will be called a "secondary" demand. Load sharing amounts to the filling in of some of the demand period (Fig. B-8) during which the base-block demand or peak-block demand is not occurring (i.e., 1-DDA(n) and 1-DDB(n), respectively). In the past, the amount of "off-peak" electricity available to be shared for each type of electric generation

---

*Where the water heaters are installed with timing devices which allow them to operate only when the primary demands are not occuring (e.g., at night).

equipment for each type of load-sharing has generally been represented by so-called off-peak constraints. Here these constraints are eliminated by redefining certain variables. This treatment reduced the computational requirements of the present model by over fifty per cent. In the present treatment, for each possible combination of compatible end-use demand categories, the electric generation facilities can be used to satisfy either the primary demand alone, or both the primary demand and the secondary demand, with the secondary demand getting as much sharable energy as the generation facilities can generate. The facilities themselves are sized to satisfy the primary demand (the equivalence of this approach and previous approaches is demonstrated in Appendix C).

The total demand for peak-load electricity (i.e., "D(3,t)") is endogenously determined from the contributions of the "peak-block" demands for all of the end-use demands. This endogenous demand is measured at the input side of the utilizing devices (note that the other end-use demands, D(n,t), are specified at the output side of the utilizing device). Thus the total peak-load electricity requirement may be shown to be

$$\sum_{\substack{u \leq t \\ (m,k)}} q(k,n) f(m,n) r(u,t) PC(m,k,u), \quad \forall t.$$

where the sum is over all (m,k) pairs and

f(m,n) = ratio of the electrical energy supplied to the "peak-block" demand to the energy supplied to the "base-block" demand for end-use demand category n when the energy is delivered by supply enterprises having input-and-process paths of type m (f(m,n)=0 if m is not an electricity generation input-and-process path);

q(k,n) = the fraction of the electrical energy supplied by energy supply enterprises with output path type k that is used to satisfy end-use demand n (q(k,n)=1 if k is not an electrical load-sharing output path).

Therefore, the demand constraint for peak-load electricity can be expressed as

$$\begin{bmatrix}\text{Endogenously deter-}\\ \text{mined average annual}\\ \text{demand for peak-}\\ \text{load electricity}\\ \text{in period t.}\end{bmatrix} \leqq \begin{bmatrix}\text{Average annual}\\ \text{electrical energy}\\ \text{supplied to peak-load}\\ \text{electricity demand}\\ \text{in period t.}\end{bmatrix}$$

$$\sum_{\substack{u \leq t\\(m,k)}} q(k,n)f(m,n)r(u,t)PC(m,k,u) \leqq \sum_{\substack{u \leq t\\(m,k)\varepsilon MKN(3)}} q(k,3)r(u,t)PC(m,k,u), \quad \forall t. \quad \text{(B-4)}$$

Demand Constraints: The General Case (Excluding Peak-Load Electricity)

Since the peak-block fraction ($f(m,n)$) of the demand profile is already accounted for in the peak-load electricity demand constraint, the PC that appears in the present end-use demand constraint must be adjusted accordingly. The appropriate adjustment is to multiply the PC by $(1+f(m,n))$. Since $f(m,n)$ equals zero if there is no peak-block, only the PC´s supplying the peak-blocks are adjusted.

The proof for this adjustment process proceeds as follows. Let $D_\alpha(n,t)$ be the portion of the end-use demand $D(n,t)$ that is satisfied by $PC(m,k,t)$ in period t. Since $[f(m,n)/(1+f(m,n))]D_\alpha(n,t)$ is the portion of this demand that is already satisfied by peak-load electric generation facilities, in order for the remaining demand to be satisfied it is sufficient to require that

$$q(k,n)d(k,n,u)r(u,t)PC(m,k,u) \geqq \frac{1}{1+f(m,n)} D_\alpha(n,t)$$

so

$$q(k,n)[1+f(m,n)]d(k,n,u)r(u,t)PC(m,k,u) \geqq D_\alpha(n,t).$$

Thus, with the admission of electricity as an energy supply source, the demand constraints (Eqn. B-3) must be replaced by

$$\begin{bmatrix}\text{Average annual pro-}\\ \text{duction of end-use}\\ \text{energy category n}\\ \text{by facilities}\\ \text{constructed}\\ \text{since 1975.}\end{bmatrix} \geq \begin{bmatrix}\text{Average annual}\\ \text{net demand for}\\ \text{energy in}\\ \text{category n in}\\ \text{period t.}\end{bmatrix}$$

$$\sum_{\substack{u \leq t \\ (m,k) \varepsilon MKN(n)}} q(k,n)[1+f(m,n)]d(k,n,u)r(u,t)PC(m,k,u) \geq D(n,t),$$

$$\forall n \neq 3, \ \forall t. \quad \text{(B-5)}$$

Refinery Constraints

In the discussion of the supply contraints, it was indicated that crude oil is assumed to be supplied to oil refineries (type "RC" supply enterprises) and that these refineries are the source of refined oil products for some of the "PC" supply enterprises. It is, therefore, necessary to include refinery balance constraints in the model in order to relate the "RC" and "PC" variables in a way that ensures that enough crude oil is supplied to each refinery type to produce the required output mix, including refining losses. Figure B-9 shows the balance constraints for a low gasoline refinery (p = 1). This refinery is assumed to produce g(1,v) Quads of oil product type v per Quad of crude oil input to the refinery. Recalling that all facilities are assumed to be utilized at full capacity throughout their lifetime, the annual requirement for crude oil that is to be supplied to this refinery type is

$$\sum_{u \leq t} r(u,t)RC(1,u)$$

The annual production of refined oil product of type v is, therefore, constrained to be less than g(1,v) times the annual crude oil requirement for this refinery type. Therefore, if MKV(p,v) is the set

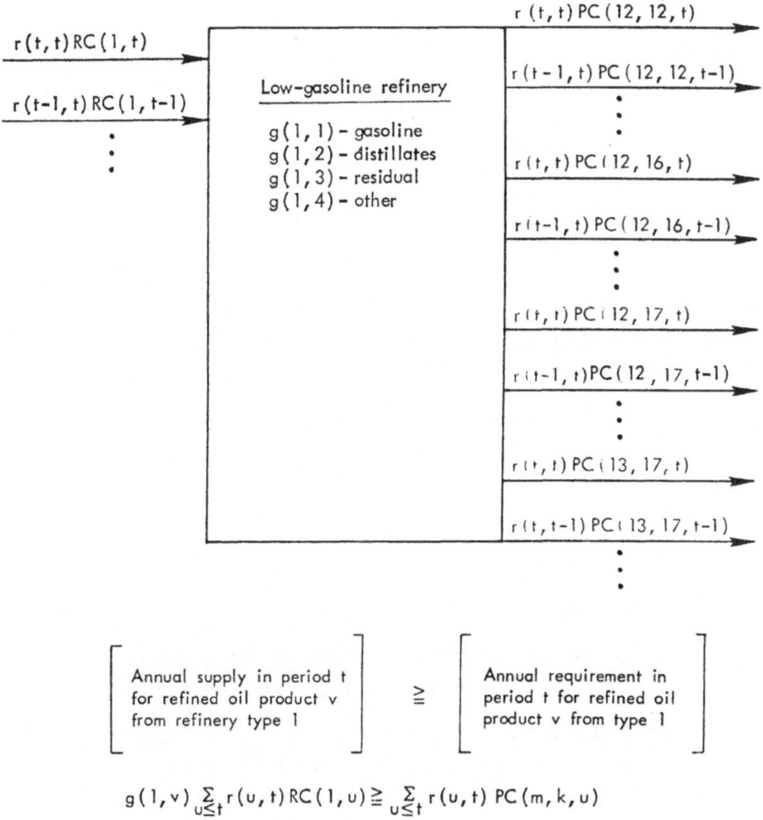

[Annual supply in period t for refined oil product v from refinery type 1] $\geqq$ [Annual requirement in period t for refined oil product v from type 1]

$$g(1,v) \sum_{u \leq t} r(u,t)\, RC(1,u) \geqq \sum_{u \leq t} r(u,t)\, PC(m,k,u)$$

$$(m,k)\, MKV(p,v) \qquad v = 1, 2, 3, 4$$

Fig. B-9— Example refinery balance constraints for refinery type 1: low-gasoline refinery

of supply enterprises that are allowed to use refined oil product v from refinery type p, then

$$\sum_{\substack{u \leq t \\ (m,k) \in MKV(p,v)}} r(u,t)PC(m,k,u)$$

is the total demand for this oil product from this type of refinery. The balance equations for refinery type 1 are shown at the bottom of Fig. B-9. The general refinery balance constraints may be written as

$$\begin{bmatrix} \text{Average annual supply} \\ \text{of refined oil} \\ \text{product v that is} \\ \text{produced by refinery} \\ \text{type p in period t.} \end{bmatrix} \geq \begin{bmatrix} \text{Average annual requirement} \\ \text{for refined oil} \\ \text{product v that is} \\ \text{produced by refinery} \\ \text{type p in period t.} \end{bmatrix}$$

$$g(p,v) \sum_{u \leq t} r(u,t)RC(p,u) \geq \sum_{\substack{u \leq t \\ (m,k) \in MKV(p,v)}} r(u,t)PC(m,k,u), \quad \forall p,\ \forall v,\ \forall t. \qquad \text{(B-6)}$$

Where:

Set

MKV(p,v) = the set of "PC" supply enterprises that require refined oil product v from refinery type p.

Coefficient Parameter

g(p,v) = the refinery efficiency and product split coefficient for refinery type p (the ratio of the energy content of the refined oil product of type v to the energy content of the crude oil that is input to the refinery).

Resource Constraints

The resource constraints require that the cumulative extraction of a resource type in a particular cost category not exceed the supply that is ultimately available in each extraction cost category. The average annual production of resource type i in extraction cost category j for period t must be multiplied by the length of the period, 1(t), in order to determine the total depletion for that resource category in period t. Since R(i,j) is the total supply that is available for resource type i in extraction cost category j, the resource constraints may be written as

$$\begin{bmatrix}\text{Total extraction} \\ \text{of resource type i} \\ \text{in cost category j.}\end{bmatrix} \leq \begin{bmatrix}\text{Total ultimately avail-} \\ \text{able supply of resource} \\ \text{type i in cost category j.}\end{bmatrix}$$

$$\sum_{t=1}^{6} l(t)DS(i,j,t) \leq R(i,j), \quad \forall i, \forall j. \qquad \text{(B-7)}$$

Where:

<u>Coefficient Parameters</u>

1(t) = the length of time period t (in years);

<u>Constants</u>

R(i,j) = the total supply of resource type i that is ultimately available in extraction cost category j (in Quads) at the beginning of the model's time horizon (i.e., beginning of 1975).

<u>Growth Constraints</u>

There are three types of growth constraints employed in the model: 1) the rate of buildup of nuclear electricity generation facilities is constrained by specifying maximum levels for new reactor construction in each period for each reactor type; 2) a maximum extraction rate is specified for both domestic oil and domestic natural gas and 3) the extraction rate of low-Btu coal is constrained to be less than double the extraction rate of high-Btu coal. The assumed maximum growth rates and corresponding references are given in Appendix D.

Growth Constraints: Nuclear Reactor Construction

The nuclear electricity generation facilities construction constraint places an upper bound on the introduction of new nuclear facilities in each period. That is,

$$\begin{bmatrix}\text{The total capacity} \\ \text{of all new reactors} \\ \text{installed during} \\ \text{period u.}\end{bmatrix} \leq \begin{bmatrix}\text{Limit on the total capacity} \\ \text{of all new reactors which} \\ \text{may be installed in} \\ \text{period u.}\end{bmatrix}$$

$$\sum_{k} \frac{PC(m,k,u)}{PF(k)} \leq gPC(m,u), \quad \forall m \in NR, \forall u. \qquad \text{(B-8)}$$

Where:

Set

NR = the set of input-and-process paths that include nuclear reactor facilities;

Coefficient Parameter

PF(k) = the plant factor at which electric generation facilities must operate when they are part of supply enterprises with an output path of type k (the plant factor is the fraction of the plant's capacity that is actually used on the average);

Constant

gPC(m,u) = the limit on the total capacity (in Quads/year) of all new reactors of type m which may be installed in period u.

Growth Constraints: Domestic Oil and Gas

The maximum extraction rate constraints for domestic oil and gas place upper bounds on the amount of domestic oil and gas that can be extracted in any period as follows:

$$\begin{bmatrix}\text{Average annual} \\ \text{extraction of} \\ \text{resource i} \\ \text{during} \\ \text{period t.}\end{bmatrix} \leq \begin{bmatrix}\text{Maximum permissable} \\ \text{average annual} \\ \text{extraction of} \\ \text{resource i in} \\ \text{period t.}\end{bmatrix}$$

$$\sum_{j=1}^{3} DS(i,j,t) \leq gDS(i,t), \quad i=4,\ 5;\ \forall t. \qquad \text{(B-9)}$$

Where:

Constant

$gDS(i,t)$ = the maximum permissible average annual extraction rate (in Quads/year) of resource i in period t.

Growth Constraints: Coal

The restriction on coal extraction limits the extraction of low-Btu coal to be less than twice the extraction of high-Btu coal. This assumption is necessitated by consideration of the geographical distribution of these two resources. Since the low-Btu coal is found predominantly in the west, the transportation cost assumed for it is not great enough to reflect transport to eastern markets. Therefore, it is assumed that some high-Btu coal must be extracted to satisfy the demands of these markets.

The constraints are:

$$\begin{bmatrix}\text{Average annual amount} \\ \text{of low-Btu coal} \\ \text{extracted during} \\ \text{period t.}\end{bmatrix} \leq \begin{bmatrix}\text{Two times the} \\ \text{average annual amount} \\ \text{of high-Btu coal} \\ \text{extracted during} \\ \text{period t.}\end{bmatrix}$$

$$\sum_{j} DS(2,j,t) \leq 2 \sum_{j} DS(3,j,t), \quad \forall t. \qquad \text{(B-10)}$$

OBJECTIVE FUNCTION

The objective function of the model represents the discounted total cost of meeting energy demands over the specified 60-year time horizon. A 10 per cent discount rate has been used. Since supply enterprise facilities are assumed to be fully utilized over a thirty-year lifetime, the discounted operational costs (not including energy resource costs) of running the facilities over their lifetimes can be added to the capital cost for the facilities in order to get a single cost coefficient for facilities built during any period. The coefficients are CPC for type "PC" supply enterprises and CRC for type "RC" enterprises.

Energy supply enterprise facilities are assumed to be constructed at a constant rate between the midpoint of the period prior to their assumed theoretical introduction into service (say u-1) and the midpoint of the period during which they are assumed to be first introduced into service (u). The net effect is that the average actual date of introduction into service approximately coincides with the beginning of the period during which they are theoretically assumed to be introduced into service (e.g., see Fig. 3-7). Thus, the unit cost stream for building and operating facilities for the supply enterprises start with a construction cost stream that originates in the middle of period u-1.

The discounted construction and operating cost per unit of annual energy production capacity* is represented by CPC(m,k,u) and CRC(m,k,u) for the type "PC" and "RC" supply enterprises respectively. The discounted "unit cost" of extracting resource type i in extraction cost category j over the duration of period t (i.e., dollars per Quad per period) is represented by CDS(i,j,t). This represents the 1974 present value of a stream of annual expenditures for the purchase of one Quad/yr of resource type i in extraction cost category j for the length of the period.

---

*Recall that the supply enterprise "capacity" is fully utilized throughout its lifetime. Of course, individual facilities within an enterprise may operate at specified percentages of the time (termed "plant factors"). Thus the supply enterprise "capacity" = "plant factor" x plant capacity.

The model's objective function may now be written as

$$\text{Min.} \left[\sum_{\substack{(m,k)\\t}} CPC(m,k,u)PC(m,k,u) + \sum_{p,u} CRC(p,u)RC(p,u) + \sum_{i,j,t} CDS(i,j,t)DS(i,j,t) \right] \tag{B-11}$$

Where:

Coefficient Parameters

CPC(m,k,u) = the discounted* unit cost [in billions of 1974 dollars/(Quad/year)] for building and operating supply enterprise facilities of type "PC" that are first introduced into service at the beginning of period u;

CRC(p,u) = the discounted unit cost [in billions of 1974 dollars/(Quad/year of refining capacity)] for building and operating supply enterprise facilities of refinery type p that are first introduced into service at the beginning of period u;

CDS(i,j,t) = the discounted cost per unit of annual production [in billions of 1974 dollars/(Quad/year)] for the consumption of resource type i (supply cost category j) for a period of l(t) years that span period t.

The objective function employed here, thus, represents the total discounted cost of those activities of the United States energy system that are represented in the model. Only marketplace economic costs are included in this objective function; nonmarketplace socio-economic costs

---

*All costs are discounted at a rate of 10 per cent to a 1974 present value.

are excluded. The use of this objective function implies perfect competition in the energy sector, as each end-use demand is satisfied by the minimum cost alternative.

The basic cost data that were used to determine the cost coefficients in the model may be found in Appendix D. This completes the algebraic formulation for the base case scenario. The complete linear programming implementation of the model for the base case scenario is described after the algebra necessary for the alternative scenarios is developed.

THE IMPROVED EFFICIENCIES IN END-USE SCENARIOS

The improved efficiencies in end-use scenarios are the easiest to describe relative to the base case scenario since they require neither the definition of new variables nor the formulation of any new constraints. For the improved efficiencies in end-use scenarios, the modifications are: 1) increases in the values for some of the end-use efficiencies (e.g., increased efficiencies for air conditioners), which are represented by d(k,n,t) and 2) reductions in some of the end-use demands (e.g., reductions in space heat demands due to improved building design) which are represented by D(n,t).

THE BREEDER SCENARIOS

An additional energy supply enterprise input-and-process path (i.e., m = 19) is required in order to specify the breeder associated supply enterprise. Rather than have this addition entered in Table B-3, Table B-6 summarizes the modifications to Table B-3 for the various scenarios. The small amount of natural uranium the breeder uses - s(19,t) in ten-thousands of short tons per Quad of delivered electricity - must be reflected in the uranium supply constraints (Eqn. B-1). Additionally, the LMFBR capacity built in each period t is restricted to be less than gPC(19,t). Finally, although the breeder is a net producer of plutonium over its lifetime, a substantial amount of plutonium is required for the initial core. This plutonium would come from light-water reactors (LWRs) during the introduction of the breeder technology and from other breeders in a mature breeder economy. These factors are accounted for in a set of plutonium balance constraints included in the model.

Table B-6

DESCRIPTION OF THE INPUT-AND-PROCESS PATHS FOR THE TYPE "PC" ENTERPRISES
(For the Breeder and Synfuels Scenarios)

Index m	Input Resource Supply		Principal Process(es) (liquefaction/gasification/ electricity generation/ transportation)	Admissible Output Paths Index k; see Table B-4)
	Energy Form	Point of Delivery		
Breeder Scenarios				
19	Uranium	Mill output	Liquid-metal fast-breeder reactor	1-4,7,8,11,12,14,16,17
Synfuels Scenarios				
20	Gasoline	Coal liquids refinery	Transportation	18,20,24
21	Jet fuel and other[a]	Coal liquids refinery	Transportation	19,24
22	Low-Btu coal	Minemouth	Liquefaction	17,24,25
23	High-Btu coal	Minemouth	Liquefaction	17,24,25
24	Low-Btu coal	Minemouth	Liquefaction + steam - electric	1-4,7,8,11,12,14,16,17
25	High-Btu coal	Minemouth	Liquefaction + steam - electric	1-4,7,8,11,12,14,16,17
26	Low-Btu coal	Minemouth	Low-Btu gas + combined cycle	1-4,7,8,11,12,14,16,17
27	High-Btu coal	Minemouth	Low-Btu gas + combined cycle	1-4,7,8,11,12,14,16,17

[a]Other jet fuel grade products.

In order to construct the plutonium balance constraint, let pU(1,u,t) represent the metric tons of plutonium that are produced in period t for each Quad of LWR electrical energy delivery capacity in period t (the LWR enterprise having been introduced into service at the beginning of period u). The breeder that is first introduced into service at the beginning of period u either adds to the supply (e.g., in the periods after introduction) in period t or subtracts from the supply (e.g., in the period during which it is introduced). The variable pU(19,u,t) represents the net balance of accumulated plutonium in metric tons per Quad of breeder electrical energy delivery capacity in period t. Hence, the general plutonium balance constraint may be written as:

$$\begin{bmatrix} \text{Plutonium inventory} \\ \text{at the end of} \\ \text{period t-1.} \end{bmatrix} + \begin{bmatrix} \text{Net balance of} \\ \text{accumulation} \\ \text{of plutonium} \\ \text{in period t.} \end{bmatrix} - \begin{bmatrix} \text{Plutonium inventory} \\ \text{at the end of} \\ \text{period t.} \end{bmatrix} \begin{matrix} > 0 \\ = \end{matrix}$$

$$PUINV(t-1) + \sum_{\substack{u \leq t \\ (m,k) \varepsilon MKPu}} pU(m,u,t)PC(m,k,u) - PUINV(t) \geq 0, \quad \forall t. \qquad (B-12)$$

Where:

<u>Set</u>

MKPu = the set of energy supply enterprises that either produce or consume plutonium;

<u>Coefficient Parameter</u>

pU(m,u,t) = the production or consumption [in metric tons/(Quad of electrical energy delivery capacity)] of plutonium in period t by supply enterprise type (m,k) that was first introduced into service at the beginning of period u;

<u>Variables</u>

PUINV(t) = the inventory of plutonium (in metric tons) at the end of period t.

THE SYNFUELS SCENARIOS

The synfuels scenarios require the most modification to the base case scenario since both high- and low-Btu coal gasification, as well as both coal and oil shale liquefaction are included in these scenarios. Table B-6 shows that eight new energy supply enterprise input-and-process paths (i.e., m=20,21,...27) need to be added. Furthermore, a new resource type (i.e., i=6) for shale oil must be added to those that are listed in Table B-1 (this resource type is described in Table B-7). The modifications to the base case scenario that are required in order to generate the synfuels scenarios are now described on an energy technology basis.

Oil Shale Liquefaction

As shown in Table B-7, oil shale is a new basic resource that is added to the menu of available basic resources for the synfuels scenario. Hence, resource constraints (for i = 6) must be added to the resource contraints (Eqn. B-7). Three cost categories (j=1,2,3) are assumed for oil shale. These cost categories include the cost of liquefying the oil shale and, therefore, are measured either at the output of the retort facility or at the minemouth in the case of in situ processing. The energy supply enterprise that is responsible for transporting and upgrading shale oil is designated by the variable SHA(u) which measures the annual energy production for the enterprise. An upper limit for this variable during the period when shale processing is first assumed to be available (period 3) is also specified. This new variable is analogous to PC and RC. Once the shale has been upgraded, the model treats the shale oil as being equivalent to crude oil. Hence, the term

$$\sum_{u \leq t} r(u,t)SHA(u)$$

must be appended to the left-hand side of the oil supply constraints (Eqn. B-2) and the cost factor

$$\sum_{u} CSHA(u)SHA(u)$$

Table B-7

SHALE OIL SUPPLY CATEGORIES FOR THE SYNFUELS SCENARIOS

Resource Type		Supply Cost Categories[a]		
Index i	Description	Index j	Cost Basis	Cost Category Number
6	Shale oil at the retort[b] (or minemouth in the case of in-situ processing)	1	Domestic extraction[c]	1
		2	Domestic extraction	2
		3	Domestic extraction	3

[a]Each supply category includes demonstrated reserves plus both inferred and expected undiscovered reserves for that category.

[b]As output from the retort facility.

[c]For in-situ. Liquefied shale oil in the case of retort recovery.

(where CSHA is analogous to CPC and CRC) must be included in the objective function (Eqn. B-11) in order to represent the availability of oil shale processing technologies.

Where:

Coefficient Parameter

CSHA(u) = the discounted unit cost [in billions of 1974 dollars/(Quad/year)] of building and operating the supply enterprise that upgrades shale oil and is first introduced into service at the beginning of period u.

Variable

SHA(u) = the average annual production (in Quads/year) by the supply enterprise that upgrades shale oil and is first introduced into service at the beginning of period u.

Coal Liquefaction

The liquefaction process for coal is assumed to produce a liquid fuel similar in characteristics to low-sulfur residual fuel oil. Both low-Btu and high-Btu coal can be liquefied. This liquefaction product can then be: 1) consumed directly by an end-use utilizing device that uses residual fuel oil, 2) used to generate electricity or 3) refined into gasoline and/or jet fuel. Type "PC" supply enterprises are used to represent the supply enterprises for the first two consumption alternatives. For the first alternative, these supply enterprises include the transport of the coal, the liquefaction of the coal and the distribution of the residual fuel oil. The PC(22,k,u) and PC(23,k,u) variables represent the supply enterprises where the product of the coal liquefaction is directly consumed as residual fuel oil. The PC(24,k,u) and PC(25,k,u) variables represent the supply enterprises where the liquefied coal is converted to electricity in a steam-electric power plant and finally transmitted to a particular end-use demand category.

For the refined products, refinery balance constraints are necessary. LCLR(u) and HCLR(u) represent production capacity for supply enterprises that are responsible for liquefying and refining high-Btu and low-Btu coal respectively. These variables are analogous to the RC variables. Since the refinery splits for the coal-liquids refineries are assumed to be the same regardless of the type of coal used as a feedstock, only the following single set of coal-liquids refinery constraints is required:

$$\begin{bmatrix}\text{Average annual}\\ \text{production of}\\ \text{refined oil product}\\ \text{type v from coal-}\\ \text{liquids refineries}\\ \text{in period t.}\end{bmatrix} \geq \begin{bmatrix}\text{Average annual}\\ \text{requirement for}\\ \text{refined oil product}\\ \text{type v from coal-}\\ \text{liquids refineries}\\ \text{in period t.}\end{bmatrix}$$

$$g(3,v) \sum_{u \leq t} r(u,t)[LCLR(u)+HCLR(u)] \geq \sum_{\substack{u \leq t \\ (m,k) \in MKV(3,v)}} r(u,t)PC(m,k,u), \quad \forall v, \forall t. \quad \text{(B-13)}$$

Additionally the terms

$$\sum_{u \leq t} r(u,t)\frac{LCLR(u)}{sLCLR(u)}$$

and

$$\sum_{u \leq t} r(u,t)\frac{HCLR(u)}{sHCLR(u)}$$

must be added to the right-hand sides of the low-Btu coal (i=2) and high-Btu coal (i=3) supply constraints (Eqn. B-1) respectively and the term

$$\sum_{u} [CLCLR(u)LCLR(u) + CHCLR(u)HCLR(u)]$$

appended to the objective function (Eqn. B-11).

Where:

Set

MKV(3,v) = the set of "PC" supply enterprises that require refined oil product v from coal-liquids refineries;

Coefficient Parameters

CLCLR(u) = the discounted unit cost [in billions of 1974 dollars/(Quad/year of refining capacity)] for building and operating the supply enterprise that liquefies and refines low-Btu coal, and is first introduced into service at the beginning of period u;

CHCLR(u) = the discounted unit cost [in billions of 1974 dollars/(Quad/year of refining capacity)] for building and operating the supply enterprise that liquefies and refines high-Btu coal, and is first introduced into service at the beginning of period u;

g(3,v) = the refinery efficiency and product split coefficient for coal-liquids refineries (the ratio of the energy content of the refined oil product of type v to the energy content of the syncrude that is input to the refinery).

sLCLR(u) = the fractional efficiency for converting low-Btu coal into residual fuel oil for facilities first introduced into service at the beginning of period u;

sHCLR(u) = the fractional efficiency for converting high-Btu coal into residual fuel oil for facilities first introduced into service at the beginning of period u;

Variables

LCLR(u) = the average annual production (in Quads/year) of residual fuel oil by the supply enterprise that liquefies low-Btu coal (to residual fuel oil) and refines the resulting residual fuel oil, and is first introduced into service at the beginning of period u;

HCLR(u) = the average annual production (in Quads/year) of residual fuel oil by the supply enterprise that liquefies high-Btu coal (to residual fuel oil) and refines the resulting residual fuel oil, and is first introduced into service at the beginning of period u.

High-Btu Gas from Coal

Both high-Btu and low-Btu coal can be used to produce high-Btu gas, which is assumed to be perfectly substitutable for natural gas. HCGS(u) and LCGS(u) are the production capacity variables for the supply enterprises responsible for the high-Btu gasification of high-Btu and low-Btu coal respectively. The supply enterprises that are responsible for high-Btu coal gasification in the model require the addition of the term

$$\sum_{u \leq t} r(u,t)[LCGS(u) + HCGS(u)]$$

to the left-hand side of the natural gas (i=4) supply constraints (Eqn. B-1), the term

$$\sum_{u \leq t} r(u,t)\frac{LCGS(u)}{sLCGS(u)}$$

to the right-hand side of the low-Btu coal (i=2) supply constraint (Eqn. B-1), the term

$$\sum_{u \leq t} r(u,t)\frac{HCGS(u)}{sHCGS(u)}$$

to the right-hand side of the high-Btu coal (i=3) supply constraint (Eqn. B-1) and, finally, the addition of the term

$$\sum_{u} [CLCGS(u)LCGS(u) + CHCGS(u)HCGS(u)]$$

to the objective function (Eqn. B-11).

Where:

Coefficient Parameters

CLCGS(u) = the discounted unit cost [in billions of 1974 dollars/(Quad/year)] for building and operating the supply enerprise that converts low-Btu coal into high-Btu gas, and is first introduced into service at the beginning of period u;

CHCGS(u) = the discounted unit cost [in billions of 1974 dollars/(Quad/year)] for building and operating the supply enerprise that converts high-Btu coal into high-Btu gas, and is first introduced into service at the beginning of period u;

sLCGS(u) = the fractional efficiency for converting low-Btu coal into high-Btu gas for facilities first introduced into service at the beginning of period u;

sHCGS(u) = the fractional efficiency for converting high-Btu coal into high-Btu gas for facilities first introduced into service at the beginning of period u;

Variables

LCGS(u) = the annual production (in Quads/year) of gas by the supply enterprise that is responsible for the gasification of low-Btu coal into a high-Btu gas and is first introduced into service at the beginning of period u;

HCGS(u) = the annual production (in Quads/year) of gas by the supply enterprise that is responsible for the gasification of high-Btu coal into a high-Btu gas and is first introduced into service at the beginning of period u.

Gasification of Coal to Low-Btu Gas for Combined-Cycle Electricity Generation

Both high-Btu and low-Btu coal can be converted to a low-Btu gas that is subsequently used to generate electricity in a combined-cycle power plant. These supply enterprises are represented by type "PC" variables with input-and-process paths m = 26 and m = 27 for the combined cycle electricity generation process using low-Btu and high-Btu coal respectively.

LINEAR PROGRAMMING IMPLEMENTATION OF THE MODEL

This section summarizes the linear programming implementation of the model for the alternative scenarios. Figure B-10 summarizes the algebra and nomenclature used in both the base case and the improved efficiencies in end use scenarios. The algebra is presented in standard linear programming format with variables pre-multiplied by coefficients (which are enclosed in brackets) on the left-hand sides of the constraints and only constants on the right-hand sides of the constraints. Tables B-1 through B-4 give the allowable values for the indices i, j, n, k, and m for these two scenarios.

Figure B-11 summarizes the model's linear programming formulation and corresponding nomenclature for the scenario that includes all three of the new technologies (i.e., end-use efficiencies plus synfuels plus breeders). From this formulation and the tables of permissible index

Given values for the constants R, rS, D, gPC, gDS and the coefficient brackets (i.e., {__}) which contain the parameters CPC, CRC, CDS, r, s, q, f, d, g, l and PF. Determine values for the variables PC, RC and DS that

$$\text{Minimize}\left[\sum_{\substack{(m,k)\\u}}\left\{CPC(m,k,u)\right\}PC(m,k,u)+\sum_{p,u}\left\{CRC(p,u)\right\}RC(p,u)+\sum_{i,j,t}\left\{CDS(i,j,t)\right\}DS(i,j,t)\right]$$

Subject to the following constraints:

<u>Supply Constraints</u>

Basic resource supply constraints (except crude oil)

$$\sum_{j}DS(i,j,t)-\sum_{\substack{u\le t\\(m,k)\in MKI(i)}}\left\{\frac{r(u,t)}{s(m,u)}\right\}PC(m,k,u)\geqq rS(i,t),\ i=1,\ldots,4;\ \forall t.$$

Crude Oil supply constraints

$$\sum_{j}DS(5,j,t)-\sum_{\substack{u\le t\\p}}\left\{r(u,t)\right\}RC(p,u)\geqq rS(5,t),\ \forall t.$$

<u>Demand Constraints</u>

End-use demand constraints (except peak electric)

$$\sum_{\substack{u\le t\\(m,k)\in MKN(n)}}\left\{q(k,n)[1+f(m,n)]d(k,n,u)r(u,t)\right\}PC(m,k,u)\geqq D(n,t),\ \forall t,\ \forall n\ne 3.$$

Endogenous peak-electric demand constraints

$$\sum_{\substack{u\le t\\(m,k)\in MKN(3)}}\left\{q(k,3)r(u,t)\right\}PC(m,k,u)-\sum_{\substack{u\le t\\(m,k)}}\left\{q(k,n)f(m,n)r(u,t)\right\}PC(m,k,u)\geqq 0,\ \forall t.$$

<u>Refinery Balance Constraints</u>

$$g(p,v)\sum_{u\le t}\left\{r(u,t)\right\}RC(p,u)-\sum_{\substack{u\le t\\(m,k)\in MKV(p,v)}}\left\{r(u,t)\right\}PC(m,k,u)\geqq 0,\ \forall p,\ \forall v,\ \forall t.$$

<u>Resource Constraints</u>

$$\sum_{t=1}^{6}\left\{l(t)\right\}DS(i,j,t)\leqq R(i,j),\ \forall i,\ \forall j.$$

<u>Growth Constraints</u>

Nuclear facility construction constraints

$$\sum_{k}\left\{\frac{1}{PF(k)}\right\}PC(m,k,t)\leqq gPC(m,t),\ \forall m\in NR,\ \forall t.$$

Crude oil and natural gas extraction rate constraints

$$\sum_{j=1}^{3}DS(i,j,t)\leqq gDS(i,t),\ \text{for } i=4,5;\ \forall t.$$

Constraints on the mix of low-Btu and high-Btu coal extraction

$$\sum_{j}DS(2,j,t)-2\sum_{j}DS(3,j,t)\leqq 0,\ \forall t.$$

Fig. B-10—Linear programming implementation for the base case and improved efficiencies in end-use scenarios

VARIABLES

DS - average annual resource consumption (Quads[a]/yr)
RC - average annual crude oil requirements for type "RC" supply enterprises (Quads/yr)
PC - average annual energy production for type "PC" supply enterprises (Quads/yr)

PARAMETERS

Resources

CDS - resource cost factor[b] (Billions of discounted 1974 dollars/(Quad[a]/yr))
R - total domestic resource supplies ultimately available (Quads[a])
rS - annual resource consumption by pre-1975 facilities (Quads[a]/yr)
gDS - maximum possible extraction rate (Quads/yr) (domestic oil and gas only)

Type "RC" Supply Enterprises

CRC - construction and operating cost factor $\left(\frac{\text{Billions of discounted 1974 dollars}}{\text{Quad of refinery capacity}}\right)$
g - refinery efficiency and product split

Type "PC" Supply Enterprises

CPC - construction and operating cost $\left(\frac{\text{Billions of discounted 1974 dollars}}{\text{Quad of energy delivery capacity}}\right)$
e - input-and-process path efficiency
q - fraction of average energy production delivered to a particular end-use demand utilizing device
PF - plant factor (fraction of time facilities are in operation[d])
gPC - maximum construction increment (nuclear reactors only) $\left(\frac{\text{Quads of energy delivery capacity}}{\text{Period}}\right)$

End-Use Demands

D - end-use demand that must be satisfied by facilities constructed after 1974 (Quads/yr)
d - end-use demand utilizing device efficiency
f - peak demand energy ratio (peak-block-demand energy requirement/base-block-demand energy requirement)

Other

r - life profile for supply enterprise (fraction of facilities still in operation)
l - length of period (years)

INDICES

i - resource type
j - resource cost category
k - supply enterprise output-path type
m - supply enterprise input-and-process-path type
n - end-use demand category
p - crude oil refinery type
t - time period
u - time period in which a supply enterprise initiates operation
v - refinery product type

SETS

MKI(i) - set of type "PC" supply enterprises (m,k) that consume resource type i
MKN(n) - set of type "PC" supply enterprises (m,k) that can satisfy demand category n
NR - set of input-and-process paths that include a nuclear reactor
MKV(p,v) - set of type "PC" supply enterprises (m,k) that may consume refinery product v from refinery type p

[a] 10,000s of short tons for uranium.

[b] Cost factor includes the length of the period.

[c] Except nuclear, where it is 10,000s of short tons of U_3O_8/Quad delivered.

[d] Facilities operate at full capacity when they are in operation.

Fig. B-10 — continued

Given values for the constants R, rS, D, gPC, gDS and the coefficient brackets (i.e., $\{\_\_\}$) which contain the parameters CPC, CRC, CDS, CLCLR, CHCLR, CLCGS, CHCGS, CSHA, r, s, SLCLR, sLCGS, sHCLR, sHCGS, g, f, d, g, l, PF and pU. Determine values for the variables PC, RC, DS, LCLR, HCLR, LCGS, HCGS and SHA that

$$\text{Minimize}\left[\sum_{\substack{(m,k)\\u}} \{CPC(m,k,u)\}PC(m,k,u) + \sum_{p,u} \{CRC(p,u)\}RC(p,u) + \sum_{i,j,t} \{CDS(i,j,t)\}DS(i,j,t) + \sum_{u} \{CLCLR(u)\}LCLR(u) + \sum_{u} \{CHCLR(u)\}HCLR(u) + \sum_{u} \{CLCGS(u)\}LCGS(u) + \sum_{u} \{CHCGS(u)\}HCGS(u) + \sum_{u} \{CSHA(u)\}SHA(u)\right]$$

Subject to the following constraints:

Supply Constraints

Uranium supply constraint

$$\sum_{j} DS(1,j,t) - \sum_{\substack{u \leq t\\(m,k)\in MKI(1)}} \left\{\frac{r(u,t)}{s(m,u)}\right\}PC(m,k,u) \geq \{rS(1,t)\}, \ \forall t.$$

Low-Btu coal supply constraint

$$\sum_{j} DS(2,j,t) - \sum_{\substack{u \leq t\\(m,k)\in MKI(2)}} \left\{\frac{r(u,t)}{s(m,u)}\right\}PC(m,k,u) - \sum_{u \leq t} \left\{\frac{r(u,t)}{sLCLR(u)}\right\}LCLR(u) - \sum_{u \leq t} \left\{\frac{r(u,t)}{sLCGS(u)}\right\}LCGS(u) \geq \{rS(2,t)\}, \ \forall t.$$

High-Btu coal supply constraint

$$\sum_{j} DS(3,j,t) - \sum_{\substack{u \leq t\\(m,k)\in MKI(3)}} \left\{\frac{r(u,t)}{s(m,u)}\right\}PC(m,k,u) - \sum_{u \leq t} \left\{\frac{r(u,t)}{sHCLR(u)}\right\}HCLR(u) - \sum_{u \leq t} \left\{\frac{r(u,t)}{sHCGS(u)}\right\}HCGS(u) \geq \{rS(3,t)\}, \ \forall t.$$

Gas supply constraint

$$\sum_{j} DS(4,j,t) + \sum_{u \leq t} \{r(u,t)\}[HCGS(u) + LCGS(u)] - \sum_{\substack{u \leq t\\(m,k)\in MKI(4)}} \left\{\frac{r(u,t)}{s(m,u)}\right\}PC(m,k,u) \geq \{rS(4,t)\}, \ \forall t.$$

Oil supply constraint

$$\sum_{j} DS(5,j,t) + \sum_{u \leq t} \{r(u,t)\}SHA(u) - \sum_{\substack{u \leq t\\p=1,2}} \{r(u,t)\}RC(p,u) \geq \{rS(5,t)\}, \ \forall t.$$

Demand Constraints

End-use demand constraints (except peak electric)

$$\sum_{\substack{u \leq t\\(m,k)\in MKN(n)}} \{q(k,n)[1 + f(m,n)]d(k,n,u)r(u,t)\}PC(m,k,u) \geq \{D(n,t)\}, \ \forall t, \ \forall n \neq 3.$$

Endogenous peak-electric demand constraints

$$\sum_{\substack{u \leq t\\(m,k)\in MKN(3)}} \{q(k,3)r(u,t)\}PC(m,k,u) - \sum_{\substack{u \leq t\\(m,k)}} \{q(k,n)f(m,n)r(u,t)\}PC(m,k,u) \geq 0, \ \forall t.$$

Fig. B-11—Linear programming implementation for the improved efficiencies improved efficiencies in end use, synfuels and breeder scenarios

VARIABLES

DS - average annual resource consumption (Quads[a]/yr)
RC - average annual crude oil requirements for type "RC" supply enterprises (Quads/yr)
PC - average annual energy production for type "PC" supply enterprises (Quads/yr)
LCLR - average annual production of residual fuel oil by the supply enterprise that liquefies (to residual fuel oil) and refines low-Btu coal (Quads/yr)
HCLR - average annual production of residual fuel oil by the supply enterprise that liquefies (to residual fuel oil) and refines high-Btu coal (Quads/yr)
LCGS - average annual production of gas by the supply enterprise that converts low-Btu coal to high-Btu gas (Quads/yr)
HCGS - average annual production of gas by the supply enterprise that converts high-Btu coal to high-Btu gas (Quads/yr)
SHA - average annual production of upgraded shale oil (Quads/yr)
PUINV - plutonium inventory at end of period (metric tons)

PARAMETERS

Resources

CDS - resource cost factor[b] (Billions of discounted 1974 dollars/(Quads[a]/yr)
R - total domestic resource supplies ultimately available (Quads[a])
rS - annual resource consumption by pre-1975 facilities (Quads[a]/yr)
gDS - maximum possible extraction rate (Quads/yr) (domestic oil, gas and shale oil only)

Type "RC" Supply Enterprises

CRC - construction and operating cost factor[c]
g - refinery efficiency and product split

Type "PC" Supply Enterprises

CPC - construction and operating cost factor[d]
s - input-and-process path efficiency[e]
q - fraction of average energy production delivered to a particular end-use demand utilizing device
PF - plant factor (fraction of time facilities are in operation[f])
gPC - maximum construction increment (nuclear reactors only) $\left(\frac{\text{Quads of energy delivery capacity}}{\text{Period}}\right)$
pU - change in plutonium inventory in period per Quad of capacity for delivered electricity (metric tons/Quad/yr) for light-water reactors and breeders only)

Other Supply Enterprises

CLCLR - construction and operating cost factor for the supply enterprise that liquefies and refines low-Btu coal[c]
CHCLR - construction and operating cost factor for the supply enterprise that liquefies and refines high-Btu coal[c]
CLCGS - construction and operating cost factor for the supply enterprise that converts low-Btu coal to high-Btu gas[d]
CHCGS - construction and operating cost factor for the supply enterprise that converts high-Btu coal to high-Btu gas[d]
CSHA - construction and operating cost factor for the supply enterprise that upgrades shale oil[d]
sLCLR - fractional efficiency for converting low-Btu coal into residual fuel oil
sHCLR - fractional efficiency for converting high-Btu coal into residual fuel oil
sLCGS - fractional efficiency for converting low-Btu coal into high-Btu gas
sHCGS - fractional efficiency for converting high-Btu coal into high-Btu gas

End-Use Demands

D - end-use demand that must be satisfied by facilities constructed after 1974 (Quads/yr)
d - end-use demand utilizing device efficiency
f - peak demand energy ratio (peak-block-demand energy requirement/base-block-demand energy requirement)

Other

r - life profile for supply enterprise (fraction of facilities still in operation)
l - length of period (years)

INDICES

i - resource type
j - resource cost category
k - supply enterprise output-path type
m - supply enterprise input-and-process-path type
n - end-use demand category
p - crude oil refinery type
t - time period
u - time period in which a supply enterprise initiates operation
v - refinery product type

SETS

MKI(i) - set of type "PC" supply enterprises (m,k) that consume resource type i
MKN(n) - set of type "PC" supply enterprises (m,k) that can satisfy demand category n
NR - set of input-and-process paths that include a nuclear reactor
MKPU - the set of supply enterprises (m,k) that produce or consume plutonium
MKV(p,v) - set of type "PC" supply enterprises (m,k) that consume refinery product v from refinery type p

---

[a] 10,000s of short tons for uranium.

[b] Cost factors include the length of the period.

[c] $\left(\frac{\text{Billions of discounted 1974 dollars}}{\text{Quad of refinery capacity}}\right)$.

[d] $\left(\frac{\text{Billions of discounted 1974 dollars}}{\text{Quad of energy delivery capacity}}\right)$.

[e] Except nuclear, where it is 10,000s of short tons of U_3O_8/Quad delivered.

[f] Facilities operate at full capacity when they are in operation.

Fig. B-11—continued

Refinery Balance Constraints

Crude oil refinery balance constraints

$$g(p,v) \sum_{u \le t} \{r(u,t)\} RC(p,u) - \sum_{\substack{u \le t \\ (m,k) \in MKV(p,v)}} \{r(u,t)\} PC(m,k,u) \geq 0, \ \forall v, \ \forall t, \ p = 1,2.$$

Coal liquids refinery balance constraints

$$g(3,v) \sum_{u \le t} \{r(u,t)\} [LCLK(u) + HCLK(u)] - \sum_{\substack{u \le t \\ (m,k) \in MKV(3,v)}} \{r(u,t)\} PC(m,k,u) \geq 0, \ \forall v, \ \forall t.$$

Resource Constraints

$$\sum_{t=1}^{6} \{l(t)\} DS(i,j,t) \leq \{R(i,j)\}, \ \forall i, \ \forall j.$$

Growth Constraints

Nuclear facility construction constraints

$$\sum_{k} \left\{\frac{1}{PF(k)}\right\} PC(m,k,u) \leq \{gPC(m,u)\}, \ \forall m \in NR, \ \forall u.$$

Crude oil, natural gas and shale oil extraction rate constraints

$$\sum_{j=1}^{3} DS(i,j,t) \leq \{gDS(i,t)\}, \ \text{for } i = 4,5,6; \ \forall t.$$

Constraints on the mix of low-Btu and high-Btu coal extraction

$$\sum_{j} DS(2,j,t) - 2 \sum_{j} DS(3,j,t) \leq 0, \ \forall t.$$

Plutonium Balance Constraints (omit for nonbreeder scenarios)

$$PUINV(t-1) + \sum_{\substack{u \le t \\ (m,k) \in MKPu}} \{pU(m,u,t)\} PC(m,k,u) - PUINV(t) \geq 0, \ t = 2,\ldots,6$$

Fig. B-11 — continued

values (i.e., Tables B-1 through B-4, B-6 and B-7) the formulation for all eight scenarios considered in the dissertation can be determined. The inclusion of the improved efficiencies in end use technologies only alters the D(n,t) and d(k,n,t) values and, hence, does not lead to any modifications in the model's algebra. The synfuels scenario includes all of the constraints shown in Fig. B-11 except for the plutonium balance constraint. Tables B-6 and B-7 show the additional index values for i, j and m that must be added to the base case possibilities for the alternative scenarios. Finally, Table B-8 is a dictionary of all of the variables, coefficient parameters, constants, indices and sets used in all the alternative scenario formulations.

Table B-8

DICTIONARY OF SYMBOLS FOR THE ALGEBRAIC FORMULATION*

Indices

i = a subscript corresponding to the basic resource categories.

j = a subscript corresponding to the extraction cost categories for the basic resources.

k = a subscript corresponding to the supply enterprise´s output path (used in defining the supply enterprises of type "PC").

m = a subscript corresponding to the energy supply enterprise´s input-and-process path (used in defining the supply enterprises of type "PC").

n = a subscript corresponding to end-use demand categories.

p = a subscript corresponding to the oil refinery types.

t = a subscripts corresponding to the time periods.

u = a subscript corresponding to the time periods when supply enterprises are first introduced into service.

v = a subscript corresponding to the types of refined oil products.

Sets

MKI(i) = the set of supply enterprises (m,k) that use basic resource i.

MKN(n) = the set of supply enterprises (m,k) that satisfy end-use demand category n.

MKPu = the set of energy supply enterprises that either produce or consume plutonium.

---

*This dictionary covers all of the scenarios that were analyzed in Chapter 4.

MKV(p,v) = the set of "PC" supply enterprises that require refined oil product v from refinery type p.

NR = the set of input-and-process paths that include nuclear reactor facilities.

Coefficient Parameters

CDS(i,j,t) = the discounted cost per unit of annual production [in billions of 1974 dollars/(Quad/year)] for the consumption of resource type i (supply cost category j) for a period of l(t) years that span period t.

CHCGS(u) = the discounted unit cost [in billions of 1974 dollars/(Quad/year)] for building and operating the supply enerprise that converts high-Btu coal into high-Btu gas, and is first introduced into service at the beginning of period u.

CHCLR(u) = the discounted unit cost [in billions of 1974 dollars/(Quad/year of refining capacity)] for building and operating the supply enterprise that liquefies and refines high-Btu coal and, is first introduced into service at the beginning of period u.

CLCGS(u) = the discounted unit cost [in billions of 1974 dollars/(Quad/year)] for building and operating the supply enerprise that converts low-Btu coai into high-Btu gas, and is first introduced into service at the beginning of period u.

CLCLR(u) = the discounted unit cost [in billions of 1974 dollars/(Quad/year of refining capacity)] for building and operating the supply enterprise that liquefies and refines low-Btu coal, and is first introduced into service at the beginning of period u.

CPC(m,k,u) = the discounted unit cost [in billions of 1974 dollars/(Quad/year)] for building and operating supply enterprise facilities of type "PC" that are first introduced into service at the beginning of period u.

CRC(p,u) = the discounted unit cost [in billions of 1974 dollars/(Quad/year) of refining capacity] for building and operating supply enterprise facilities of refinery type p that are first introduced into service at the beginning of period u.

CSHA(u) = the discounted unit cost [in billions of 1974 dollars/(Quad/year)] of building and operating the supply enterprise that upgrades shale oil and is first introduced into service at the beginning of period u.

d(k,n,u) = the efficiency for the supply enterprise with output path k that is first introduced into service at the beginning of period u and can deliver energy to end-use demand category n.

f(m,n) = ratio of the electrical energy supplied to the "peak-block" demand to the energy supplied to the "base-block" demand for end-use demand category n when the energy is delivered by supply enterprises having input-and-process paths of type m (f(m,n)=0 if m is not an electricity generation input-and-process path).

g(p,v) = the refinery efficiency and product split coefficient for refinery type p (the ratio of the energy content of the refined oil product of type v to the energy content of the crude oil that is input to the refinery).

l(t) = the length of time period t (in years).

PF(k) = the plant factor at which electric generation facilities must operate when they are part of supply enterprise with an output path of type k (the plant factor is the fraction of the plant's capacity that is actually used on the average).

pU(m,u,t) = the production or consumption [in metric tons/(Quad of electrical energy delivery capacity)] of plutonium in period t by supply enterprise type (m,k) that was first introduced into service at the beginning of period u.

q(k,n) = the fraction of the electrical energy supplied by energy supply enterprises with output path type k that is used to satisfy end-use demand n (q(k,n)=1 if k is not an electrical load-sharing output path).

r(u,t) = the fraction of capacity first available for use in period u that remains available for use in period t.

s(m,u) = for non-nuclear supply enterprises: the efficiency of energy resource supply facilities for the supply enterprise with input-and-process path m that was first introduced into service at the beginning of period u.

s(m,u) = for nuclear supply enterprises: the U_3O_8 requirement (10,000s of short tons/year) for one Quad of delivered electricity from the supply enterprise with input-and-process path m that was first introduced into service at the beginning of period u.

sHCGS(u) = the fractional efficiency for converting high-Btu coal into high-Btu gas for facilities first introduced into service at the beginning of period u.

sHCLR(u) = the fractional efficiency for converting high-Btu coal into residual fuel oil for facilities first introduced into service at the beginning of period u.

sLCGS(u) = the fractional efficiency for converting low-Btu coal into high-Btu gas for facilities first introduced into service at the beginning of period u.

sLCLR(u) = the fractional efficiency for converting low-Btu coal into residual fuel oil for facilities first introduced into service at the beginning of period u.

Constants

D(n,t) = the average annual net demand (in Quads/year) for end-use energy form n in period t.

gDS(i,t) = maximum permissible average annual extraction rate (in Quads/year) of resource i in period t.

gPC(m,u) = the limit on the total capacity (in Quads/year) of all new reactors of type m which may be installed in period u.

R(i,j) = the total supply of resource type i that is ultimately available in extraction cost category j (in Quads) at the beginning of the time horizon (i.e., beginning of 1975).

rS(i,t) = the average annual consumption (Quads/year) of basic resource i in period t by facilities built prior to 1975.

Variables

DS(i,j,t) = the average annual consumption (in Quads/year) during period t of basic resource type i in supply cost category j.

HCGS(u) = the annual production (in Quads/year) of gas by the supply enterprise that is responsible for the gasification of high-Btu coal into a high-Btu gas and is first introduced into service at the beginning of period u.

HCLR(u) = the average annual production (in Quads/year) of residual fuel oil by the supply enterprise that liquefies high-Btu coal (to residual fuel oil) and refines the resulting residual fuel oil, and is first introduced into service at the beginning of period u.

LCGS(u) = the annual production (in Quads/year) of gas by the supply enterprise that is responsible for the gasification of low-Btu coal into a high-Btu gas and is first introduced into service at the beginning of period u.

LCLR(u) = the average annual production (in Quads/year) of residual fuel oil by the supply enterprise that liquefies low-Btu coal (to residual fuel oil) and refines the resulting residual fuel oil, and is first introduced into service at the beginning of period u.

PC(m,k,u) = the average annual energy production (in Quads/year) for the supply enterprise specified by the (m,k) pair first introduced into service at the beginning of period u;

PUINV(t) = the inventory of plutonium (in metric tons) at the end of period t.

RC(p,u) = the annual crude oil requirement (in Quads/year) for refinery type p that is first introduced into service at the the beginning of period u.

SHA(u) = the average annual production (in Quads/year) by the supply enterprise that upgrades shale oil and is first introduced into service at the beginning of period u.

Appendix C

THE ADVANTAGE OF THE PRESENT TREATMENT OF LOAD SHARING

This appendix shows that the representation of the load sharing of electrical generation capacity by compatible pairs of primary and secondary demands that was used in the present model is equivalent to, but considerably more efficient than, previous representations.

THE BASIC CONCEPT

Suppose in this simple example that there is only one type of electrical generating equipment in the energy economy, with design plant factor* PF and a plant capacity of Q units of energy per year. Suppose further, that there is a primary (in the sense of Table B-5) electrical demand that posseses only a base-block (see Fig. B-8). The demand factor (DF) is defined as the demand duration (DDA(n) in Fig. B-8) for this case since there is no peak-block (Fig.B-8). Then, for this system, the top of Fig. C-1 is a schematic diagram of the load-sharing representation used in previous (e.g., the Brookhaven; Hoffman, 1972; Cherniavsky, 1974; and Bodin, 1974) energy models. The bottom part of the figure is a schematic diagram of the representation of the load-sharing potential used in the present model. The immediate objective here is to show that: 1) these two representations are equivalent, and 2) the representation employed in the current model is computationally more efficient, since it does not require the use of an explicit constraint on the amount of "off-peak" electricity that is generated.

In the top part of Fig. C-1, P units of electrical energy per year are supplied to the primary demand, while OP units of electrical energy per year are supplied to the secondary demand. Since the generating equipment is assumed to be sized to meet the demand rate profile of the primary demand, P = DFxQ in this case. Now, in the Brookhaven formulation, with these variable definitions, it is necessary to introduce a constraint on the amount of electrical energy that can be

---

*The design plant factor is defined here as the maximum fraction of the time that the equipment could be in commercial operation at full capacity (assuming that whenever the plant is in operation, it is always operated at full capacity).

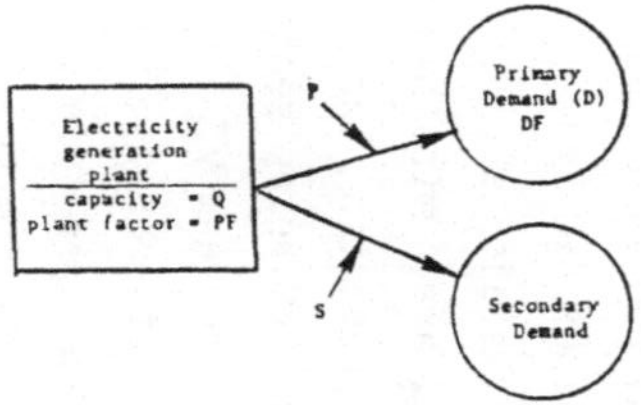

<u>BROOKHAVEN APPROACH</u>

- Given P and S as average annual energy flow variables, the plant capacity is sized to meet the primary demand

$$Q = \frac{D}{DF} = \frac{P}{DF}$$

where

$P = D$
and DF is the demand factor (e.g., DDA(n) in Fig. B-8 for the case DDB(n) = 0).

- Then, the average annual energy flow that goes to the secondary demand must satisfy the constraint

$$S \leq \frac{PF - DF}{DF} P. \qquad (1)$$

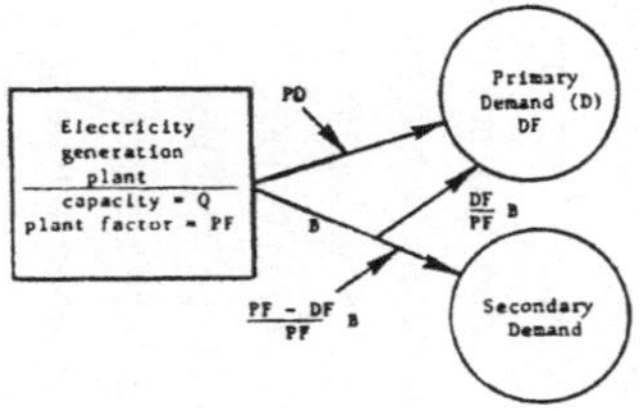

<u>WEYANT APPROACH</u>

- Given PO and B as average annual energy flow variables, the plant capacity is still sized to meet the primary demand

$$Q = \frac{D}{DF} = \frac{PO}{DF} + \frac{B}{PF}, \qquad (2)$$

and the average annual energy flow supplied to the primary demand is

$$PO + \frac{DF}{PF} B \qquad (3)$$

and to the secondary demand

$$\frac{PF - DF}{PF} B. \qquad (4)$$

- In order for there to be equivalence between the approaches, the Brookhaven load-share constraint (1) must be satisfied; so from (1)

$$\left[\begin{array}{c}\text{Electrical energy supplied to the}\\ \text{secondary demand utilizing device}\end{array}\right] \leq \frac{PF - DF}{DF} \times \left[\begin{array}{c}\text{Electrical energy supplied to the}\\ \text{primary demand utilizing device}\end{array}\right]$$

and after substituting (3) and (4);

$$\frac{PF - DF}{PF} B \leq \frac{PF - DF}{DF} \times \left[PO + \frac{DF}{PF} B\right]$$

substituting (2);

$$\frac{PF - DF}{PF} B \leq \frac{PF - DF}{DF} \times \left[DF \cdot Q - \frac{DF}{PF} B + \frac{DF}{PF} B\right]$$

$$\frac{B}{PF} \leq Q$$

$B \leq PF \cdot Q$ which must hold since $PF \cdot Q$ is the maximum energy output for the plant.

Fig. C-1 — Comparison of load-sharing representations

supplied to the secondary demand by the underutilized electric generation equipment that was sized to satisfy the primary demand. Since Q=P/DF, the maximum possible amount of energy available for the secondary demand is (PF-DF)xQ.

The bottom part of the figure shows how, in the current model, a redefinition of variables eliminates the need for the Brookhaven constraint. An amount of electrical energy PO is sent each year to the primary demand only, while an amount B is sent to both the primary and the secondary demands, with (DF/PF)xB going to the primary demand and [(PF-DF)/PF]xB going to the secondary demand. First, the plant capacity relation for a plant capacity of Q units of energy per year is shown in the bottom of Fig. C-1 for the new variable definitions. Next, it is shown that the Brookhaven constraint must be satisfied by any solution in the present formulation by showing that it is equivalent to the constraint B $\leq$ PFxQ, which must always hold since PFxQ is the maximum energy output for the plant. Finally, in this formulation, the amount of electrical energy that is generated for the primary demand is again DFxQ, and the amount of electrical energy that is supplied to the secondary demand can be anywhere from 0 (when B = 0) to (PF-DF)xQ (when PO=0).

The representation described here exploits the convexity property of linear pogramming solutions; that is, given that any two solutions to a linear programming problem are feasible (say, for values B=0 and B=PFxQ), any convex combination of these two solutions is also a feasible solution (i.e., all values of B from 0 to PFxQ are admissible). In the present application, although only variables representing the minimum (zero) and maximum possible amount (PFxQ) of energy being sent to the secondary demands are employed in the model, the convexity property allows solutions involving intermediate levels of energy going to the secondary demand to be represented by weighted averages (i.e., convex combinations) of the values of these variables. The simple example described showed how exploiting this property can lead to an improved computational efficiency for the models of the present type (including the Brookhaven model).

EXTENDING THE BASIC CONCEPT

Thus far, only a single end-use demand has been considered. It is possible for electrical energy from generating equipment that is sized for a particular primary demand to be used to satisfy more than one secondary demand. Furthermore, many types of electric generation equipment can be used to generate electricity for the secondary demands. Finally, two different types of so-called electrical "load-sharing" are possible (see Appendix B). First, electrical generation facilities that are sized to meet end-use demands with a demand period of one week and a random demand duration interval (e.g., miscellaneous intermediate-load electricity and peak-load electricity) can be used to satisfy end-use demand categories that can be satisfied at any time during the week (e.g., water heat and the peak-load electricity demand via pumped storage facilities). The second type of load-sharing involves electrical generation facilities that are sized to meet the winter space heat demands that can also be used to satisfy air conditioning demands in the summer. To handle all of these possibilities, however, it is only necessary to define an analogous pair of variables for electricity supplied to each pair of primary and possible secondary demands for each type of load-sharing for each type of electric generation equipment. The convexity property of linear programming solutions again allows for all possible solutions in terms of both the possible destinations and the amounts of all electricity delivered to secondary demands.

THE COMPUTATIONAL ADVANTAGE

Some idea of the computational advantages of this formulation can be gained by considering the computational savings it led to in the current model formulation. If the Brookhaven representation had been used, an off-peak constraint would have been necessary for each type of electric generation equipment for each type of load sharing considered in each time period. Since there are at least 5 types of electric generation equipment suitable for load sharing represented in the present model (see Table B-4), this means that at least 60 constraints would have to be added to the 200 constraint, 6 period formulation.

Since the computational burden of a linear programming formulation increases approximately with the cube of the number of constraints in the model, the adoption of the representation suggested here more than halved the computer costs for the model.

MODELING WASTE HEAT UTILIZATION

A scheme similar to that suggested here could be employed to explicity model the potential for waste heat utilization.* In this case, a variable representing only electric generation (with no waste heat utilization) and variables involving waste heat utilization at the maximum level for each end-use demand that can use the waste heat, would be required for each type of electric generation equipment. This contrasts with the formulation suggested by Hoffman (1972), in which a constraint limiting the total amount of waste heat utilized must be defined for each type of electric generating equipment. If this representation were combined with the off-peak representation suggested above, order of magnitude computational savings relative to previous representations could be expected.

---

*Waste heat utilization was not explicitly represented in the current model because of the lack of adequate data on the costs and efficiencies of waste-heat delivery and utilization systems.

Appendix D

DATA USED IN THE EXAMPLE APPLICATION

This Appendix presents the basic data used in the example application of the model in Chapters 4 and 5. The data are also related to the model's coefficient parameters and constants that were described in Appendix B. The data is presented in the following order:

1) Energy supply availability data for the alternative resource cases
   - o Table D-1 and Figure D-1
   - o This table and figure present the data for the resource supplies (R(i,j)) and the data used to construct the resource supply cost coefficient parameters (CDS(i,j,t)).*
2) End-use demand data
   - o Tables D-2 to D-9
   - o These tables culminate in a determination of the net end-use demand values (D(n,t)).
3) Energy conversion/supply process and end-use utilizing device efficiency data
   - o Tables D-10 to D-14
   - o These tables culminate in a determination of the efficiency data for the energy supply enterprises (s(m,u), sLCLR(u), sHCLR(u), sLCGS(u), sHCGS(u)) and the end-use utilizing devices (d(k,n,u)).
4) Energy resource supplies required to operate energy supply facilities existing prior to 1975
   - o Tables 15 to 18
   - o These tables culminate in a determination of the energy resource supplies required to operate pre-1975 energy supply enterprises until retirement (rS(i,t)).

---

*The symbols are the coefficient parameters and constants used in the algebraic formulation of the model (Appendix B). These coefficients constitute the input for the model.

5) Energy supply enterprise cost data
   - o Tables D-19 to D-21
   - o These tables provide the basic cost data that were used to construct the supply enterprise cost coefficient parameters (CRC(m,k,u), CPC(p,u), CSHA(u), CLCLR(u), CHCLR(u), CLCGS(u), CHCGS(u)).

6) Retirement fraction data
   - o Table D-22
   - o This table presents data for the retirement fractions (r(u,t)).

7) Growth constraint data
   - o Tables D-23 and D-24
   - o This table presents the data for the limits on new capacity additions for nuclear reactor supply enterprises (gPC(m,t)) and on the extraction of the basic domestic energy resources (gDS(i,t)).

8) Electrical load sharing data.
   - o Table D-25
   - o This section presents data for the electrical load-sharing fraction coefficient parameters (q(n,t)).

9) Plutonium balance data
   - o Table D-26
   - o This table presents data for the plutonium accumulation coefficient parameters (pU(m,u,t)).

10) Conversion Factors
   - o Table D-27
   - o This table presents the conversion factors used in the study.

RESOURCE AVAILABILITY DATA

This section describes the resource supply data used in the study. The data for the nominal resource case (defined in Fig. 4-1) are described first. Then, the data for the alternative resource cases are described.

The Nominal Resource Case

The resource supply availability data for the nominal resource case are shown in Table D-1. The resource supply term (R(i,j)) and the associated indices that are used in the algebraic formulation of the model (Appendix B) are described in Table B-1.

The uranium supply data for the first three cost categories is from ERDA-1 (1975). However, the "forward" costs for the three cost categories given there are scaled up to reflect sunk costs and return on investment in accordance with data given in Palmer, et al. (1975). The low-Btu coal, high-Btu coal, and oil shale extraction cost data are all derived from the Synfuels Interagency Task Force Report (1975), although total coal supplies are taken from an FEA source (Federal Energy Administration, 1974b).

The apportionment of the domestic oil and natural gas resources among the cost categories is also based on the task force report, however, the supplies for the two lower cost categories were modified to reflect more recent (USGS) estimates for "low-cost" oil and natural gas supplies (United States Geological Survey, 1975). These estimates include expected undiscovered, as well as measured, inferred, and indicated reserves.

The price of imported crude oil was specified as a time stream in accordance with data extracted from the Synfuels Interagency Task Force Report (1975). The unit costs shown in Table D-1 must be discounted and multiplied by the approriate period lengths to get the resource cost coefficient parameters (CDS(i,j,t)) used in the study. Thus, Table D-1 provides the values for the resouce supply constants (R(i,j)) and the unit cost data used to derive the resource supply cost coefficient parameters (CDS(i,j,t)) used in the study for the nominal resource case.

Table D-1

AVAILABILITY OF ENERGY RESOURCE SUPPLIES BY EXTRACTION COST CATEGORY

Resource	Cost Category number	Available Supplies in the Model Units of Measure (in TeT[a]/Quad[b] as indicated)	Resource Supply Cost: Common Units	Resource Supply Cost: $ x 10^8 per model unit of measure (1974) dollars)	Basis for the Resource Supply Cost	Sources
Uranium	1	73 Tet[a]	$12.50/lb	2.5	Output from mill	ERDA-1 (1975) Palmer, et al. (1975)
	2	122 TeT	$27.5/lb	5.5		
	3	154 TeT	$52.5/lb	10.5		
	4	Unlimited	$100/lb	20.0		
Low-Btu Coal[e]	1	1023 Quads[b]	$5.95/ton	3.5	Minemouth	Synfuels Report (1975) FEA (1974)
	2	1061 Quads	$9.35/ton	5.5		
High-Btu Coal[f]	1	1500 Quads	$15.00/ton	5.8	Minemouth	
	2	1980 Quads	$24.7/ton	9.5		
	3	Unlimited	$35/ton	13.5		
Gas[g]	1	362 Quads	$.446/mcf[c]	4.37	Wellhead	Synfuels Report (1975) USGS (1975)
	2	580 Quads	$1.01/mcf	9.9		
	3	467 Quads	$3.36/mcf	32.9		
Oil[h]	1	421 Quads	$5.48/bbl	9.86	Wellhead	
	2	381 Quads	$8.95/bbl	16.1		
	3	511 Quads	$22.73/bbl	40.9		
	4[i]	Unlimited	($11.50/bbl)[d]	(20.7)[d]	Port of Entry	Synfuels Report (1975)
Shale Oil[h]	1	600 Quads	$10.00/bbl	18.0	Wellhead for in-situ (output of retort facility otherwise)	Synfuels Report (1975)
	2	600 Quads	$12.00/bbl	21.6		
	3	Unlimited	$15.00/bbl	27.0		

(a) TeT = 10,000 short tons.

(b) 1 Quad = 10^{15} Btu.

(c) mcf = thousand cubic feet.

(d) assumed 1974 import price.

(e) 17 x 10^6 Btu/ton.

(f) 24 x 10^6 Btu/ton.

(g) 1020 Btu/Cu. ft..

(h) 180 x 10^6 bbl/Quad.

(i) Oil (4) = imports - prices represented as a time stream:

1978 - $12.00/bbl = $20.7 x 10^8/Quad

1985 - $13.00/bbl = $21.6 x 10^8/Quad

1992 - $14.00/bbl = $23.4 x 10^8/Quad

2000 - $15.00/bbl = $27.0 x 10^8/Quad

2012 - $18.00/bbl = $32.4 x 10^8/Quad

2027 - $20.00/bbl = $36.0 x 10^8/Quad.

Alternative Resource Cases

This section describes the resource availability sensitivity data used in the study. These consist of low, nominal, and high values for both domestic oil and natural gas availability, and the price of imported oil.

Recall that the nominal values for low-cost domestic oil and gas resources are the "expected values" for these reserves determined in a recent USGS study (United States Geological Survey, 1975). The values used for the sensitivity analysis here are the 5th and 95th percentile assessments made in that study. In other words, there is thought to be only a five per cent chance that the availability of low-cost domestic oil and gas will be less than the low availability case examined here, and similarly, only a five per cent chance that the availability of low-cost oil and gas will be greater than that assumed for the high availability case. Figure D-1(a) provides the values for the domestic oil and gas supply constants (R(4,j) and R(5,j) for j=1,2 and 3) provided to the model for the various resource cases.

The nominal values assumed for the price of imported oil over time are the nominal values for this parameter given in the Synthetic Fuels Commercialization Task Force Report (Synfuels Interagency Task Force, 1975). High and low values for the price of imported oil are also included in this report and are used as the high and low import prices here. The low price case involves a break in the world oil cartel, the nominal price case, the continuance of the current cartel; and the high price case, an immediate increase of 3 dollars per barrel in the price of imported oil (the bottom portion of Figure 4-1 summarizes the resource cases considered in the study). Figure D-1(b) provides the unit cost data used in deriving the price of imported oil coefficient parameters (CDS(5,4,t)) provided to the model for the various scenarios.

END-USE DEMAND DATA

The derivation of the net end-use demand data used in the study are described in this section. Only two different sets of end-use demand data were required; one set for the base case scenario, which was also used in the SYN, BRE, and SYN+BRE scenarios, and a second set for the improved efficiencies in end-use (END) scenario, which was also used in the SYN+END, SYN+END+BRE and BRE+END scenarios. Consequently, the

Low Domestic Supply Case			Nominal Domestic Supply Case			High Domestic Supply Case		
Resource	Cost Category Number	Available Supplies (Quads)	Resource	Cost Category Number	Available Supplies (Quads)	Resource	Cost Category Number	Available Supplies (Quads)
Gas	1	292	Gas	1	362	Gas	1	420
	2	469		2	580		2	674
	3	467		3	467		3	467
Oil	1	326	Oil	1	421	Oil	1	551
	2	296		2	381		2	499
	3	511		3	511		3	511

(a) Domestic resource reserves for oil and gas

Low Import Price Case		
Year	Dollars (1974) per bbl	$\$ \times 10^8$ (1974) per Quad
1978	8.50	15.3
1985	7.50	13.5
1992	8.50	15.3
2000	9.00	16.2
2012	10.50	18.9
2027	12.00	21.6

Nominal Import Price Case		
Year	Dollars (1974) per bbl	Dollars (1974) per Quad
1978	12.00	20.7
1985	13.00	21.6
1992	14.00	23.4
2000	15.00	27.0
2012	18.00	32.4
2027	20.00	36.0

High Import Price Case		
Year	Dollars (1974) per bbl	Dollars (1974) per Quad
1978	14.50	26.1
1985	16.50	29.7
1992	18.00	32.4
2000	19.50	35.1
2012	21.00	37.8
2027	22.50	40.5

(b) Imported oil price

Fig. D-1 — Data for the alternative resource assessment cases

current section refers only to the end-use demand data for the base case and improved efficiencies in end-use scenarios.

Base Case Scenario

The sequence of calculations necessary to calculate the net end-use demands, which serve as the model's input, is schematically depicted in Fig. D-2 for the base case scenario (see Fig. 3-1 for another illustration of the net end-use demand concept). First, projections of gross end-use demands (Table D-2) were developed by starting with 1972 demand levels (ERDA-48, 1975) and applying projected end-use demand growth rates derived from ERDA-48 for the time intervals 1972 to 1985 and 1985 to 2000. Additional data from Brookhaven's forthcoming revised reference energy systems* was used to refine and extend this projection.**

Next, the retirement of facilities existing prior to 1975 is treated in Tables D-3, D-4, and D-5. Recall, from Chapter 3, that the demands that continue to be satisfied by pre-1975 facilities are subtracted from the gross end-use demands in determining the net end-use demands (e.g., see Fig. 3-1).

The facilities that are assumed to be associated with a particular end-use demand are assumed to have been built up at the historical growth rate for that end-use demand (see the last column of Table D-3). Knowing the historical percentage growth rate (gr) for the facilities built to satisfy a particular end-use demand and assuming that such facilities have a 30-year lifetime, the fraction of the initial capacity remaining t years into the future is:

$$\text{fraction of the pre-1975 facilities remaining after t years} = 1 - \frac{1 - \left(1 + \frac{gr}{100}\right)^{t}}{1 - \left(1 + \frac{gr}{100}\right)^{30}}$$

---

*Personal communication, Andre Doernberg, Brookhaven National Laboratory.

**The "peak-load electricity" demand is determined by the model (i.e. it is determined endogenously) from the demand duration characteristics (e.g., see Fig. B-8) of the end-use demand categories that have peak-block demands for electricity.

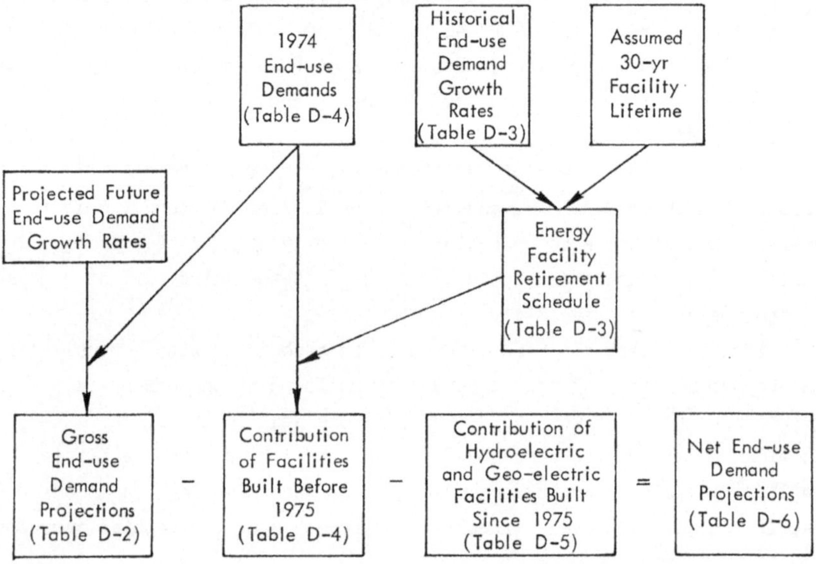

Fig. D-2 — Calculation of net end-use demand projections

Table D-2

GROSS END-USE DEMANDS FOR THE BASE CASE SCENARIO[a]
(in Quadrillion Btus/year)

End-Use Demands	Period 1 (1978)	Period 2 (1985)	Period 3 (1992)	Period 4 (2000)	Period 5 (2012)	Period 6 (2027)
Misc. Base-Load Electricity	4.34	5.84	7.42	9.77	14.16	23.21
Misc. Int.-Load Electricity	.93	1.22	1.54	2.04	2.95	4.86
Peak-Load Electricity	Endogenous	Endogenous	Endogenous	Endogenous	Endogenous	Endogenous
Iron and Steel	.7	.9	1.07	1.17	1.42	1.8
Air Conditioning	1.56	2.78	4.08	4.82	5.76	7.20
Space Heat	5.72	6.33	7.07	7.88	9.35	10.74
Water Heat	2.17	2.41	2.7	3.01	3.61	4.01
Industrial Process Heat	9.36	11.3	13.90	18.49	26.36	41.07
Automobile	9.61	10.48	11.39	12.84	14.78	16.59
Air Transportation	2.96	4.7	6.34	8.63	11.22	13.10
Gasoline for Other Transportation	3.50	4.15	5.09	5.97	6.73	7.78
Distillates for Other Transportation	2.03	2.46	3.01	3.5	4.03	4.73
Gas for Petrochemicals	.9	1.26	1.45	1.7	2.16	2.90
Coal for Petrochemicals	.17	.24	.27	.32	.40	.54
Oil Products for Petrochemicals	4.55	6.4	7.35	9.52	10.92	14.70
Residual Fuel Oil for Ships	.57	.76	.94	1.01	1.34	1.68
TOTAL	49.07	61.23	73.62	90.37	115.2	155.0

[a]Derived from ERDA-48 (1975).

Table D-3

FRACTION OF THE PRE-1975 FACILITIES REMAINING

(Based on 30 Year Life and Historical Growth Rates)

End-Use Demand	Period 1 (1978)	Period 2 (1985)	Period 3 (1992)	Period 4 (2000)	Historical[a] Growth Rate
Misc. Base-Load Electricity	.91	.73	.51	.19	3.0%
Misc. Intermediate-Load Electricity	.91	.73	.51	.19	3.0%
Peak-Load Electricity	.91	.73	.51	.19	3.0%
Iron and Steel	.91	.73	.51	.19	3.0%
Air Conditioning	.97	.88	.72	.37	9.0%
Space Heat	.89	.68	.45	.16	1.5%
Water Heat	.89	.68	.45	.16	1.5%
Industrial Process Heat	.91	.73	.51	.19	3.0%
Automobile	.91	.72	.49	.18	2.5%
Air Transportation	.95	.82	.62	.26	6.5%
Gasoline for Other Transportation	.91	.72	.49	.18	2.5%
Distillates for Other Transportation	.91	.72	.49	.18	2.5%
Gas for Petrochemicals	.91	.73	.51	.19	3.0%
Coal for Petrochemicals	.94	.79	.58	.23	5.0%
Oil Products for Petrochemicals	.94	.79	.58	.23	5.0%
Residual Fuel Oil for Ships	.92	.76	.54	.21	4.0%

[a]Derived from ERDA-48 (1975) and Associated Universities (1972).

This formula was used to calculate the fraction of the former facilities still remaining at the representative year for each period (Table D-3). These fractions were then multiplied by the 1974 end-use demand levels (first column of Table D-4) to determine the end-use demand satisfaction of the remaining facilities (remaining columns of Table D-4).

The demand satisfaction contributions of facilties built before 1975 (Table D-4), as well as the assumed contribution of new hydroelectric and geothermal-electric facilities (Table D-5) must be subtracted from the gross end-use demands (Table D-2) to get the net end-use demand constants (D(n,t); shown in Table D-6) which were provided to the model for the base case scenario.

Improved Efficiencies in End Use Scenarios

The sequence of calculations required to calculate the net end-use demands for the improved efficiencies in end-use scenario is essentially the same as that for the base case scenario except for two small modifications. First, the gross end-use demands for the base case scenario (Table D-2) are reduced to reflect improved end-use efficiencies that can't be reflected in the end-use efficiency coefficient parameters (e.g., improved building design is assumed to reduce space heat requirements). These reduced demands (Table D-7) are then the gross demands for the improved end-use efficiencies scenarios.

Second, improved efficiency contributions from new geothermal-heat, waste heat, and solar heating and cooling facilities (Table D-8) must be netted out. These modifications lead to the net end-use demands shown in Table D-9 for the improved efficiencies in end-use scenarios. This table provides the values for the end-use net demand constants (D(n,t)) which were provided to the model for the improved efficiencies in end-use scenarios.

ENERGY CONVERSION EFFICIENCY DATA

Table D-10 shows the end-use utilizing device efficiencies that were used for both the base case and the improved efficiencies in end-use scenarios.

Table D-11 presents the energy conversion process efficiencies for the individual processes represented in the model. Table D-12 lists the

Table D-4

END-USE DEMAND SATISFACTION CAPACITY OF PRE-1975 FACILITIES
(in Quadrillion Btus)

End-Use Demand	Initial Demand[a] (1974)	Period 1 (1978)	Period 2 (1985)	Period 3 (1982)	Period 4 (2000)
Misc. Base-Load Electricity	3.86	3.51	2.82	1.92	.71
Misc. Intermediate-Load Elec.	.80	.73	.58	.41	.15
Peak-Load Electricity	Endogenous	Endogenous	Endogenous	Endogenous	Endogenous
Iron and Steel	.62	.56	.45	.32	.12
Air Conditioning	1.1	1.07	.97	.79	.41
Space Heat	5.39	4.80	3.67	2.43	.86
Water Heat	2.05	1.83	1.39	.92	.33
Industrial Process Heat	8.31	7.56	6.07	4.24	1.58
Automobile	8.78	7.99	6.32	4.30	1.58
Air Transportation	2.32	2.20	1.90	1.44	.6
Gasoline for Other Transportation	3.17	2.86	2.28	1.55	.57
Distillates for Other Transportation	1.84	1.67	1.33	.90	.33
Gas for Petrochemicals	.75	.68	.55	.38	.14
Coal for Petrochemicals	.14	.13	.11	.08	.03
Oil Products for Petrochemicals	3.76	3.53	2.97	2.18	.86
Residual Fuel Oil for Ships	.56	.52	.43	.30	.12

[a]Derived from ERDA-48 (1975), Associated Universities (1972), Ford Energy Policy Project (1974), and Hittman Associates (1974).

Table D-5

CONTRIBUTION OF NEW HYDROELECTRIC AND GEOTHERMAL-ELECTRIC FACILITIES IN EACH REPRESENTATIVE YEAR[a]
(in Quadrillion Btus/yr)

End-Use Demand	Period 1 (1978)	Period 2 (1985)	Period 3 (1992)	Period 4 (2000)	Period 5 (2012)	Period 6 (2027)
Misc. Base-Load Electricity	.12	.41	.67	1.06	1.28	1.70
Misc. Intermediate-Load Electricity	.03	.09	.14	.23	.28	.35

[a]Derived from ERDA-48 (1975) and Associated Universities (1972).

Table D-6

NET END-USE DEMANDS FOR THE BASE CASE SCENARIO[a]
(in Quadrillion Btus/yr)

End-Use Demand	Period 1 (1978)	Period 2 (1985)	Period 3 (1992)	Period 4 (2000)	Period 5 (2012)	Period 6 (2027)
Misc. Base-Load Elec.	.71	2.61	4.83	8.0	12.88	21.61
Misc. Int.-Load Elec.	.17	.55	.99	1.66	2.67	4.51
Peak-Load Electricity	Endogenous	Endogenous	Endogenous	Endogenous	Endogenous	Endogenous
Iron and Steel	.14	.45	.75	1.05	1.42	1.8
Air Conditioning	.49	1.81	3.29	4.41	5.76	7.2
Space Heat	.92	2.66	4.64	7.02	9.35	10.74
Water Heat	.34	1.02	1.78	2.68	3.61	4.01
Process Heat	1.80	5.23	9.66	14.25	26.36	41.07
Automobile	1.62	4.16	7.09	11.26	14.78	16.59
Air Transportation	.76	2.80	4.90	8.03	11.22	13.10
Gasoline for Other Transportation	.64	1.87	3.54	5.40	6.73	7.78
Distillates for Other Transportation	.36	1.13	2.11	3.17	4.03	4.73
Gas for Petrochemicals	.22	.71	1.07	1.56	2.16	2.90
Coal for Petrochemicals	.04	.13	.19	.29	.4	.54
Oil Products for Petrochemicals	1.02	3.43	5.17	8.66	10.92	14.70
Residual Fuel Oil for Ships	.05	.33	.64	.89	1.34	1.68

[a]Gross end-use demands (Table D-2) net of demands that are satisfied by:

(1) remaining pre-1975 facilities (Table D-4)

(2) new (i.e., post-1974 hydroelectric and geothermal-electric facilities (Table D-5).

Table D-7

GROSS END-USE DEMANDS FOR THE IMPROVED EFFICIENCIES IN END-USE SCENARIOS[a]
(in Quadrillion Btus/yr)

End-Use Demand	Period 1 (1978)	Period 2 (1985)	Period 3 (1992)	Period 4 (2000)	Period 5 (2012)	Period 6 (2027)
Misc. Base-Load Elec.	4.31	5.30	6.44	8.11	11.49	18.50
Misc. Int.-Load Elec.	.9	1.11	1.34	1.69	2.39	3.86
Peak-Load Electricity	Endogenous	Endogenous	Endogenous	Endogenous	Endogenous	Endogenous
Iron and Steel	.7	.9	.96	.94	1.07	1.26
Air Conditioning	1.53	2.64	3.77	4.34	5.07	6.26
Space Heat	5.41	5.38	6.01	6.46	7.66	8.70
Water Heat	2.17	2.41	2.70	3.01	3.61	4.01
Industrial Process Heat	9.36	11.30	13.9	18.49	26.36	41.07
Automobile	9.11	9.81	9.29	9.17	10.16	11.61
Air Transportation	2.94	4.00	5.39	7.34	9.54	11.14
Gasoline for Other Transportation	3.37	3.75	4.38	4.78	5.25	5.84
Distillates for Other Transportation	1.66	2.26	2.66	2.91	3.30	3.77
Gas for Petrochemicals	.88	1.20	1.24	1.28	1.57	2.03
Coal for Petrochemicals	.17	.23	.23	.24	.29	.38
Oil Products for Petrochemicals	4.46	6.08	6.28	6.48	7.95	10.28
Residual Fuel Oil for Ships	.57	.76	.94	1.01	1.34	1.68
TOTAL	47.54	57.13	65.53	76.25	97.05	130.4

[a]Derived from ERDA-48 (1975).

Table D-8

CONTRIBUTION OF NEW GEOTHERMAL-HEAT, WASTE HEAT, AND SOLAR HEATING AND COOLING CAPACITY FOR THE IMPROVED EFFICIENCIES IN END-USE SCENARIOS[a]
(in Quadrillion Btus/yr)

End-Use Demand	Period 1 (1978)	Period 2 (1985)	Period 3 (1992)	Period 4 (2000)	Period 5 (2012)	Period 6 (2027)
Air Conditioning	0	0	.2	.5	1.0	1.5
Space Heat	0	.35	.5	1.0	1.5	2.0
Water Heat	0	.20	.4	1.0	1.25	1.5
Industrial Process Heat	0	.3	1.5	5.0	8.0	10.00

[a] Derived from ERDA-48 (1975).

Table D-9

NET END-USE DEMANDS FOR THE IMPROVED EFFICIENCIES IN END-USE SCENARIOS[a]

(in Quadrillion Btus/yr)

End-Use Demand	Period 1 (1978)	Period 2 (1985)	Period 3 (1992)	Period 4 (2000)	Period 5 (2012)	Period 6 (2027)
Misc. Base-Load Elec.	.68	2.07	3.85	5.13	10.21	16.80
Misc. Int.-Load Elec.	.14	.44	.79	1.31	2.11	3.51
Peak-Load Electricity	Endogenous	Endogenous	Endogenous	Endogenous	Endogenous	Endogenous
Iron and Steel	.14	.45	.64	.82	1.07	1.26
Air Conditioning	.46	1.67	2.78	3.43	4.07	4.76
Space Heat	.61	1.36	3.08	4.60	6.16	6.70
Water Heat	.34	.82	1.38	1.68	2.36	2.51
Industrial Process Heat	1.80	4.93	8.16	11.91	18.36	31.07
Automobile	1.12	3.49	4.99	7.59	10.16	11.61
Air Transportation	.74	2.10	3.95	6.74	9.54	11.14
Gasoline for Other Transportation	.51	1.47	2.83	4.21	5.25	5.84
Distillates for Other Transportation	.00	.93	1.76	2.58	3.30	3.77
Gas for Petrochemicals	.20	.65	.86	1.14	1.57	2.03
Coal for Petrochemicals	.04	.12	.15	.21	.29	.38
Oil Products for Petrochemicals	.93	3.11	4.10	5.62	7.95	10.28
Residual Fuel Oil for Ships	.05	.33	.64	.89	1.34	1.68

[a]Gross end-use demands (Table D-2) net of demands that are satisfied by:

(1) remaining pre-1975 facilities (Table D-4)

(2) new (i.e., post-1975) hydroelectric and geothermal-electric facilities (Table D-5)

(3) new geothermal-heat, waste heat, and solar heating and cooling facilities (Table D-8)

(4) improvements in end-use device efficiencies not otherwise explicitly represented in the model (i.e., the difference between Tables D-7 and D-2). For example, improved home insulation decreases the demand for space heat.

Table D-10

END-USE UTILIZING DEVICE EFFICIENCIES[a]

Utilizing Device Process	Efficiency for Base Case Scenario (Efficiency for Improved Efficiencies in End-Use Scenario)						
	Period (representative year)						
	0(1974)[b]	1(1978)	2(1985)	3(1992)	4(2000)	5(2012)	6(2027)
Coal to Iron and Steel	.24 (.24)	.24 (.26)	.24 (.26)	.24 (.29)	.24 (.29)	.24 (.30)	.24 (.30)
Air Conditioning	3.00 (3.00)	3.00 (3.30)	3.00 (3.30)	3.00 (3.60)	3.00 (3.60)	3.00 (3.90)	3.00 (3.90)
Oil to Space Heat	.45 (.45)	.45 (.47)	.45 (.47)	.46 (.48)	.46 (.48)	.46 (.49)	.46 (.49)
Gas to Space Heat	.49 (.49)	.49 (.51)	.49 (.51)	.51 (.54)	.51 (.54)	.51 (.56)	.51 (.56)
Electricity to Space Heat	1.00 (1.00)	1.00 (1.00)	1.00 (1.00)	1.00 (1.00)	1.00 (2.00)	1.00 (2.00)	1.00 (2.00)
Oil to Water Heat	.63 (.63)	.63 (.63)	.63 (.63)	.63 (.63)	.63 (.63)	.63 (.63)	.63 (.63)
Gas to Water Heat	.55 (.55)	.55 (.61)	.55 (.61)	.55 (.66)	.55 (.66)	.55 (.70)	.55 (.70)
Coal to Industrial Process Heat	.70 (.70)	.70 (.77)	.70 (.77)	.70 (.77)	.70 (.77)	.70 (.77)	.70 (.77)
Oil to Industrial Process Heat	.68 (.68)	.68 (.75)	.68 (.75)	.68 (.75)	.68 (.75)	.68 (.75)	.68 (.75)
Gas to Industrial Process Heat	.64 (.64)	.64 (.70)	.64 (.70)	.64 (.70)	.64 (.70)	.64 (.70)	.64 (.70)

[a] Derived from ERDA-48 (1975).

[b] Initial period - 1974.

Table D-11
SUPPLY PROCESS EFFICIENCIES[a]

Supply Process	Efficiency						
	Period (representative year)						
	0(1974)	1(1978)	2(1985)	3(1992)	4(2000)	5(2012)	6(2027)
Conversion to Synfuels							
Coal liquefaction	-	-	-	.66	.66	.66	.66
Coal to low-Btu gas	-	-	-	.75	.75	.75	.75
Coal to high-Btu gas	-	-	-	.66	.66	.66	.66
Shale upgrading	-	-	-	1.00	1.00	1.00	1.00
Conversion to Electricity							
Coal-fired steam electric	.34	.38	.38	.38	.38	.38	.38
Oil-fired steam electric	.32	.38	.38	.38	.38	.38	.38
Gas-fired steam electric	.32	.38	.38	.38	.38	.38	.38
Combined cycle	.36	.40	.40	.40	.40	.40	.40
Gas turbine	.22	.25	.25	.25	.25	.25	.25
LWR[b]	.31	.33	.33	.33	.33	.33	.33
HTGR[b]	.39	.40	.40	.40	.40	.40	.40
LMFBR[b]	-	-	-	.39	.39	.39	.39
Hydroelectric	.32	.32	.34	.34	.37	.37	.37
Pumped storage	.75	.75	.75	.75	.75	.75	.75
Refining							
Coal liquids refinery	-	-	-	.97	.97	.97	.97
Low-gasoline refinery	.91	.86	.86	.86	.86	.86	.86
High-gasoline refinery	.91	.97	.97	.97	.97	.97	.97
Transmission and Transport							
Oil	1.0	1.0	1.0	1.0	1.0	1.0	1.0
Natural gas	.91	.91	.91	.91	.91	.91	.91
Coal	.97	.97	.97	.97	.97	.97	.97
Electricity	.90	.91	.91	.91	.91	.91	.91

[a]Derived from ERDA-48 (1975), Bechtel Corporation (1975), and Cherniavsky (1974).

[b]The thermal efficiency of a nuclear reactor is defined as the electrical energy output at the busbar divided by the thermal output of the nuclear process.

refinery product splits and efficiencies for the three types of refineries used in the model. Finally, Table D-13 combines the individual process efficiencies into composite efficiencies for the energy supply enterprises. The data in Table D-13 provide the values for the supply enterprise efficiency coefficient parameters (s(m,u), sLCLR(u), sHCLR(u), sLCGS(u), sHCGS(u)) which were provided to the model for the various scenarios. The major components of these supply enterprise efficiencies are the input-and-process-path efficiencies (see Tables B-3 and B-6 for a description of the supply enterprise input-and-process paths). The supply enterprise output-path (see Table B-4) efficiencies are typically final distribution efficiencies, except as otherwise noted in the subsequent section on "Electrical Generation Load-Sharing Data."

The reader will note that the composite efficiencies for the energy supply enterprises that include nuclear reactors in Table D-13 are incomplete since they omit consideration of the "efficiencies" of pre-reactor nuclear fuel-upgrading processes. Since the equivalent energy content of uranium is highly sensitive to the type of nuclear process being considered, the model accounts for uranium resources in terms of 10,000 of short tons of U_3O_8 supplied by the mill (Table D-14). This is in contrast to the other basic energy resources that are accounted for in terms of their thermal energy content (specifically in terms of quadrillion Btus) in order to simplify the model's bookkeeping procedures. This turns out to be a practical procedure because the thermal energy content for the fossil fuel resources (i.e., coal, gas, crude oil, and shale oil) is determined by measuring the heat generated when the resource of interest is burned in a standard apparatus called a calorimeter. Unfortunately, a nuclear reactor must be used to determine the "heat content" of uranium. The value that is obtained is highly sensitive to the reactor process, unlike the fossil fuel cases where the standard calorimeter is appropriate.

To get the milled U_3O_8 requirement for a nuclear reactor per Quad of delivered electricity, the U_3O_8 requirement per Quad of reactor thermal output (Table D-14) must be multiplied by the inverse supply efficiency for the electricty conversion and transmission process shown (Table D-13). Therefore, 3.33x.241 = .803 ten-thousands of short tons

Table D-12

REFINERY PRODUCT SPLITS AND EFFICIENCIES[a]

Refined Products	Product Split (the fraction of the energy in one barrel of crude/syncrude that can be converted to the indicated product)	Efficiency	Combined Split and Efficiency
Coal Liquids Refinery			
Gasoline	.63	.97	.61[b]
Jet fuel and other products	.37	.97	.36
Low Gasoline Refinery			
Gasoline	.25	.86	.21
Distillates	.30	.86	.26
Residual	.45	.86	.39
High Gasoline Refinery			
Gasoline	.63	.97	.61
Jet fuel and other products	.37	.97	.36

[a]Derived from ERDA-48 (1975) and Bechtel Corporation (1975).

[b]E.g., one Btu of syncrude input yields .61 Btu of gasoline.

Table D-13

EFFICIENCIES FOR THE SUPPLY ENTERPRISES[a]

Class of Supply Enterprises	Efficiencies for 1975-2034 (Efficiencies for 1974)						Inverse Efficiency (for 1974)
	Fuel Transport	Synfuels Processing	Refining	Electric Conversion	Electric Transmission	Total	
Coal							
Low-Btu coal transport	.97 (.97)	-	-	-	-	.97 (.97)	1.03 (1.03)
Low-Btu coal/steam electric	.97 (.97)	-	-	.38 (.34)	.91 (.91)	.34 (.30)	2.98 (3.37)
Low-Btu coal/low-Btu gas/combined cycle	.97	.75	-	.40	.91	.27	3.78
Low-Btu coal/high-Btu gas	.97	.66	-	-	-	.64	1.56
Low-Btu coal/liquefaction/residual	.97	.66	-	-	-	.64	1.56
Coal liquids refinery products	-	-	.97	-	-	.97	1.03
Low-Btu coal/liquefaction/residual/steam electric	.97	.66	-	.38	.91	.22	4.52
High-Btu coal transport	.97 (.97)	-	-	-	-	.97 (.97)	1.03 (1.03)
High-Btu coal/steam electric	.97 (.97)	-	-	.38 (.34)	.91 (.90)	.34 (.30)	2.99 (3.37)
High-Btu coal/low-Btu gas/combined cycle	.97	.75	-	.40	.91	.27	3.78
High-Btu coal/high-Btu gas	.97	.66	-	-	-	.64	1.56
High-Btu coal/liquefaction/residual	.97	.66	-	-	-	.64	1.56
High-Btu coal/liquefaction/residual/steam electric	.97	.66	-	.38	.91	.22	4.52
Natural Gas							
Natural gas transport	.91 (.91)	-	-	-	-	.91 (.91)	1.10 (1.10)
Natural gas/combined cycle	.91 (.91)	-	-	.40 (.36)	.91 (.90)	.33 (.29)	3.03 (3.39)
Natural gas/gas turbine	.91 (.91)	-	-	.25 (.22)	.91 (.90)	.21 (.18)	4.83 (5.55)
Natural gas/steam electric	.91 (.91)	-	-	.38 (.32)	.91 (.90)	.32 (.26)	3.17 (3.82)
Oil							
Low gasoline refinery products	-	-	.86 (.91)	-	-	.86 (.91)	1.16 (1.10)
Distillate/combined cycle	-	-	-	.40 (.36)	.91 (.90)	.36 (.32)	2.75 (3.09)
Distillate/gas turbine	-	-	-	.25 (.22)	.91 (.90)	.23 (.20)	4.40 (5.05)
Residual/steam electric	-	-	-	.38 (.32)	.91 (.90)	.35 (.29)	2.89 (3.47)
High gasoline refinery products	-	-	.97 (.91)	-	-	.97 (.91)	1.03 (1.10)
Shale upgrading	-	-	1.00	-	-	1.00	1.00
Uranium							
LWR	-	-	-	.33 (.31)	.91 (.90)	.30 (.28)	3.33 (3.58)
HTGR	-	-	-	.40 (.39)	.91 (.90)	.36 (.35)	2.75 (2.85)
LMFBR	-	-	-	.39 (.39)	.91 (.90)	.36 (.35)	2.82 (2.85)

[a] Does not include the efficiencies for refineries and load share facilities.

Table D- 14

MILLED URANIUM REQUIREMENTS FOR THE NUCLEAR REACTOR PROCESSES

Nuclear Reactor Process	Milled Uranium Required per Quad of Thermal Output (10,000 short tons of U_3O_8/quadrillion Btu)
Light-water	.241
High-temperature gas-cooled	.163
Liquid-metal fast breeder	.0022

of milled U_3O_8 are required per Quad of delivered LWR-generated electricity, 2.75x.163 = .448 ten-thousands of short tons of milled U_3O_8 are required per Quad of delivered HTGR generated electricity, and 2.82x.0022 = .0062 ten-thousands of short tons of milled U_3O_8 are required per Quad of delivered LMFBR-generated electricity.

RESOURCES REQUIRED TO OPERATE PRE-1975 FACILITIES

Since it is assumed here that some of the end-use demands are satisfied by energy conversion facilities that were built prior to 1975, it is necessary to deplete the resources required to run these facilities until they are retired from the energy system. This is accomplished by tracing the 1974 end-use demands back through the energy system to the basic energy resources.

Table D-15 provides a breakdown of the fuels that were used to supply the 1974 end-use demands. It is assumed that this pattern continues to be applicable for the pre-1975 energy supply enterprises until their facilities are retired. Since electricity is not a basic energy resource, it is also assumed that the 1974 split (Table D-16) between basic energy resources that are used to generate electricity continues to be applicable until the pre-1975 electric generation facilities are retired. The data in Tables 15 and 16, in conjunction with these assumptions, then serve as the basis for the determination of how much of each end-use demand was satisfied in 1974 by pre-1975 facilities using the specified basic energy resources (Table D-17).

The depletion of basic energy resources in 1974 can then be determined by multiplying the results in Table D-17 with the inverse of the supply enterprise's efficiency for 1974 given in Table D-13.* A similar calculation is performed to calculate the resources required to run the pre-1975 facilities after 1975. However, the calculations must start by multiplying the fuel splits (categorized by end-use demand) in Table D-15 by the fraction of pre-1975 facilities (also categorized by end-use demand) that are still remaining (Table D-3) in order to determine annual basic resource requirements (for pre-1975 facilities) for each period (Table D-18). These requirements can be multiplied

*Recall, however, that uranium requirements are measured in ten-thousands of short tons (see the preceeding section for a description of how uranium resources are accounted for in the model).

Table D-15

END-USE DEMAND SATISFACTION IN 1974 BY FUEL FORM[a]
(in Quadrillion Btus/yr)

Fuel Form	End-Use Demand Category[b]														
	1	2	5	6	7	8	9	10	11	12	13	14	15	16	17
Electricity	3.86	.80	.14	1.1	.33	.61	0	0	0	0	0	0	0	0	0
Coal	0	0	.48	0	0	0	1.21	0	0	0	0	.14	0	0	0
Oil	0	0	0	0	1.87	0	1.83	8.78	2.32	3.17	1.84	0	0	3.76	.56
Natural gas	0	0	0	0	3.19	1.44	5.28	0	0	0	0	0	.75	0	0
Total Demand Satisfied in 1974	3.86	.80	.62	1.10	5.39	2.05	8.31	8.78	2.32	3.17	1.84	.14	.75	3.76	.56

[a]Derived from ERDA-48 (1975).

[b]End-use demand categories:

1. Miscellaneous base-load electricity
2. Miscellaneous intermediate-load electricity
5. Iron and steel
6. Air conditioning
7. Space heat
8. Water heat
9. Industrial process heat
10. Automobile
11. Air transport
12. Gasoline for other transportation
13. Distillates for other transportation
14. Gas for petrochemicals
15. Coal for petrochemicals
16. Oil products for petrochemicals
17. Residual fuel oil for ships

Table D-16

ELECTRICITY GENERATION IN 1974 BY BASIC ENERGY RESOURCE TYPE[a]

Basic Energy Resource	Type of Generating Equipment	Fraction of Total Electricity Generated in 1974
Uranium	Light-water reactor	.0560
	High-temperature gas-cooled reactor	.0015
Coal	Steam electric	.4446
Gas	Steam electric	.1700
	Gas turbine and combined cycle	.01015
Oil	Steam electric	.1576
	Gas turbine and combined cycle	.01015
Hydroelectric	Hydroelectric facility	.1498

[a]Derived from ERDA-48 (1975), Ford Energy Policy Project (1974), and Federal Energy Administration (1974b, 1974c).

Table D-17

END-USE DEMAND SATISFACTION IN 1974 BY BASIC RESOURCE AND ENERGY SUPPLY PROCESS
(in Quadrillion Btu/yr)

Basic Energy Resource	Energy Supply Process	End-Use Demand Category[a]														
		1	2	5	6	7	8	9	10	11	12	13	14	15	16	17
Oil	Gas turbine and combined cycle	.039	.008	.0014	.011	.003	.006	0	0	0	0	0	0	0	0	0
	Steam electric	.608	.126	.022	.173	.052	.096	0	0	0	0	0	0	0	0	0
	Refinery	0	0	0	0	1.87	0	1.83	8.78	2.32	3.17	1.84	0	0	3.76	.56
Gas	Transport	0	0	0	0	3.19	1.44	5.28	0	0	0	0	0	.75	0	0
	Gas turbine and combined cycle	.039	.008	.0014	.011	.003	.006	0	0	0	0	0	0	0	0	0
	Steam electric	.656	.136	.0238	.187	.056	.104	0	0	0	0	0	0	0	0	0
Coal	Transport	0	0	.48	0	0	0	1.21	0	0	0	0	.14	0	0	0
	Steam electric	1.716	.356	.062	.489	.147	.271	0	0	0	0	0	0	0	0	0
Uranium	Light-water reactor	.216	.045	.0078	.062	.018	.034	0	0	0	0	0	0	0	0	0
	High-temperature gas-cooled reactor	.006	.001	.0002	.002	.0005	.0009	0	0	0	0	0	0	0	0	0
Hydroelectric	Hydroelectric	.578	.120	.021	.165	.049	.091	0	0	0	0	0	0	0	0	0
Total Demand Satisfied in 1974		3.86	.8	.62	1.1	5.39	2.05	8.31	8.78	2.32	3.17	1.84	.14	.75	3.76	.56

[a] See footnote b for Table D-15 for a numbered list of the end-use demand categories.

Table D-18

BASIC ENERGY RESOURCES REQUIRED TO OPERATE PRE-1975 FACILITIES UNTIL RETIREMENT[a]

	Average Annual Requirement (Quads[b]/yr) by Period (Representative Year)				Total Requirement (Quads) by Period (Representative Year)			
Basic Energy Resource	1 (1978)	2 (1985)	3 (1992)	4 (2000)	1 (1978)	2 (1985)	3 (1992)	4 (2000)
Uranium	.30	.24	.24	.07	2.10	1.70	1.68	.63
Low-Btu coal	6.84	5.65	5.18	2.06	47.88	39.55	36.26	18.54
High-Btu coal	6.84	5.65	5.18	2.06	47.88	39.55	36.26	18.54
Oil	30.96	24.88	14.46	6.64	216.70	174.20	101.22	59.76
Gas	22.07	17.43	11.94	4.39	154.50	122.00	83.6	39.51

[a]Based on the pre-1975 facilities remaining and the historical contribution of these basic resources to the satisfaction of the end-use demands satisfied by these facilities.

[b]1 Quad = 1 quadrillion Btu.

by the lengths of the periods to get the total resources required to operate the pre-1975 facilities (Table D-18) in each period. The data in Table D-18 provides the resources that are needed annually (rS(i,t)) in each period to meet the requirements of the pre-1975 facilities that are still remaining.

ENERGY SUPPLY PROCESS COST DATA

This section presents the cost data for the energy supply facilities represented in the model. Basic data are first presented for the individual energy supply facilities represented in the model. Next, the manner in which these costs are combined to determine energy supply enterprise costs is discussed. Finally, the derivation of the energy supply enterprise cost coefficient parameters that are provided to the model for the various scenarios is discussed.

Individual Facility Costs

This section presents the cost data for the energy supply facilities represented in the model. The capital cost data used in the study were derived primarily from a recent study by the Bechtel Corporation (1975), while the operating costs were derived primarily from recent Brookhaven (Cherniavsky, 1974) and Jet Propulsion Laboratory (Smith, Weyant, and Holdren, 1975) studies. The capital costs for all the individual energy supply facilities represented in the model are shown in the first column of Table D-19. These capital costs are for "representative" facilities sized as indicated in the second column of the table. In the third column, these costs are scaled to the costs for facilities to provide one Quad of energy output (energy input in the case of refineries). Finally, the operating costs for one Quad of output from the facilities are shown in the last column of the table. Note, however, that the capital costs for electrical generation facilities are calculated at the assumed design plant factor of .65. For supply enterprises that involve operating plant factors other than the assumed design plant factor, these costs must be appropriately scaled. For example, if a low-Btu coal/steam-electric power plant is used at the design plant factor, the $27.4 billion per generated Quad/yr capital cost is appropriate. However, if the supply enterprise involves utilizing the plant to provide miscellaneous intermediate-load

Table D-19

SUPPLY PROCESS COST DATA[a]

Supply Process	Capital Cost[b] (millions of 1974 dollars/plant)	Plant Size (MWe or output/year)	Capital Cost per Quad of Capacity[c] (billions of 1974 dollars/Quad/yr)	Operating Cost[d] per Quad of Output[c] (millions of 1974 dollars/Quad)
Electric Conversion[e] (excluding nuclear)				
High-Btu coal steam electric	375.0[f]	800 MWe	24.20	382.5
Low-Btu coal steam electric	425.0[f]	800 MWe	27.40	382.5
Combined cycle	82.5	400 MWe	10.60	382.5
Gas turbine	18.7	133 MWe	7.23	896.0
Gas steam electric	137.5	800 MWe	8.84	382.5
Oil steam electric	225.0	800 MWe	14.40	382.5
Pumped storage	321.2	1000 MWe	107.40	965.0
Nuclear Reactors				
LMFBR[e]	770.0[g]	1000 MWe	39.60	396.0
Reprocessing	311.0	950 MTH[h]	.28	9.0
Fabrication	105.0	315 MTH	.30	101.0
Total LMFBR	-	-	40.18	506.0
LWR[e]	644.0	1100 MWe	30.10	323.0
Conversion	64.5	14,690 MTUF6	.04	11.0
Enrichment	3459.0	8,750 KgSWU	1.79	221.0
Fabrication	62.4	600 MTU	.12	34.4
Reprocessing	325.0	1500 MTU	.24	6.6
Total LWR	-	-	32.29	596.0
HTGR[e]	945.0	1500 MWe	32.30	323.0
Conversion	64.5	14,690 MTUF6	.02	8.5
Enrichment	3459.0	8750 KgSWU	1.38	170.0
Fabrication	208.0	450 MTH	.17	35.4
Reprocessing	143.0	300 MTH	.15	36.1
Total HTGR	-	-	34.02	573.0
Refining				
Low-gasoline	537.5	72×10^6 bbl	1.34	201.0
High-gasoline	600.0	72×10^6 bbl	1.50	128.0
Coal-liquids	387.5	36×10^6 bbl	1.94	150.0
Synfuels Processing				
Coal gasification to high-Btu gas	937.5	82.13×10^9 scf	11.20	239.0
Coal gasification to low-Btu gas	843.8	9.26×10^{13} Btu	9.11	284.0
Coal liquefaction	412.5	7.88×10^6 bbl	9.42	541.0
Shale-oil upgrading	204.0	32×10^6 bbl	1.15	173.0
Coal Transport				
Unit train to petrochemicals, electric conversion, iron and steel, gasification and liquefaction	-	-	-	88.9
Conventional train to process heat	-	-	-	295.0
Crude Transport (to refineries)	-	-	-	311.0
Electric Transmission and Distribution[e]	265.0	1000 MWe	15.00	660.0
Natural Gas Distribution				
To space heat	-	-	-	1040.0
To water heat	-	-	-	1040.0
To process heat	-	-	-	267.0
To petrochemicals	-	-	-	267.0
To electric conversion	-	-	-	127.0
Oil Product Distribution				
Distillates to space heat	-	-	-	686.0
Distillates to water heat	-	-	-	686.0
Distillates to process heat	-	-	-	191.0
Residual to process heat	-	-	-	330.0
Gasoline to automobile	-	-	-	1120.0
Gasoline to other transportation	-	-	-	1030.0
Distillates to other transportation	-	-	-	1030.0
Oil products to petrochemicals	-	-	-	191.0
Residual to ships	-	-	-	191.0
Oil products to electric conversion	-	-	-	191.0
Jet fuel to air transportation	-	-	-	191.0
Coal-Liquids Product Distribution				
Gasoline to automobile	-	-	-	1120.0
Gasoline to other transportation	-	-	-	1030.0
Jet fuel to air transportation	-	-	-	191.0
Residual to ships	-	-	-	191.0
Residual to process heat	-	-	-	191.0
Residual to petrochemicals	-	-	-	191.0
Gasoline and jet fuel to petrochemicals	-	-	-	191.0

[a] Derived from Bechtel Corporation (1975), Cherniavsky (1974), Smith, Weyant, and Holdren (1974) and Synfuels Interagency Task Force (1975).

[b] A blank in this column does not imply that the corresponding facility has no capital cost, but rather that the capital cost was amortized and included in the corresponding "operating cost" total.

[c] I.e., per Quad of average annual energy flow out of the facility (except for refineries, where the cost is per Quad of average energy flow into the facility and nuclear fuel processing facilities, where the costs are for enough processing to produce the fuel required to generate one Quad of electricity).

[d] Operation and maintenance costs which exclude the cost of the primary energy input to the facility.

[e] A .65 plant factor is assumed, except for pumped storage which is assumed to have a .10 plant factor.

[f] Includes $100/KWe for a scrubber.

[g] 770 for period 3
744 for period 4
694 for period 5
644 for period 6

Cost reductions based on learning at a rate approximately equal to that suggested in Cochran, et al., 1975; and Alexander and Rice, 1975.

[h] Metric tons of heavy metal (i.e., uranium and plutonium).

electricity (i.e., at an operating plant factor of .50), then the appropriate capital cost for the power-plant facilities would be (27.4)(.65/.50) = $35.6 billion per generated Quad/yr.

Supply Enterprise Costs

Recall from the discussion in Appendix B that an energy supply enterprise represents a sequence of energy conversion facilities. Table D-20 gives the capital and operating costs for the individual facilities for the input-and-process paths for the supply enterprises, while Table D-21 gives the output path costs. In order to derive the total costs of the supply enterprise, the individual facility capital and operating costs must be combined in a manner that reflects the costs for facilities sized in accordance with the supply enterprise efficiencies shown in Table D-13, and the capital cost of electric conversion facilities operated at a non-design plant factor included in the supply enterprise must be adjusted to reflect this lower plant factor.

For example, consider the low-Btu coal/steam-electric/miscellaneous intermediate-load electricity enterprise depicted in Fig. B-5. To calculate the capital and operating costs for one Quad of electricity delivered by this supply enterprise, the $88.9 million/Quad coal transport cost (Table D-20) must be multiplied by 2.89 (Table D-13), which is the composite inverse efficiency for coal-steam electric generation, and electric transmission and distribution. This yields a coal transport cost of $.257 billion/Quad. Next, the power-plant capital and operating costs must be multiplied by 1.10 to account for the assumed .91 efficiency of electric transmission. Additionally, the capital cost for the power plant must be adjusted to reflect the .50 plant factor at which it must operate to satisfy the miscellaneous intermediate-load electricity demand (Table B-5). Thus, the capital cost for this facility is (27.4)(1.10)(.65/.50) = $39.2 billion/(Quad/yr) and the power-plant operating cost is (.381)(1.10) = $.418 billion/Quad. Finally, miscellaneous intermediate-load electricity requires a capital cost of $19.5 billion/(Quad/yr) and an operating cost of $.66 billion/Quad for transmission and distribution (Table D-21). Since these facility costs have now been adjusted to reflect an appropriately sized sequence of facilities, they may be added

Table D-20

SUPPLY ENTERPRISE INPUT-AND-PROCESS-PATH FACILITY COSTS

Supply Enterprise Input-and-Process Path	Facility Costs (billions of 1974 dollars/Quad of energy delivery capacity): Coal transport to electric conversion		Liquefaction, gasification and shale upgrading		Natural gas transport to electric conversion		Crude transport		Refining		Oil product transport to electric conversion		Electric conversion		Nuclear	
	Capital	Annual Operating	Capital	Annual Operating	Capital	Annual Operating	Capital	Annual Operating	Capital	Annual Operating	Capital	Annual Operating	Capital	Annual Operating	Capital	Annual Operating
Coal																
Low-Btu coal/steam electric	-	.089	-	-	-	-	-	-	-	-	-	-	27.4	.38	-	-
Low-Btu coal/low-Btu gas/combined cycle	-	.089	9.11	.28	-	-	-	-	-	-	-	-	10.6	.38	-	-
Low-Btu coal/high-Btu gas	-	.089	11.20	.24	-	-	-	-	-	-	-	-	-	-	-	-
Low-Btu coal/liquefaction/residual	-	.089	9.42	.54	-	-	-	-	-	-	-	-	-	-	-	-
Coal liquids refinery	-	.089	9.42	.54	-	-	-	-	1.94	.15	-	-	-	-	-	-
Low-Btu coal/liquefaction/residual/steam electric	-	.089	9.42	.54	-	-	-	-	-	-	-	.19	14.4	.38	-	-
High Btu-coal/steam electric	-	.089	-	-	-	-	-	-	-	-	-	-	24.2	.59	-	-
High-Btu coal/low-Btu gas/combined cycle	-	.089	9.11	.28	-	-	-	-	-	-	-	-	10.6	.38	-	-
High-Btu coal/high-Btu gas	-	.089	11.20	.24	-	-	-	-	-	-	-	-	-	-	-	-
High-Btu coal/liquefaction/residual	-	.089	9.42	.54	-	-	-	-	-	-	-	-	-	-	-	-
High-Btu coal/liquefaction/residual/steam electric	-	.089	9.42	.54	-	-	-	-	-	-	-	.19	14.4	.38	-	-
Gas																
Natural gas/combined cycle	-	-	-	-	-	.13	-	-	-	-	-	-	10.6	.38	-	-
Natural gas/gas turbine	-	-	-	-	-	.13	-	-	-	-	-	-	9.2	.90	-	-
Natural gas/steam electric	-	-	-	-	-	.13	-	-	-	-	-	-	8.9	.38	-	-
Oil																
Low gasoline refinery	-	-	-	-	-	-	-	.31	1.34	.20	-	-	-	-	-	-
Distillate/combined cycle	-	-	-	-	-	-	-	-	-	-	-	.19	10.6	.38	-	-
Distillate/gas turbine	-	-	-	-	-	-	-	-	-	-	-	.19	7.2	.90	-	-
Residual/steam electric	-	-	-	-	-	-	-	-	-	-	-	.19	14.4	.38	-	-
Shale upgrading to crude	-	-	1.15	.17	-	-	-	-	-	-	-	-	-	-	-	-
High gasoline refinery	-	-	-	-	-	-	-	.31	1.50	.13	-	-	-	-	-	-
Uranium																
LWR	-	-	-	-	-	-	-	-	-	-	-	-	-	-	32.2	.60
HTGR	-	-	-	-	-	-	-	-	-	-	-	-	-	-	34.0	.57
LMFBR[a]	-	-	-	-	-	-	-	-	-	-	-	-	-	-	40.2	.51

[a]Basic cost data changes over time periods due to learning (see Table D-19).

Table D-21

SUPPLY ENTERPRISE OUTPUT-PATH FACILITY COSTS

Supply Enterprise Output Path	Facility Costs (billions of 1974 dollars/Quad of energy delivery capacity)												Plant Factor
	Coal Transport		Electric transmission and distribution		Pumped storage		Natural gas distribution		Coal liquid product distribution		Oil product distribution		
	Capital	Annual Operating	Capital	Annual Operating	Capital	Annual Operating	Capital	Annual Operating	Capital	Annual Operating	Capital	Annual Operating	
Misc. Base-load elec.	-	-	15.0	.66	-	-	-	-	-	-	-	-	.65
Misc. Intermediate-load electricity	-	-	19.5	.66	-	-	-	-	-	-	-	-	.50
Misc. Intermediate-load electricity and pumped storage	-	-	15.0	.66	107.4[a]	.965	-	-	-	-	-	-	.65
Misc. Intermediate-load electricity and water heat	-	-	15.0	.66	-	-	-	-	-	-	-	-	.65
Peak-load electricity	-	-	97.5	.66	-	-	-	-	-	-	-	-	.10
Peak-load electricity and pumped storage	-	-	15.0	.66	107.4[a]	.965	-	-	-	-	-	-	.65
Peak-load electricity and water heat	-	-	15.0	.66	-	-	-	-	-	-	-	-	.65
Iron and steel	-	.089	15.0	.66	-	-	-	-	-	-	-	-	.65
Air conditioning	-	-	29.6	.66	-	-	-	-	-	-	-	-	.33
Space heat	-	-	23.2	.66	-	-	-	1.04	-	.69	-	-	.42
Space heat and air conditioning	-	-	15.0	.66	-	-	-	-	-	-	-	-	.65
Water heat	-	-	15.0	.66	-	-	-	1.04	-	.69	-	-	.65
Process heat	-	.295	15.0	.66	-	-	-	.27	-	.19[b]	-	.19	.65
Automobile	-	-	-	-	-	-	-	-	-	1.12	-	1.12	-
Air transport	-	-	-	-	-	-	-	-	-	.19	-	.19	-
Gasoline for other transportation	-	-	-	-	-	-	-	-	-	1.03	-	1.03	-
Distillates for other transportation	-	-	-	-	-	-	-	-	-	-	-	1.03	-
Gas for petrochemicals	-	-	-	-	-	-	-	.27	-	-	-	-	-
Coal for petrochemicals	-	.089	-	-	-	-	-	-	-	-	-	-	-
Oil for petrochemicals	-	-	-	-	-	-	-	-	-	.19	-	.19	-
Residual fuel oil for ships	-	-	-	-	-	-	-	-	-	.19	-	.19	-

[a]Assumed plant factor for pumped storage is .10

[b]This is the operating cost for distillate to process heat; for residual to process heat, the cost is .33 to reflect the added costs of a scrubber.

to arrive at a total capital cost (say, CC(m=4, k=2, u)) of $58.7 billion/(Quad/yr) and a total supply enterprise operating cost (say, OC(m=4, k=2, u)) of $1.34 billion/Quad.

Cost Coefficient Parameters

To derive the supply enterprise cost coefficient parameters actually used in the model, the capital and operating costs for the supply enterprises must be combined to reflect the operating life of the facilities and discounting. The facilities of a particular vintage for a supply enterprise are assumed to be built up at a constant rate between representative years. Let dl(u) be the number of years between representative years u - 1 and u.* Whenever facilities are built, both the capital cost and a discounted 30-year stream of operating costs are assumed to be incurred. The cost coefficient CPC(m,k,u) may thus be expressed in general** as:

$$\mathrm{CPC}(m,k,u) = \frac{1}{\left[(1.10)^{\left(\sum_{n=0}^{u-1} dl(n)\right)}\right]}\left[\frac{1}{dl(u)}\left(\sum_{n=0}^{dl(u)-1}\frac{1}{(1.10)^n}\right)\mathrm{CC}(m,k,u) + \frac{1}{dl(u)}\left(\sum_{n=0}^{dl(u)-1}\frac{1}{(1.10)^n}\right)\left(\sum_{n=1}^{30}\frac{1}{(1.10)^n}\right)\mathrm{OC}(m,k,u)\right]$$

For the low-Btu coal/steam-electric/miscellaneous intermediate-load electricity example the cost coefficient for the first period (u=1) is:

$$\begin{aligned}\mathrm{CPC}(2,4,1) &= (.872)\mathrm{CC}(2,4,1) + (8.22)\mathrm{OC}(2,4,1)\\ &= (.872)(\$58.7 \text{ billion}) + (8.22)(\$1.34 \text{ billion})\\ &= \$62.2 \text{ billion }/(\text{Quad/yr})\end{aligned}$$

---

*Representative year u = 0 is assumed to be 1974.

**Some of the facilities that initiate operation during the last two periods have remaining useful lives at the end of the time horizon of the model (2034). This is accounted for in two ways in the derivation of the cost coefficient parameters. First, the stream of operational costs is terminated in 2034 and, secondly, a terminal value credit equal to the discounted value of the facilities in 2034 is given for facilities that are still operational after 2034.

RETIREMENT FRACTION DATA

Table D-22 shows the facility retirement data used in the study. These data represent the fraction of the facilities of a particular vintage assumed to be available for use in each succeeding period. These fractions were calculated by taking into account both the assumed linear buildup of capacity between representative years and the assumed 30 year lifetime for these facilities. For example, facilities that initiate operation in period 2 are actually built up at a constant rate between 1979 and 1985 and hence are retired at a constant rate between 2009 and 2015. Therefore, only three-sevenths of these facilities remain in operation by the representative year for period 5 (2012). Table D-22 provides the values for the retirement fraction coefficient parameters (r(u,t)) provided to the model for the various scenarios.

GROWTH CONSTRAINT DATA

Table D-23 presents restrictions on nuclear reactor generating capacity growth rates provided to the model. This table presents, for each reactor type, the maximum new capacity that can be added in a particular period. The resulting maximum total capacity that could be available in each time period if the maximal additions were made are shown in Table D-24. The data in Table D-23 provides the values for the maximum new reactor construction constants (gPC(m,t)) which were provided to the model for the various scenarios.

The maximum extraction rates (gDS(i,t)) for domestic oil and gas were the maximum values for these rates given in ERDA-48 (1975). The assumed maximum rate for domestic oil extraction was 22 Quads per year (11 million barrels per day), while the maximum rate for natural gas extraction was 25 Quads (24.5 trillion cubic feet) per year. Finally oil shale extration during its initial availability period (period number 3) was limited to 8 quads per year (4 million barrels per day). This was the value used in ERDA-48 (1975) for the year 2000.

The restriction on coal extraction limits the extraction of low-Btu coal to be less than twice the extraction rate of high-Btu coal. This assumption is necessitated by consideration of the geographical

Table D-22

FACILITY RETIREMENT FRACTIONS

Period of Initial Facility Operation	Fraction of These Facilities Still in Operation During					
	Period 1 (1978)	Period 2 (1985)	Period 3 (1992)	Period 4 (2000)	Period 5 (2012)	Period 6 (2027)
Period 1	1	1	1	1	0	0
Period 2	-	1	1	1	3/7	0
Period 3	-	-	1	1	1	0
Period 4	-	-	-	1	1	1/2
Period 5	-	-	-	-	1	1
Period 6	-	-	-	-	-	1

Table D-23

RESTRICTIONS ON THE GROSS ADDITIONS TO NUCLEAR CAPACITY[a]

Reactor Type	Restrictions on the Gross[b] Additions to Nuclear Reactor Capacity by Period [GWe per period (Quads/yr per period)]					
	Period 1 (1978)	Period 2 (1985)	Period 3 (1992)	Period 4 (2000)	Period 5 (2012)	Period 6 (2027)
Light-water	30 (.90)	118 (3.53)	149 (4.45)	311 (9.30)	638 (19.07)	1595 (47.68)
High-temperature gas-cooled	.30 (.01)	4.70 (.14)	13 (.39)	62 (1.85)	66 (1.98)	111 (3.32)
Liquid-metal fast breeder			149 (4.45)	311 (9.30)	638 (19.07)	1595 (47.68)

[a]Derived from ERDA-48 (1975) and Atomic Energy Commission (1974a).

[b]Includes replacements for retiring capacity.

Table D-24

MAXIMUM POSSIBLE NUCLEAR REACTOR GENERATING CAPACITY

Reactor Type	Maximum Possible Nuclear Reactor Generating Capacity [GWe/(Quads/yr)]					
	Period 1	Period 2	Period 3	Period 4	Period 5	Period 6
Light-water	63 (1.88)	180 (5.38)	329 (9.84)	640 (19.13)	1149 (34.35)	2389 (71.42)
High-temperature gas-cooled	.30 (.01)	5.00 (.15)	18 (.54)	80 (2.39)	144 (4.28)	208 (6.22)
Liquid-metal fast breeder	-	-	149 (4.45)	460 (13.75)	1098 (32.83)	2389 (71.42)

distribution of these two resources. Since the low-Btu coal is found predominantly in the west, the transportation cost assumed for it is not great enough to reflect transport to eastern markets. Therefore, some high-Btu coal must be extracted to satisfy the demands of these markets.

ELECTRICAL GENERATION LOAD-SHARING DATA

The fraction of the supply enterprise's output path energy that is delivered to the primary and secondary end-use demands for load-sharing combinations are shown in Table D-25. The fraction going to the primary end-use demand category is its base-block demand duration (see Table B-5) divided by the electric generation plant factor (.65; Table D-19). The fraction going to the secondary end-use demand is one minus the fraction going to the primary demand adjusted by the efficiencies of pumped storage and hydroelectric facilities (Tables B-5 and D-11) where appropriate. Table D-25 provides the values for the electrical facility load-sharing coefficient parameters (q(k,n)) provided to the model for the various scenarios.

PLUTONIUM MASS BALANCE DATA

Table D-26 presents the plutonium mass balance data used in the study. For each possible period of initial operation this table gives the net change in the plutonium balance in each period attributable to facilities for one Quad of delivered LWR(or LMFBR)-generated electricity. For the LMFBR, the initial negative values represent initial core requirements, while the succeeding positive values represent net LMFBR operational plutonium production and finally salvaged plutonium from the decommissioned LMFBRs. Table D-26 provides the values for the plutonium mass balance coefficient parameters (pU(m,u,t)) provided to the model for the various scenarios.

CONVERSION FACTORS

Table D-27 is a compilation of the various conversion factors used in the study (from ERDA-48, 1975). Many of these conversion factors represent widely accepted standards, while others vary from study to study. However, wide variations between the values used in particlar studies would not be expected.

Table D-25

ELECTRICAL GENERATION LOAD SHARING DATA

End-Use Demand Categories Primary --Secondary	Fraction of Output-Path Energy that is Delivered to:	
	Primary End-Use Demand	Secondary End-Use Demand
Miscellaneous intermediate-load electricity -- Peak-load electricity	$\frac{.50}{.65} = .77$	$\left(\frac{.15}{.65}\right) (.75)\ (.34) = .06$
Miscellaneous intermediate-load electricity -- Water heat	$\frac{.50}{.65} = .77$	$\frac{.15}{.65} = .23$
Peak-load electricity -- Peak-load electricity	$\frac{.10}{.65} + \left(\frac{.55}{.65}\right) (.75)\ (.34) = .37$	
Peak-load electricity -- Water heat	$\frac{.10}{.65} = .15$	$\frac{.55}{.65} = .85$
Space heat -- Air conditioning	$\frac{.42}{.65} = .65$	$\frac{.23}{.65} = .35$

Table D-26

PLUTONIUM MASS BALANCE DATA[a]

Period of Initial LWR (LMFBR) Operation	Change (+/-) in the Plutonium Inventory Attributable to LWR (LMFBR) Capacity for the Annual Delivery[b] of One Quad of Electricity in Period (in Metric Tons/Quad)					
	Period 1 (1978)	Period 2 (1985)	Period 3 (1992)	Period 4 (2000)	Period 5 (2012)	Period 6 (2027)
1	+85.75	+ 85.75	+ 85.75	+ 110.30		
2		+ 85.75	+ 85.75	+ 110.30	+ 78.75	
3		—— (- 64.69)	+ 85.75 (- 3.92)	+ 110.30 (+ 57.33)	+ 183.80 (+ 95.55)	—— (+ 113.2)
4			—— (- 56.60)	+ 110.30 (+ .73)	+ 183.8 (+ 95.55)	+ 91.88 (+ 104.4)
5				—— (- 47.17)	+ 183.80 (+ 29.52)	+ 183.80 (+ 95.55)
6					—— (- 60.37)	+ 183.80 (+ 42.72)

[a]Derived from Smith, Weyant, and Holdren (1975).

[b]That is, electricity that has already been transmitted and distributed to an end-use utilizing device.

Table D-27

CONVERSION FACTORS USED IN THE EXAMPLE APPLICATION

To Convert from:	To:	Multiply by
Quads	Btus	1.00×10^{15}
Barrels of Oil	Btus	5.56×10^{6}
Cubic Feet of Natural Gas	Btus	1020
Tons of Low-Btu Coal	Btus	17.0×10^{6}
Tons of High-Btu Coal	Btus	24.0×10^{6}
Kilowatt Hours of Electricity	Btus	3413
Barrels of Shale Oil	Btus	5.56×10^{6}
Tons of Shale	bbl	.714

To Convert from:	To:	Multiply by
Btus	Quads	1×10^{-15}
Quads	Barrels of Oil	180×10^{6}
Quads	Cubic Feet of Natural Gas	$.98 \times 10^{12}$
Quads	Tons of Low-Btu Coal	58.82×10^{6}
Quads	Tons of High-Btu Coal	41.67×10^{6}
Quads	Kilowatt Hours of Electricity	293×10^{9}

REFERENCES

Alexander, A. J. and D. B. Rice, "Comments on LMFBR Cost-Benefit Analysis," Rand Corporation, Report P-5498, August 1975.

American Gas Association, "TERA: Total Energy Resource Analysis Model," system description, 1 August 1974.

Anderson, D., "Models for Determining Least-Cost Investments in Electricity Supply," Bell Journal of Economics and Management Science, Vol. 3, No.1, Spring 1972.

Anderson, K.P., "A Simulation Analysis of U.S. Energy Demand, Supply and Prices," Rand Corporation, Report R-1591, 1976.

Argonne National Laboratory, "Social Costs for Alternative Means of Electrical Power Generation for 1980 and 1990," Report ANL-8093, March 1973.

Associated Universities, Inc., "Reference Energy Systems and Resource Data for Use in Assessment of Energy Technologies," April 1972.

Atomic Energy Commission, "Nuclear Power Growth: 1974-2000," Wash-1139, February, 1974a.

Atomic Energy Commission, "Proposed Final Environmental Impact Statement for the Liquid-Metal Fast Breeder Reactor Program," WASH-1535R, December 1974b.

Austin, A.L., and S.D. Winter, "U.S. Energy Flowcharts for 1950, 1960, 1970, 1980, 1985, and 1990," Lawrence Livermore Laboratory, Report UCRL-51487, 16 November 1973.

Baughman, M. L., "Dynamic Energy System Modeling - Interfuel Competition," MIT Energy Laboratory, Report MIT-EL-01, August 1972.

Bechtel Corporation, "The Energy Supply Planning Model," Final Report to the National Science Foundation Office of Energy R&D Policy, 2 vols., August 1975.

Benenson, P., et al. editors, "Proceedings of the Conference on Energy Modeling and Forecasting," Lawrence Berkeley Laboratory, Report LBL-3635, June 1974.

Berg, C. A., "A Technical Basis for Energy Conservation," Technology Review, February 1974.

Bodin, L., et al. "A Study to Assess the Application of Shadow Pricing Techniques to National Energy Resource Planning," Brookhaven National Laboratory, Report BNL-19438, October 1974.

Boffey, P. M., "Energy Research: A Harsh Critique Says Federal Effort May Backfire," Science, Vol. 190, 7 November 1975.

Bullard, C.W. and D.A. Pilati, "Direct and Indirect Requirements For A Project Independence Scenario", Center For Advanced Computation, University of Illinois, CAC document no. 178, 1975.

Bushnell, R. C., et al., "The Michigan Linear Programming Fuel-Energy Planning Models," paper presented at the National Meetings of the Econometric Society, San Francisco, Ca., 30 December 1974.

Cherniavsky, E. A., "Energy Systems Analysis and Technology Assessment Program," Brookhaven National Laboratory, Report BNL-19569, November 1974.

Cochran, T. B., J. G. Speth, and A. Tamplin, "Bypassing the Breeder: A Report on Misplaced Federal Energy Priorities," National Resources Defense Council, March 1975.

Committee on Aeronautical and Space Sciences, "Solar Heating and Cooling," United States Senate, 1975.

Committee on Commerce, "Energy Waste and Energy Efficiency in Industrial and Commercial Acitivities," United States Senate, Serial No. 93-102, 1974a.

Committee on Commerce, "Industry Efforts in Energy Conservation," United States Senate, 1974b.

Congressional Research Service, "Readings on Energy Conservation," United States Senate, Serial No. 94-1, 1975.

Day, M.C., " Nuclear Energy: A Second Round of Questions," Bulletin of the Atomic Scientists, December 1975.

Duchesneau, T., Competition in the Energy Industry, Ballinger Publishing, 1974.

Electric Power Research Institute, "Energy Systems, Environment, and Conservation Division Progress Report Report", Report EPRI ES-1, December 1974.

Energy Research and Development Administration, "Report of the Liquid Metal Fast Breeder Reactor Program Review Group," Report ERDA-1, January 1975.

Energy Research and Development Administration, "A National Plan for Energy Research, Development, and Demonstration: Creating Energy Choices for the Future," 2 vols., Report ERDA-48, June 1975.

Energy Research and Development Administration, "Information from ERDA," Reference Information, November 1975a.

Environmental Protection Agency (EPA), "Energy Conservation Strategies," Report EPA-R5-73-021, July 1973.

Federal Energy Administration, "Project Independence Report," GPO, November 1974a.

Federal Energy Administration, "Project Independence Blueprint Final Task Force Report: Coal," November, 1974b.

Federal Energy Administration, "Project Independence Blueprint Final Task Force Report: Nuclear Energy," November, 1974c.

Ford Energy Policy Energy Project, A Time to Choose: America's Energy Future, Ballinger, 1974.

Haefele, W., "The Fast Breeder as a Cornerstone of Future Large Energy Supplies," IIASA, Report RR-73-5, September 1973.

Haefele, W., and A. S. Manne, "Strategies for a Transition from Fossil to Nuclear Fuels," Energy Policy, March 1975.

Hagerton, J.F., "U.S. Uranium Supply and Demand, Near Term and Long Range," Nuclear News, May 1975.

Herendeen, R. A., "Use of Input-Output Analysis to Determine the Energy Cost of Goods and Services," in Macrakis (1974).

Hittman Associates, Incorporated, "Environmental Impacts, Efficiency, and Cost of Energy Supply and End Use," Volume 1, November, 1974; Volume 2, January 1975.

Hoffman, K. C., "The United States Energy System: A Unified Planning Framework," unpublished doctoral dissertation, Polytechnic Institute of Brooklyn, June 1972.

Hoffman, K.C., et al., "Coupled Energy System - Economic Models," in Benenson, et al. (1974).

Holdren, J.P., "Uranium Availabilty and the Breeder Decision", Environmental Quality Laboratory, California Institute of Technology, Memorandum No. 8, January 1974.

Holloman, J. H., et al., Energy Research and Development, Ballinger, 1975.

Hudson, E.A. and D.W. Jorgenson, "U.S. Energy Policy and Economic Growth 1975-2000," Bell Journal of Economics and Management Science, Autumn 1974.

Institute for Contemporary Studies, No Time to Confuse: A Critique of the Final Report of the Energy Policy Project of the Ford Foundation, 1975.

International Business Machines, "Mathematical Programming System/360 Version 2, Linear and Seperable Programming User's Manual," 1969.

International Institute for Applied Systems Analysis, Proceedings of the IIASA Planning Conference on Energy Systems, Laxenberg, Austria, July 20, 1973.

Just, J. J., "Impacts of New Energy Technology Using Generalized Input-Output Analysis," MIT Energy Laboratory, Report MIT-EL-01, February 1973.

Limaye, D. R., et al., "Quantitative Energy Studies and Models: A State of the Art Review," chapter 14 of D.R. Limaye, editor, Energy Policy Evaluation: Modeling and Simulation Approaches, Lexington, 1974.

Macrakis, M. S., editor, Energy: Demand, Conservation and Institutional Problems, MIT Press, 1974.

Manne, A. S., "Energy System Modeling," in Mitre Corporation, "An Agenda for Research and Development on Energy Systems," Report mtr-6605, February 1974a.

Manne, A. S., "Waiting for the Breeder," in a special issue of the American Economic Review on the Depletion of Natural Resources, December 1974b.

Meadows, D. H., et al., The Limits to Growth, Signet 1972.

Metz, W.D., "European Breeders (1): France Leads the Way," Science Vol. 190, 26 December 1975.

Morrow, W. E., "Solar Energy: Its Time is Near", Technology Review, December 1973.

Moyers, J. C., "The Room Air Conditioner as an Energy Consumer," Oak Ridge National Laboratory, Report ORNL-NSF-EP-59, October 1973.

Mutch, J. J., "Residential Water Heating: Fuel Conservation Economics and Public Policy," The Rand Corporation, Report R-1998-NSF, May 1974.

National Science Foundation, "Energy Modelling", comprising papers presented at a special workshop organized by the U.S. National Science Foundation and the Energy Research Unit, Queen Mary College, London, 15-19 October, 1973.

Palmer, R. S., "An Assessment of Economic Incentives for the Liquid Metal Fast Breeder Reactor," report presented to the Breeder Reactor Corporation, Chicago, Ill., March 1975.

Perry, H., "Energy Research and Development - Problems and Prospects," U.S. Congress, Senate Committee on Interior and Insular Affairs, 93rd Congress, 1st Session, 1973.

Ray, D. L., "The Nation's Energy Future," a report to Richard M. Nixon, President of the United States, Wash-1281, 1 December 1973.

Searl, M.F., editor, Energy Modeling: Art, Science and Practice, Resources for the Future, March 1973.

Searl, M. F., et al., "Uranium Resources to Meet Long Term Uranium Requirements," Electric Power Research Institute EPRI Special Report No. 5, November 1974.

Smith, K. R., J. P. Weyant and J. P. Holdren, "Evaluation of Conventional Power Systems," Energy and Resources Group, University of California at Berkeley, Report ERG 75-5, Jet Propulsion Laboratory, July 1975.

Stanford Research Institute, "SRI-Gulf Energy Model: Overview of Methodology," January 1975.

Synfuels Interagency Task Force, "Recommendations for a Synthetic Fuels Commercialization Program," report submitted to the President's Energy Resources Council, June 1975.

Tilton, J. E., U.S. Energy R&D Policy: the Role of Economics, Resources for the Future, 1974.

United States Geological Survey, "Geological Estimates of Undiscovered Recoverable Oil and Gas Resources in the United States," Geological Survey Circular 725, 1975.

Weyant, J.P. and E.S. Ojdana, "A Critical Analysis of Selected Benefit Contribution Models used in Military R&D Planning," The Rand Corporation, Report R-1857-PR, 1976.